DIVIDENDS DON'T LIE

FINDING VALUE IN BLUE-CHIP STOCKS

DIVIDENDS DON'T LIE

FINDING VALUE IN BLUE-CHIP STOCKS

GERALDINE WEISS/JANET LOWE

Longman Financial Services Publishing
a division of Longman Financial Services Institute, Inc.

“A lucid and powerful presentation of one of the *best* documented investment theories.”

Peter Brimelow
Senior Editor, *FORBES*, and
Author, *The Wall Street Gurus*

“Finally, an investment book that deals with values! Values ultimately rule the market and a knowledge of values is always based first and last on dividends. This book should be "the bible of dividends." I recommend *Dividends Don't Lie*—in spades.”

Richard Russell
Publisher, Dow Theory Letters

“The leading advocate of value investing has created the definitive book about making money from stocks using the only number that can't be cooked—the number you can put in your pocket and spend—the dividend yield.”

Norman G. Fosback
Editor, Market Logic

“Buy low, sell high strategies require a value-based approach that incorporates historical perspective and current conditions. Dividend-yield analysis is an important tool in the fundamental analysis of stock and no one does it better than Geraldine Weiss. Understanding the material in *Dividends Don't Lie* will improve both your stock-selection process and your market-timing outlook.”

Al Frank
The Prudent Speculator

“This investment strategy has stood the test of time. It is easy to understand and easy to apply. The investor is shortchanging his own chances for success if he is not familiar with Weiss' approach. It has proven to be a reliable guide in all kinds of markets.”

Dick Davis
Dick Davis Digest

“When it comes to value investing, few market observers have a better handle on how to profit in the real world of successful money management. This book provides hard, useful data for serious investors rather than the usual market pablum.”

Charles Allmon
Editor, Growth Stock Outlook

“Weiss and Lowe have written what is perhaps the first readable book on fundamental analysis. The first dividend accrues to the reader when you buy *Dividends Don't Lie*. It is a superb value!”

Bob Gross
Editor and Publisher,
The Professional Investor

“*Dividends Don't Lie* is the truth. Weiss and Lowe have developed an investment philosophy that got them out of the stock market long before the crash of 1987—and the beauty of it is that it is as simple as it is effective.”

Bill Griffeth
Financial News Network

“*Dividends Don't Lie* provides a tried-and-true formula for buying and selling the best of the blue-chip stocks—a safe and sane way to invest in the stock market. Highly recommended as an excellent learning experience for beginning investors and a great refresher course for the pros!”

Monte M. Korn
Host of the National Money
Time Radio Show

“I have a lot of respect for the common-sense approach of an investment strategy based on dividends. There is a wonderful order and simplification in this long-term skill which tends to achieve profits by patience rather than clever short-term market moves which do not create income or build capital.”

James L. Fraser, CFA
President, Fraser Management Associates

While a great deal of care has been taken to provide accurate and current information, the ideas, suggestions, general principles and conclusions presented in this book are subject to local, state and federal laws and regulations, court cases and any revisions of same. The reader is thus urged to consult legal counsel regarding any points of law—this publication should not be used as a substitute for competent legal advice.

Executive Editor: Kathleen A. Welton
Project Editors: Chris Christensen, Ellen Allen
Copy Editor: Regina Wells
Interior Design: Edwin Harris
Cover Design: Renee Klyczek

Published by Longman Financial Services Publishing
a division of Longman Financial Services Institute, Inc.

Printed in the United States of America.

89 90 10 9 8 7 6 5 4 3 2

Library of Congress Cataloging-in-Publication Data

Weiss, Geraldine.
Dividends don't lie.

Bibliography: p.
Includes index.
1. Investments—Handbooks, manuals, etc. 2. Stocks—Handbooks, manuals, etc. I. Lowe, Janet II. Title.
HG4521.L825 1989 332.63'22 8308
ISBN 0-462-115-4

DEDICATION

I have written this book with love for my husband, Richard; my children, Gabriel, Martin, Kathi and Gregory; and my grandchildren, Aaron, Benjamin, Brandon, Jasmine and Shenandoah—all of whom are my life's finest dividends.

Geraldine Weiss

To Austin, Beth, Risé, Tarah and Brandon, who have been wonderfully patient with the writer holed up in her office.

Janet Lowe

Table of Contents

List of Figures

Figures prepared by Investment Quality Trends—Katherine Turkeltaub, graphic artist.

List of Dow Stocks

Preface

Dividends Don't Lie is about investment strategy. Our purpose is to help investors find bargains in the stock market at any time. We will show how to take maximum advantage of a rising market, and how to insulate against a falling market. In short, this book takes most of the risk and much of the anxiety out of investing in stocks.

An enlightened investor, one who can recognize value and quality, will survive in virtually any investment climate. Our philosophy is that dividend yield can tell a lot about the value of a stock and the direction of the market. *Dividends Don't Lie* was written for the individual investor, although the principles are fundamental and intended to be used by both layman and professional alike.

The game plan outlined here has been used in Geraldine Weiss' investment advisory letter, **Investment Quality Trends**, for 25 years to predict what the market will do and how individual stocks will perform. The theory is based on the fact that a stock's underlying value is in its dividends, not in its earnings or in its prospects for capital gains. Years of research have shown that blue-chip companies, those with long records of distinguished performance, are more predictable in every way than those of newcomers or companies with erratic records of earnings and dividend payments. Though the dividend-yield theory is a common sense approach, it has led to spectacular long-term results.

Investment Quality Trends has consistently ranked in the top ten percent of the 280 investment advisory letters tracked between 1981 and 1985 by the respected analytical organization, Select Information Exchange. Frequently, it was number one in their ratings and Investment Quality Trends continues to rank in the top ten percent of other analytical organizations. Those who adhered to the dividend-yield theory during the volatile peak of the bull market in 1987 ended that year as winners. But the theory's track record goes back much earlier than that. For a 19 month period from June 1981 through January 1983, Investment Quality Trends scored the amazing annual portfolio gain of 51.2 percent. For the five year period between 1981 and 1986, Investment Quality Trends achieved an average annual return of 30 percent. By applying the same concept to the Dow Jones Industrial Average, Investment Quality Trends called the market bottoms of 1970, 1974, 1978, 1980 and 1982; and the tops, too, including the market reversal of 1987.

As the bull market of the early to mid 1980's steadily clambered toward levels that both frightened and excited investors, we both agreed that the top of the market was in full view. Calculations based on dividend yield signaled the apex of the market and Investment Quality Trends warned its clients to sell their overvalued stocks in the spring of 1987. The ominous signals continued through the summer. "Among the thirty stocks which now comprise the Dow Jones Industrial Average," warned the mid-September 1987 edition of Investment Quality Trends, "only General Motors remains undervalued. The Dow (then at 2608 and climbing) would be out of line until it dropped below 2312."

It came as no surprise to us, then, that some investors lost their shirts when the bull market lost its power. Many of those investors were big players in the market such as financial institutions, pension funds and mutual funds. They probably should have known better. But many of those caught in the market's backwash were individual investors, people who were just trying to take care of their own financial security.

Most of the losers had entered the market late in the game because, by then, the upward-spiraling stock market was big news. These investors jumped on the proverbial band wagon at the end of the parade, paying too much for what they got. Then when their stock either went flat, or worse, plummeted, they decided the stock market was not for them. It was too risky, they came to believe. Other investors got in the market at the right time, but tried to ride the crest too long. They didn't get out in time. Whichever mistake was made, both groups of investors shared the same disillusionment.

It was early on, when we anticipated that shock and disappointment would chase a lot of individual investors out of the market, that we decided to write this book. What investors needed, we felt, was a philosophy and an understanding of equity investments that would see them through all the cycles that are typical of the stock market. Even with the warnings that were published by Investment Quality Trends that the market was overvalued and would soon decline, it was a surprise to many to see the Dow plummet 508 points on a single unforgettable day, October 19. It was a reminder that the stock market sometimes can startle even the most ardent market scholar.

A lesson learned long before that fateful day is that the stock market is only a friend to investors who can recognize and appreciate good values: investors who have the courage to buy stocks when they are undervalued, the patience to hold them until the price moves upward, and the wisdom to sell when the stock becomes overvalued.

The trick is in knowing when these times have come. Investors decide, collectively, by responding either in a positive or negative way to the returns, either in terms of dividends or share price appreciation. By researching records dating back into the 19th century and charting historic yields of stocks, the unique, historical and intrinsic relationship between dividend yield and the price of an individual stock emerges.

Charles Dow, a wise market observer and one of the founders of the Dow Jones market indicators, has written that, "values, when applied to stocks, are determined in the end by the return to the investor, and nothing is more certain than that the investor establishes the price of the stocks." We will explain how that is done, and how even fairly small participants in the market can become successful players.

Geraldine Weiss
Janet Lowe

The Dividend–Yield Strategy

1

Dividends Are Fundamental

"Chance favors only the mind that is prepared."

—LOUIS PASTEUR

The venerable Wall Street mogul Bernard Baruch claimed to have cashed out of the stock market in time to avoid the crash of 1929. In fact, the legend of Baruch and the high regard in which he was held through the Depression and World War II years was built largely on his reputation for timing the market crash. While Baruch's fleet-footedness may have been a little overblown, James Grant's biography, *Bernard Baruch: The Adventures of a Wall Street Legend,* showed that in 1931 Baruch held $3.6 million in stocks, $3.1 million in bonds and an incredible $8.7 million in cash. In the 1930s, that was an amazing amount, indicating that Baruch had indeed done something right.

Baruch also used his remarkable intuition to help his close friend Winston Churchill recover several losses and exit the big bear market in a rally in 1932. Grant also notes that Baruch associates slipped a tip to Irving Berlin early in the autumn of 1929, hinting that he should get out of the stock that they had once advised him to purchase.

STOCK MARKET SUCCESS IS SLIPPERY

While all of us would like to trade as skillfully as Baruch did, most private investors can better emphathize with Churchill and Berlin. Those who are successful, perhaps even brilliant, in other fields may have little success when it comes to the stock market. Or while occasionally lucky, they have been unable to ensure consistently good returns through changing market cycles.

Not many people have a friend as shrewd as Bernard Baruch to come to the rescue. So they give up in despair.

A SERIOUS GAME

And that's too bad. What few investors understand is that the stock market is much like a game, and it can be as much fun to play as baseball, chess or Monopoly®. But, as in any other game, rules exist. And like any other challenging pursuit, the best players—the winners—are those who have knowledge and a strategy.

The difference, of course, between investing in the stock market and a mere pastime is that the stakes are higher. This is no Trivial Pursuit®. At risk are hard-won earnings, savings and security both now and in the future.

But for the winner, the rewards are also higher. The thrill of the hunt, the joy of discovery, the lasting satisfaction of victory are heightened because of the importance of this endeavor. And winning is much easier with the right strategy.

THE STRATEGY

This book teaches a value-based approach to investing, one that uses a stock's dividend yield as the primary measure of value. Because price on its own, without other factors, means nothing, an investor must find some way to determine whether the price of any given company is high, low or just about what it should be.

Even though most investors put their money in the market with the hope of reaping a good rate of return, the most tangible source of return, the dividend, is too often underemphasized in this process.

According to the dividend-yield theory, the price of a stock is driven by its yield. When a stock offers a high dividend yield, investors will buy, which pushes the price up and gradually erodes the yield. When the yield falls, the stock is shunned, until an absence of demand allows its price to fall. It then descends to a price level at which, again, the yield is attractive to investors.

So rather than emphasize the price cycles of a stock, the company's products, market strategy or other factors, this book stresses dividend-yield patterns. Investors will learn to buy and sell when dividend yields instruct them to do so. The dividend yield lets the investor know, with very little doubt, when a share's price is genuinely high, low or on the move between those two points.

To more deeply understand this line of reasoning, it is useful to examine the way an investor collects the rewards for the money placed at risk.

THE WAYS TO WIN

The return on a stock market investment is twofold. First is the dividend, which pays the stockholder an ongoing cash return on investment capital. The second is the growth in the price of the shares, which offers the investor the possibility of selling at a profit.

What is a dividend?

It is a distribution of the earnings of a company to its owners, the shareholders. The amount of dividend a company issues can vary, depending on the class of shares (various preferred classes or common). Dividends most often are paid in money or additional shares of stock, though they could be paid in scrip, company products or property. The board of directors decides on the form and amount; ordinarily, dividends are paid quarterly.

Because the directors have the option of not paying dividends on common stock, the number of companies offering dividends varies from year to year. In 1987, however, 76 percent of the 2,244 companies listed on the New York Stock Exchange paid dividends. In aggregate, they distributed about $84.4 billion dollars in dividends to investors.

The combination of the two financial rewards (dividend and the eventual profitable sale of shares) constitutes the "total return" available in the stock market.

Even at this elementary stage of our discussion, the importance of the dividend becomes apparent.

A BIRD IN THE HAND

Between the two profit paths, only dividend payment provides an element of certainty. A company's dividend is tangible. The probable appreciation of its stock is just that—a probability—or worse yet, a possibility.

The share price of even the finest-looking company can be affected by any number of events. A young and charismatic chief executive officer can die in an automobile crash. A sudden rebellion in a far-off country can strangle the supply of an essential commodity.

A good example of an unexpected event torpedoing a stock price occurred in 1985, when a judge announced that Pennzoil had won $11 billion in damages in its suit against Texaco. Stunned, Texaco not long after filed for Chapter 11 protection in bankruptcy court. Its share price fell more than 25 percent within six months. While it was public knowledge that the companies were involved in a legal wrangle as an aftermath of a takeover battle for Getty Oil, no one expected such drastic results.

Whether dividend or share price appreciation is selected as the source of return, investors must first find a way of measuring the value of the shares they plan to buy.

MEASURES OF VALUE

Three fundamental measures of value are:

- dividend yield,
- price/earnings ratio and
- price/book-value ratio.

Again, dividend yield—calculated by dividing the dividend by the price—is the most telling yardstick.

FIGURE 1.1 Dividend Yield

A stock that sells for $20 and pays a $1 dividend has a five percent dividend yield. A $40 stock with a $2 dividend also has a five percent yield. So even though the $40 stock is twice the price of the $20 stock, they represent identical values in terms of dividend yield. Here are additional examples of how the dividend yield is calculated. Note that the yield is calculated on the price paid for the stock, so until the dividend changes, the yield stays the same no matter what the stock's current price is. The company names used in this example are fictitious.

Company	*Price*	*Dividend*	*Dividend Yield*
Brandon Power	$40	$2.92	7.3%
La Jolla, Inc.	34	2.50	7.4
Tarah Corporation	40	.60	1.5
Jasmine Industries	26	.40	1.5

The dividend yield is the most revealing measure of value because in addition to producing income, dividends tell something about a company's state of health that earnings and book values may not show.

QUALITY OF EARNINGS

Earnings are often subject to those vague bookkeeping practices such as depreciation, cash flow, inventory adjustments and reserves. A skillful accountant can make good earnings appear not-so-good, and vice versa, depending on tax considerations.

Or the motive for manipulating earnings may be much more sinister than the minimization of tax liability. A company may want to puff up its quarterly earnings to enhance the share price of a pending stock offering. Certain companies have even been accused of depressing earnings in one quarter to allow officers and directors to earn their stock options at a lower price and sell them at a higher price when subsequent delayed earnings are heftier.

DIVIDENDS DON'T LIE

Dividends, on the other hand, are real money—not just figures on a balance sheet. Once a dividend is paid it is gone forever from that company. Subterfuge cannot be used in the bookkeeping department over a dividend. Either it is paid or it is not paid. And if it is not paid, there is a reason.

The managers and directors of large corporations know, far better than anyone else, the financial condition of their companies and the directions that future earnings will take. Directors of the nation's most responsible blue-chip companies are not going to pay or increase a dividend unless the payout is fiscally justified and sound.

Therefore, a consistently rising dividend trend dramatically reveals a company's profitable progress. And this leads to a pleasant surprise. While searching for a reliable return, we discover a predictor for growth as well. (See figure 4.5.)

RISING DIVIDENDS BOOST SHARE PRICE

Much more so than earnings, dividend-yield trends can show whether a stock's price is likely to appreciate. When a dividend is increased, the price of a stock (which generally represents current value) rises to reflect the increased value of the investment. Conversely, when a dividend is lowered, the price declines to reflect reduced investment value and retarded corporate growth, not to mention the loss of anticipated income to the investor.

Even the suggestion that a dividend might be lowered will send ripples of fear through the hearts of investors who understand the influence of dividends on stock prices.

The importance of dividends also is understood well by the managers and directors of blue-chip companies, who generally go to great lengths to avoid reducing an indicated payout, even in periods of cyclical stress. They know that a lowered dividend results in a lower price tag on their stock and reduced investment quality for the company.

For example, American Telephone and Telegraph's then-chairman, the late James E. Olsen, asserted in the company's 1987 annual report that AT&T was paying out too high a percentage of its earnings in dividends. In 1986, AT&T had earned $1.88 per share and paid a dividend of $1.20 per share. That is a payout ratio of almost 64 percent. Yet rather than trim dividends, Olsen promised stockholders that AT&T would reduce its payout ratio by improving earnings.

TAXES AND DIVIDENDS

Dividends became even more important with the enactment of the Tax Reform Act of 1986, which taxed capital gains and dividend income at the same rate as regular income. Under the changed law, capital gains were no longer given preferential tax treatment.

MARKET INDICATOR

The dividend-yield theory also can point to the direction of the stock market as a whole. In early 1987, the powerful bull market of the 1980s exhibited ominous mood swings, but the August 25 market top and the October 19 crash were still months away. Yet analysts and economists began to observe an interesting phenomenon. While 9,812 corporate dividends were declared in the first quarter of the year, only 626 showed increases over the year before, according to Standard & Poor's Corporation.

In a *New York Times* article, Michael Flament, vice president of Wright Investor's Service, explained why this was alarming news. "Part of the case for a continuing bull market this year has been the expectation of a big increase in corporate dividends," Flament said. He expressed consternation that among the companies in the S&P 500 index that declared dividends in 1987's first quarter, increases averaged "a paltry three percent."

The composite dividend for the 30 stocks in the Dow Jones Industrial Average rose only two percent during the same period. Though earnings were up and a favorable tax law passed, corporate leaders were exhibiting caution and uncertainty about the future by keeping a tight rein on the money allowed to creep out of the company coffers.

Without a vote of confidence for the economy by business leaders, the market highs reached by the 1987 bull market would be unsustainable. So it should not have been a surprise when the market topped, struggled slowly downward awhile, then abruptly plunged in the fall of 1987.

THE DJIA TOPS AND BOTTOMS

In fact, our own studies of dividend yield show that when the Dow Jones Industrial Average has a price-to-yield ratio of three percent, bull markets historically have ended—dating back to and including the one that peaked in 1929.

The threatening three percent yield appeared again, for the first time since the market top in 1973, in the spring of 1987. From that point on, the end of the long bull market of the 1980s seemed inevitable.

QUALITY TELLS

While the dividend-yield theory can be applied to any company paying dividends long enough to establish a pattern, for maximum safety to investors it is best applied to blue-chip stocks.

Twenty-five years of stock market research show that the dividend-yield philosophy, when utilized with high-quality stocks with long track records, provides a powerful tool for building personal wealth.

A NATURAL LAW

The philosophy that the dividend yield of a quality company can reveal volumes about a stock's future performance does not lend itself merely to a certain tax climate or a particular market cycle. It is a basic principle, one that serves as a faithful guide through even the most confounding stock market phases.

"The underlying principles of sound investment should not alter from decade to decade," pointed out Benjamin Graham in his classic text, *The Intelligent Investor,* "but the application of these principles must be adapted to significant changes in the financial mechanisms and climate."

To get the most benefit from the dividend-yield philosophy and adapt it to any stock market "mechanisms and climate" requires the mastering of several illuminating concepts.

An investor must:

- confirm the value of a stock,
- identify quality and
- grasp the significance of cycles.

And finally, the investor must apply the concepts explained here to the process of building a portfolio, managing the portfolio through various market cycles and anticipating future share price and market directions.

These subjects, and a great many others that hone investor skills, are covered in more detail in the chapters ahead.

2

The Confirmation of Value

"The sweetness of low price is soon forgotten; but the bitterness of poor quality is long remembered."

—ANONYMOUS

The dictionary tells us that value is "proper price; the quantity of money that an article is likely to command in the long run, as distinct from its price in an individual instance." This wisdom sometimes escapes investors in relating their holdings to price. In fact, the very essence of successful investing involves an identification of value. As stated earlier, the most fundamental representation of value in the stock market is the receipt of dividends.

To fully understand the significance of dividend yield, it is necessary to analyze two other important measures of value in stocks: book value and price/earnings ratio.

While dividend yield expresses the "bottom line," or the ultimate measure in the worth of a company's shares, these two measures, however imperfect they may be, can be of great use. They can fill in some of the details as to what is happening in the stock market and with an individual stock, and they can confirm the conclusion reached by assessing the dividend. In turn, this leads to a re-evaluation of the term *total return* when determining the value of a stock.

BOOK VALUE

Some particularly interesting observations on book value were offered in a 1974 interview we conducted with Benjamin Graham, which was published in the *San Diego Union.* Graham, the author of *Security Analysis, The Intelligent Investor* and numerous other financial and investment texts, is looked upon as the father of modern security analysis. He taught at Columbia University's Graduate School of Business and at the University of California at Los Angeles.

The occasion for the interview was Mr. Graham's 80th birthday. Though his health was failing, he was brilliantly articulate, and on that day he wanted to talk about the stock market. His favorite subject was book value, which he used as a tool to identify value. It was his guide to bargain hunting.

Graham advised investors to purchase stocks as if they were buying a business: examining a company's fundamental situation, its assets, liabilities, financial condition, etc., and carefully noting the company's price in relation to its book value figure.

In the world of certified public accounting, the net asset value of a company is the same as the book value figure. That figure reflects all of the company's assets, minus intangible assets such as goodwill and patents, minus current and long-term liabilities and minus equity issues that have a prior claim. It is the liquidating or redemption value.

Book value is the bare-bones worth of a company, below which, if the stock market were rational, no company's price would fall.

But the stock market is not always rational. And, it should be noted, most accounting techniques overlook the effects of inflation on assets. Therefore, book value figures can be vastly understated; and stock prices sometimes fall even below those bargain basement levels.

Graham's preference was for stocks that demonstrated a combination of favorable investment factors, including asset values of at least two-thirds of the market price. In those stocks, he was most comfortable.

The major theme of his work reminds investors that the greater the premium above book value, the less certain the basis for determining intrinsic value, and the more this "value" depends on the changing moods and measurements of the stock market. According to Graham, an investor should concentrate on issues selling reasonably close to asset value, but certainly at no more than 30 percent above that figure. "Purchases made at such levels, or lower, may with logic be regarded as related to the company's balance sheet, and as having a justification or support independent of the fluctuating market prices," he said.

Book value, therefore, can be a significant measure of investment value in the stock market. But there are no guarantees that stocks purchased near book value will immediately rise. Other fundamental measures also should be applied to each stock selection, especially those regarding the safety of the dividend.

OTHER FUNDAMENTALS ALSO IMPORTANT

In his book *The Intelligent Investor,* Benjamin Graham cautioned that a stock does not become a sound investment merely because it can be bought close to asset value. The investor also should demand a satisfactory ratio of earnings to price, a sufficiently strong financial position and the prospect that earnings will at least be maintained over the years. However, the investor with a stock portfolio of low price-to-book-value ratios can take a much more independent and detached view than those who had paid high multiples of both earnings and tangible assets.

"As long as the earning power of his holdings remains satisfactory, he can give as little attention as he pleases to the vagaries of the stock market. More than that, at times he can use these vagaries to play the master game of buying low and selling high."

THE VALUE OF PATIENCE

Benjamin Graham enlarged on one other point during that interview that may help others put the stock market into its proper perspective: He lamented the fact that investors always are so anxious to see stock prices rise quickly. "It's hard enough to find good values," he said. "When a stock rises slowly, intrinsic value can keep pace with the gradual increase in the price of the stock. However, when the price escalates quickly, faster than the fundamental development of the company, then the stock must be sold and a new investment decision must be made." He concluded, "Every new investment decision bears the risks of being a mistake."

THE IMPORTANCE OF EARNINGS

The importance of earnings as a measure of corporate growth and an indicator of investment value cannot be denied. That is, it couldn't be, if an investor could be certain that corporate earnings reports mean what they appear to mean.

However, as emphasized before, earnings are nebulous figures on an income statement, numbers that can be doctored, disguised or distorted by clever accounting techniques. To some extent, earnings are whatever some accountant says they are. And who knows what secrets are locked in the "cash flow" of a company's annual report?

"The long and short of it was that generally accepted accounting practices weren't as generally accepted as I thought."

SOURCE: Reprinted by permission of UFS, One.

This means that from the very beginning, because earnings are unreliable, the price/earnings ratio is also somewhat suspect. Even so, the P/E ratio is a widely discussed element in the investment world, and a better understanding of how it works is worthwhile.

While the paying and increasing of dividends confirm the validity of earnings, so can the P/E ratio, to some extent, confirm the message of the dividend-yield trend.

PRICE/EARNINGS RATIOS

A Price/Earnings, (P/E), ratio relates the price of a stock to the underlying company. The figure is derived by dividing the stock price by the company's previous 12-month per-share earnings. If, for example, the price is $26 per share and the earnings are two dollars per share, the P/E ratio is 13 to 1. The ratio tells how much must be paid for one dollar of earnings power.

Obviously, a low P/E ratio is preferable to a high one. The lower the ratio, the more earnings for the money. A P/E ratio of 20 or more is high, a P/E of 15 is average, and a P/E of ten or less is low. However, a P/E ratio that is too low (below five) can be a sign of danger.

As a measure of the market in particular, earnings and P/E ratios can be dangerously misleading. In September of 1983, for example, the DJIA was priced at 105 times its latest 12-months' earnings. The extraordinary P/E ratio was the result of deficit earnings in a handful of Dow stocks.

When the economy improved, corporate earnings rose, dramatically reducing the high P/E ratios. In September 1986, the DJIA was priced at 12 times earnings. By September 1987, it was 21 times earnings.

Obviously, there are times when earnings do not give a true picture of investment value in the stock market. This observation leads to the further study of dividends as an indicator.

FIGURE 2.1 Price/Earnings Ratios

Company	*Price*	*Annual EPS*	*P/E Ratio*
Shenandoah Co.	$51	$1.75	29 to 1
Benjamin Industries	18	1.75	10.3 to 1
Aaron Corporation	7	1.70	4.1 to 1

(The corporation names listed above are fictitious.)

WHY DIVIDENDS ARE SO IMPORTANT

There is no more accurate indication of fiscal achievement in a publicly held corporation than a trend of rising dividends. Dividends are real money, a spendable return on one's investment. Dividends are the surest confirmation of a company's profitability, since dividends can arise only from the reality of earnings.

Enlightened investors have grasped the point that it is usually one condition—higher earnings or management's reasonable expectation of higher earnings—that prompts a dividend increase.

Even an investor who does not require income from his or her stocks should realize that dividends provide a floor of safety under the price of the stock. Because so many investors in the stock market pay close attention to dividend yield, when the price of a stock falls to a level that creates an attractive return, large sums of long-term investment capital are drawn into the market and the decline is halted. A stock that pays no dividend has no such safeguard on its price.

For the dividend of a blue chip to be boosted, strong prospects for improvement in earnings must exist. In addition, the foreseeable future must hold good growth potential. A dividend will not be raised if future earnings are in doubt. A corporation may declare an "extra" dividend in a windfall year but is loathe to increase the regular cash dividend unless it can be maintained. A rising dividend trend is so important, in fact, that it should be included in calculations of total return.

TOTAL RETURN REVISITED

Some features of investing in common stocks seem so obvious, so elementary, that it hardly appears necessary to spend much time discussing them. The concept of total return is one of those. And yet the dividend-yield theory adds a critical element to the basic concept of total return, an element that all investors need to take into account.

As it is popularly conceived, the notion of total return refers to the dividend yield, plus the potential for capital gain.

Dividend yield + capital gains = total return

If, for example, a stock moves from $20 per share to $40 per share over a three-year period, the capital gain is $20 per share, or 100 percent. Assuming that the dividend was $1 per share the first year, $1.15 per share in the second year and $1.25 per share in the third year, stockholders can add $3.40 to their $20 per share for a total gain of $23.40 per share. To calculate a percentage return, divide the total gain by the original price ($20). The result is 117 percent, which is the "total return" on this investment over the three years. The average annual return is 39 percent.

The dividend-yield theory would add another factor to that equation—dividend growth.

Dividend yield + dividend growth + capital gains = real total return

The idea of real total return is, has been and always will be the underlying reason why investors the world over are willing to risk their capital in common stocks. It has been the fundamental attraction of stock market investments ever since they began.

The bond market can offer a fixed return and, depending on the trend in interest rates, some potential for capital gains. But growth of dividend income is available only in the stock market. Dividend growth accompanies and inspires rising stock prices. Hence, only in the stock market can real total return be so munificently rewarding.

Look at it this way: When we add a current dividend yield of four percent, five percent or more to conservative dividend growth that perhaps will average five percent per year (and which frequently averages ten percent per year), to an average capital gain of ten percent per year, we find the real reason why long-term investment capital is better off in the stock market than in a savings bank or in the bond market.

Take, for example, a stock that is selling for $20 per share and is paying a $1 per-share annual dividend. The current yield on that investment is five percent.

If, over a period of 12 months, the stock rises only two points (net) for a ten percent capital gain, the total return on that investment in the year will be 15 percent.

This is certainly a better return than is generally available in a bond, savings account or any other investment vehicle that comes to mind. If the $20 stock that pays a $1 per-share dividend rises four points in a year, the total return will be 25 percent, and so on.

But if the stock is held for several years, during which time there are dividend increases in addition to price appreciation, the total return can escalate to heights that are virtually impossible to reach in any other investment vehicle. Again, all of this assumes that the purchase has been made at undervalued levels, from which price appreciation and dividend growth is a reasonable expectation over a reasonable period of time.

The total return from stocks that are held long enough for the concept to work will outpace inflation, even after taxes. It has been calculated that to beat an inflation rate of five percent per year, the investor who is in a 28 percent tax bracket must average 6.95 percent per year, just to stay even with taxes and inflation. With the reasonable objective of 15 percent per year as an average total return, an investor can stay well ahead of the game. This cannot be done in the bond market. It can be accomplished only in the stock market.

The reasoning behind real total return is a long-term investment concept that will not appeal to short-term traders. It deals with averages—an average dividend yield, average dividend growth and average annual price appreciation.

Figure 2.2, comparing the total return of stocks, Treasury bills and gold back to 1871, paints a vivid picture of the long-term advantage of stocks.

We cannot be sure that dividends will rise in each and every year. We cannot be sure when and to what extent stock prices will rise. However, if stocks are purchased at historically undervalued price levels, and if those stocks have a long, uninterrupted history of dividend payments and of frequent dividend increases, over a period of years the total return on that investment is likely to outperform the total return on any other kind of investment.

Obviously, dividends count, as does dividend growth. The higher the dividend yield becomes on an original investment, the less capital appreciation is necessary to reach that 15 percent average annual total return. With a current annual dividend yield of five percent, capital appreciation must average ten percent per year, but if the dividend yield climbs to seven percent, capital appreciation can fall to eight percent to achieve the same goal.

From historical tracking of stocks purchased using the principles outlined here, investors can have a reasonable expectation that sometime during a five-year period, a stock that is purchased at an undervalued price in terms of dividend yield will rise *at least* 50 percent. Dividend increases along the way will provide an even greater total return. But patience is required.

There is no sure road to investment riches. If there were, everyone would trod that path. But to the enlightened investor, the stock market offers not only the best map for the road to riches, but also the safest and most likely place where capital can be *conserved.* The dividend-yield theory, especially when applied to investment-grade stocks (those appropriate for purchase by a prudent investor), reduces much of the mystery and anxiety that so often accompany stock market investing.

FIGURE 2.2 Comparison of Total Returns

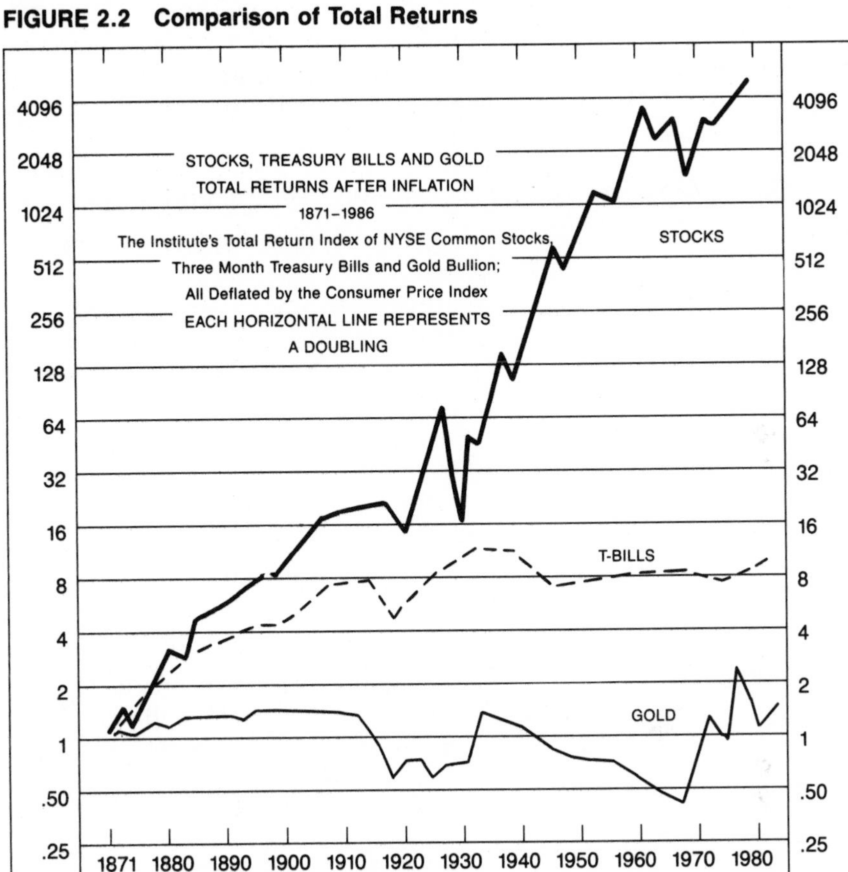

Over the long run, the stock market far outpaces alternative investments, especially if dividends are taken into consideration. This chart, produced by Norman Fosback of the Institute for Econometric Research, reflects the average Investor's experience. Fosback figures that over the long term, dividends account for almost half the return on common stocks.

SOURCE: Market Logic, 3471 N. Federal Highway, Fort Lauderdale, FL 33306.

3

Identifying Quality

"Take calculated risks. This is quite different from being rash."

GEORGE SMITH PATTON

Oscar Wilde described a cynic as a man who knows the price of everything and the value of nothing. The same description applies to all too many investors. Recognizing true value and being able to identify quality are two of the greatest forces investors can have behind them in the stock market.

QUALITY

Many ways of measuring the quality of a stock exist, but the most persuasive characteristic of all is a company's standing as a blue-chip operation.

To save time and turmoil, to pave the way to profits and, most of all, to minimize risk, the dividend-yield theory should be applied only to the most prosperous and progressive corporations on the stock exchanges—the blue chips.

Why concentrate on blue-chip stocks when searching for quality? Don't some young, growing companies have high-quality characteristics and potential for paying outstanding dividends? Aren't there good values to be found in formerly troubled, turnaround companies under new and better management?

Perhaps. Sometimes the company on the brink of disaster does save itself. Small companies sometimes emerge from the pack and achieve spectacular success.

But with these companies, risk runs high. There is no way to be certain they will achieve their goals. Talk comes easy; evidence is harder to produce. A lot of young companies in growing industries have not been able to survive the competition. Even a chief executive with a brilliant record may not be able to pull a sinking ship out of deep, dark waters.

The world of blue-chip stocks offers fewer unpleasant surprises. These companies are managed by the best, the most experienced leaders that money can buy. Their products and services are well known and widely distributed. They often are sold on international markets, especially in the lesser-developed countries, where growth potentials still are extraordinary. Blue-chip companies have the most sophisticated research centers, the most elaborate advertising programs, the largest sales organizations and the longest histories of profitable progress.

They are the most willing to share profits with their stockholders, paying dividends that can help investors keep pace with inflation and provide a safety net under the prices of stocks.

And our research has shown that there is just as much profit potential in high-quality stocks as there is in low-quality stocks. So why take any risk?

Consequently, there is no reason to follow each of the nearly 2,244 stocks on the New York Stock Exchange. You do just fine sticking to the blue chips.

TIMING

For reasons explained in an upcoming section, understanding the cycles of blue chips will help you be positioned at the right place in the market at the right time. Blue-chip stocks are in the forefront of every major market move. They are the first stocks to rise in a bull market and the last stocks to fall when the market declines.

In good times, blue-chip companies outperform both their lesser competitors and the economy. In bad times, they resist adversity best. Time and time again, experience has shown, there is no profitable substitute for quality.

WHAT IS A BLUE CHIP?

It has been said that any stock that goes up is a blue-chip stock. To some investors, any stock they own is a blue chip.

Confusion over the definition of *blue chip* in the stock market abounds. Maybe it is the term itself that gets our thinking off track. As you may have guessed, the expression comes from the blue chips used in a poker game. The blue chips are the highest denomination of money. They are the most expensive tokens—the most valuable chips in the game.

In the stock market, however, price has little to do with value, and even less to do with the definition of a blue-chip stock. Only as it relates to the dividend, to earnings or to book value is price an important measure of blue-chip quality.

Okay, so what is a blue chip? The term really refers to the quality of the company on which the stock is issued. A blue-chip company is one that has a long history of corporate excellence.

Six criteria define blue-chip quality. These guidelines mainly weigh dividends, earnings, profitability, institutional interest and liquidity.

Litmus Test for a Blue-Chip Company

1. The dividend has been raised at least five times in the past 12 years.
2. At least five million shares are outstanding.
3. At least 80 institutions hold the stock.
4. Earnings have improved in at least seven of the last 12 years.
5. There have been at least 25 years of uninterrupted dividends.
6. The stock carries a Standard & Poor's ranking of "A" or higher.

By studying each blue-chip characteristic on its own, it is easier to understand the rationale behind it. Explanations of the six criteria follow.

A RECORD OF DIVIDEND INCREASES

Few investors are in a position to know by personal contact if the management of a business is good or bad. Even if it were possible to meet every chief executive officer, president and corporate director, personality factors would influence one's opinion, perhaps inaccurately.

The only reliable way to recognize good management is by its long-term performance, by its proven ability to score successive gains in the net earnings of its company, gains that also are reflected by a substantial upward trend of increased dividends.

Of the utmost importance is a continuity of performance, the historic, steady rise in both the fortunes of the corporation and the dividends it pays. Dramatic ups and downs may be exciting, but they do not create a bulwark of investment confidence, nor do they create an admirable pattern of corporate growth. The trend also shows a willingness by management to share the company's good fortune with its stockholders, increasing the return on investment capital, enlarging their dividend income, boosting the value of their holdings and thereby contributing to superior total returns. The proof is in the payout.

AT LEAST FIVE MILLION SHARES OUTSTANDING

With enough common shares outstanding, a stock is assured of liquidity. Institutional investors purchase only companies that are liquid, with many shares outstanding, so that they can establish large investment positions without disturbing the price of the stock. Also, when the time comes to sell, they want to know that there will be buyers. An illiquid company leaves little room for an orderly entrance, or exit, by investors with large sums of capital at their disposal.

In other words, even institutional investors can buy and sell large blocks of stock without significantly moving the share price up or down. Sufficient liquidity guards against manipulation of share price.

AT LEAST 80 INSTITUTIONAL INVESTORS

To deny the importance of institutional interest on the trends of stock prices is to close one's eyes to the market's most influential group of investors, the real movers and shakers in the stock market. Like it or not, it is a fact of investment life that institutions (mutual funds, banks, insurance companies, pension and retirement funds) dominate approximately 80 percent of all stock trading in the market on any given day.

Because professional money managers bear a fiduciary responsibility to their clients, their conduct in the stock market is carefully scrutinized. They are accountable to the institutions for which they work, the Securities and Exchange Commission, the state commissioner of corporations and the clients for whom they manage money. They *must* invest in high-quality stocks.

It is also true that institutional investors tend to associate with, listen to and behave like other institutional investors. Consequently, institutional interest in a stock can be a mixed blessing. The professional investors can bid prices up too high when they favor a particular company or industry group, but they also can pull the rug out from under a stock when the news is bad and they all decide to sell at the same time.

Even so, when a stock is undervalued, institutions are more likely to be buying than selling. They are more apt to do their rug pulling when a stock is overvalued.

Of the six criteria for blue chips, the level of institutional ownership is the least rigid. And there is nothing magical about the number 80. What *is* important is evidence of widespread interest in a stock, that it has attracted a broad and diverse institutional following.

From the viewpoint of price stability, it would be preferable to find that 80 or more different institutions hold 50 percent of the common shares outstanding, rather than one or several institutions holding the same amount. There is safety in diversity. Information on institutional investors can be obtained from a full-service stockbroker. It also is included in some investor databases now available for home computers.

EARNINGS IMPROVED SEVEN OUT OF THE LAST 12 YEARS

Even under the finest management, corporate earnings can falter. There may be surprises in the economy, or problems in the industry, or changes that require a period of adjustment. A consistent record of earnings growth is very difficult to achieve, let alone sustain over a long period.

Still, we are looking for well-managed blue chips, not ordinary companies. To qualify, our standards insist that out of the most recent 12 years, corporate earnings should have improved in at least seven.

Such an earnings history shows us that a company can survive the hard times, as well as prosper and grow in the easy times. It also indicates that the reins of management are in good hands. It is no trick to succeed when times are right; but to succeed when times are bad requires intelligence, experience, foresight and superior leadership qualities.

AT LEAST 25 YEARS OF UNINTERRUPTED DIVIDENDS

This requirement is not etched in stone. Some companies listed in the "Investment Quality Trends" roster of 350 select blue chips have not yet been in business for 25 years. However, *most* of the companies on the list have paid dividends for 25 years or more.

Abbott Laboratories, for example, has paid uninterrupted dividends for 60 years. American Brands has paid dividends for more than 80 years. American Express has been rewarding its stockholders with uninterrupted dividends for 115 years. Citicorp has paid dividends for 172 years. Longest of all, Bank of Boston has paid its stockholders uninterrupted dividends since 1786—202 years.

Though this is not a hard and fast rule, in order for it to be relaxed, dividends at least must have been paid long enough for several cycles of undervalue and overvalue to be established, so that extremes of high and low dividend yield can be observed. (See figure 3.1.)

Another remarkable blue chip is Bristol-Myers. Bristol-Myers has an exemplary record. The company is more than 100 years old and has been paying dividends for 85 years with unfailing annual increases for the past 29 years. A diversified pharmaceutical and cosmetics company, more than 1,000 of Bristol-Myers products are marketed in 100 countries worldwide. The company holds first or second place in 16 of its 21 product categories.

The company's record shows that it has been able to continue dividend payments, keep company sales on a continual growth path, nurture the creation of new products, and at the same time compensate investors for their financial support by issuing dividends. (See figure 3.2.)

When Bristol-Myers's dividend yield indicates that it is undervalued, you can count on it to be a good buy.

STANDARD & POOR'S "A" RANKING

Standard & Poor's classifies common stock on a ranking based on earnings and dividends. The S&P Stock Guide explains the rankings: (See figure 3.3.)

FIGURE 3.1 Champion Dividend Payers

Among companies that have paid uninterrupted dividends far in excess of 25 years are the following blue-chip luminaries.

Company	*Years of Uninterrupted Dividends*
American Electric Power	77
American Home Products	66
Amoco	91
Baltimore Gas & Electric	75
Bankers Trust	70
Borden	86
Campbell Soup	83
Carter Wallace	103
Chase Manhattan	137
Chemical New York Bank	158
Chevron	73
Coca-Cola	92
Colgate-Palmolive	90
Commonwealth Edison	95
Consolidated Edison	101
Deluxe Check Printing	64
R. R. Donnelley	74
Dow Jones & Company	79
Du Pont	81
Eastman Kodak	83
Exxon	103
Fort Howard	63
Gannett Company	56
General Electric	86
General Mills	87
Gillette	79
Hawaiian Electric	84
Houston Industries	63
IBM	69
Imperial Oil	94
Jefferson-Pilot	73
Johnson & Johnson	80
K-Mart	72
Kellogg	62
Kroger	83
Eli Lilly	100
Manufacturers Hanover	133
Marsh & McLennan	62

FIGURE 3.1 Champion Dividend Payers (continued)

Company	*Years of Uninterrupted Dividends*
May Department Stores	74
Mellon Bank	90
Melville Corporation	68
Minnesota Mining & Manufacturing	69
Mobil Corporation	83
J. P. Morgan	93
National Fuel Gas	82
Norfolk & Southern	84
Oklahoma Gas & Electric	77
Pacific Lighting	76
J. C. Penney	63
Pfizer	84
Philadelphia Electric	83
Potomac Electric	83
PPG Industries	86
Procter & Gamble	94
Quaker Oats	79
RJR Nabisco	84
St. Paul Companies	113
San Diego Gas & Electric	76
Scott Paper	70
Sears, Roebuck	50
Security Pacific	104
SmithKline Beckman	62
Southern California Edison	76
Squibb Corporation	83
Stanley Works	108
Sun Company	81
Teco Energy	85
Texas Utilities	68
Times-Mirror	93
Travelers Corporation	121
Union Pacific	85
Unisys Corporation	90
Unocal	70
Upjohn	76
USG Corporation	66
Warner-Lambert	60
Westvaco	93
Wm. Wrigley Jr.	72

"The investment process involves assessment of various factors—such as product and industry position, corporate resources and financial policy—with results that make some common stocks more highly esteemed than others," says the guide. "Standard & Poor's believes that earnings and dividend performance is the end result of the interplay of these factors and that, over the long run, the record of this performance has a considerable bearing on relative quality."

A ranking, continues the stock guide, "is not a forecast of future market price performance, but is basically an appraisal of past performance of earnings and dividends, and relative current standing."

FALTERING ANGELS

Sometimes it makes sense to track stocks that no longer meet the six criteria relating to dividend payout, shares outstanding, institutional investors, earnings and ranking.

For example, a stock that originally carried an S&P "A" rating can run into temporary or cyclical difficulties. At least in the beginning of a rough phase, a blue-chip company receives the benefit of doubt. It is hoped that problems will be conquered and the quality rank will improve. Any company that slips below "B+," however, is deleted.

FALLEN ANGELS

Economic disasters of one kind or another have struck many industry groups in recent years.

Automobile manufacturers and steel companies are good examples of once-venerable stocks that have become tattered angels.

General Motors and Ford were, for many years, clearly qualified to be listed among the blue chips. So was Inland Steel and Armco. No longer are there any blue-chip investments in the auto industry due to its extremely cyclical nature and the inroads foreign manufacturers have made. Neither are there any blue chips in the old-technology steel industry.

Stocks such as Caterpillar Tractor, Union Carbide and Woolworth, which were industry leaders of the highest caliber, now wear the stigma of flawed investment quality. As in the case of International Harvester, such a fall from grace can lead to a major restructuring. The company

FIGURE 3.2 Dividend-Yield Chart

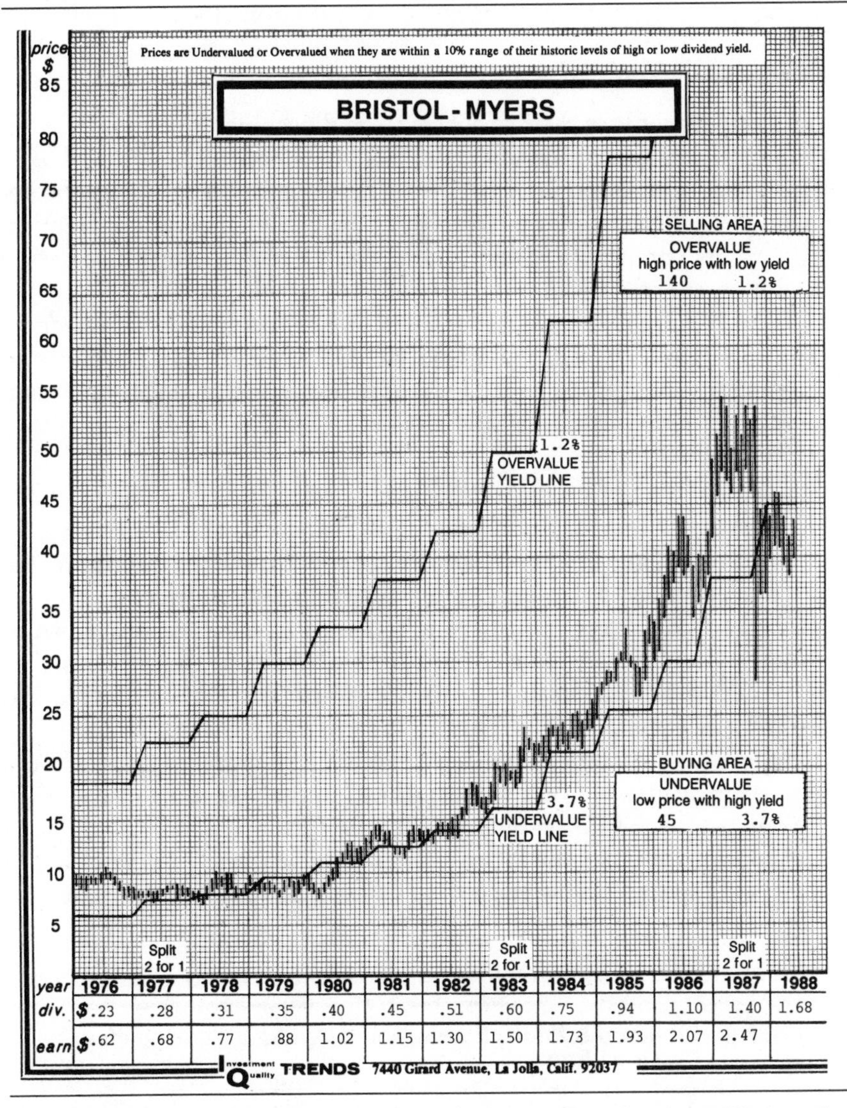

After establishing a base of undervalue (1977 through 1979), Bristol-Myers' stock rose 558 percent from 1980 to 1987. Frequent dividend increases paced the rising trend and kept the price near its undervalued yield line. The October 1987 crash carried the stock below undervalue, where historically good value became available.

sold off many divisions and changed its name to Navistar, to indicate its changed nature.

ANGELS UNAWARE

Stocks sometimes lose their select status and become impossible to evaluate for quality for reasons beyond their own control.

In 1983, for example, when AT&T was restructured and the regional telephone subsidiaries (the "Baby Bells") were divested, eight essentially new companies were formed. The telephone companies passed through an era of tremendous turmoil.

Though AT&T and the Baby Bells offer good quality, it is impossible to figure out the right dividend yield at which to buy or sell, since not enough time has passed to establish extremes of undervalue and overvalue in terms of dividend yield.

VALUE

But recognizing quality is not enough to guarantee profits in the stock market. Even a top-quality product can be overpriced.

Without conscious effort, we automatically measure relationships of price and value every day of our lives. It takes no genius to realize that $1,000 is an undervalued price for a new car, but an overvalued price for a new hat.

Once a high-quality, blue-chip stock is identified, investors should apply the measures of good value outlined in the preceding chapters. In this way, both safety of capital and total return are maximized.

If concern about value persists, it makes sense to buy stocks as if buying a company itself—as close to its net asset value (book value) as possible.

FIGURE 3.3 Standard & Poor's Earnings and Dividend Rankings for Common Stocks

A+	Highest	B+	Average	C	Lowest
A	High	B	Below average	D	In reorganization
A–	Above average	B–	Lower		

NR signifies no ranking because of insufficient data or because the stock is not amenable to the ranking process.

Measures of Good Value

Rule 1. A dividend yield that is historically high for that particular stock, and that repeatedly has signaled the bottom of a major declining trend in the price of that stock.

Rule 2. A price/earnings ratio that is historically low for that particular stock, and that is below the multiple for the Dow Jones Industrial Average. The only exceptions to this rule would be growth stocks with consistent records of rising earnings that are advancing faster than the market average and therefore can command higher-than-average price/earnings ratios.

Rule 3. A strong financial position with a ratio of current assets to current liabilities of at least two to one, and a debt-to-equity ratio of no more than 50 percent debt to equity.

Utility stocks are excluded from this debt ratio rule due to the special debt situation in force because of their regulated status.

Rule 4. A price that is no higher than one-third above the book value of the company—and the closer to book value, the better.

Again, this fourth rule can be broken in the case of companies with proven, superior, long-term growth characteristics. Such companies often are priced at many times book value, especially in a bull market.

The Dow Jones Industrial Average also has established significant price-to-book-value ratios over the years that can be used as indicators of stock market value.

Whenever the Dow Jones Industrial Average has been priced below book value, as it was in 1974 and other pivotal bear market years, stock prices generally were undervalued, and bargains abounded for discriminating investors. The bull market that began in December 1974 and did not end until 13 years later owed its longevity to its deep initial level of undervalue.

Conversely, we find that whenever the price of the Dow Jones Industrial Average rises 100 percent above book value, as a price-to-book-value ratio of two to one, the market is ready to top and investors had better beware. On August 25, 1987, at the peak of the bull market, the price-to-book-value ratio was 2.7 to one, one of the highest such readings in stock market history.

ATTENTION TO FUNDAMENTALS

To emphasize a point made earlier, the linking of quality and value in the stock market can help investors select timely, undervalued stocks. Close attention to fundamental investment precepts may not be the most glamorous approach to the stock market, but it is the safest and most sane way to ensure long-term investment success. And having money grow is glamorous, making patience quite worth the effort.

Now that quality and value can be spotted, become thoroughly acquainted with the cyclical forces that propel stocks and the stock market.

Bargains Come in Cycles

4

Bargains Come in Cycles

"Nature, to be commanded, must be obeyed."

—FRANCIS BACON

The solar system itself, with moons circling around planets and planets whirling around the sun, is built upon a series of cycles. Cycles are everywhere, from the wonderfully mysterious birth, growth, aging and death pattern of our lives to the mundane consumer's durable goods cycle. Even history seems to follow some cycles. While the past does not always repeat itself in exactly the same way, history does provide important lessons on which to base future expectations.

The past very often is repeated in the stock market, where prices are influenced strongly by human responses and reactions to financial and economic events that occur time after time.

CYCLES OF DIVIDEND YIELD

As you already have noticed, the dividend-yield theory, too, has a cyclical aspect. And these cycles are interconnected with the ebb and flow of the stock market and the great surging rhythms of national and world economies.

Before delving into the cyclical aspect of the dividend-yield theory, this is a good place to review the basic concept behind it: when all other factors that merit analytical consideration have been digested, the underlying value of dividends, which determines yield, will in the long run also determine price.

Tracking the price of a stock, as so many investors do, is meaningless. A company may have been overvalued at ten dollars per share five years ago, but if dividends have risen dramatically, the same stock could be undervalued at $25 today. So price is significant only as part of the formula for determining dividend yield.

Years of stock market research have shown that stocks generally fluctuate between repetitive extremes of high dividend yield and low dividend yield. These recurring extremes of yield can be used to establish a channel of undervalued and overvalued price levels.

The tops and bottoms of cycles are determined simply by charting the dividend yield of a stock over a long enough period of time for the dividend-yield pattern to emerge. By calculating the historic points at which a stock turns down, or reverses a slide and turns up, the future behavior of that stock can be anticipated.

Because charting stocks over a long stretch can be time-consuming and cumbersome, the charts for all 30 of the Dow Jones Industrial Average stocks, plus 40 others, are provided in this book, along with a brief analysis of their dividend patterns (see appendix).

The shares of Tyler Corporation, a company that supplies products and services to industry ranging from explosives to industrial and residential pipe, have followed a predictable fluctuating pattern for more than a decade.

The Tyler chart, figure 4.1, has two major horizontal lines. The solid line at the top represents a 2.2 percent dividend yield, where the stock is overvalued and a sale should be considered. The solid line at the bottom represents a 4.5 percent yield, where the price of Tyler is undervalued and a purchase can be made. The vertical lines indicate the actual monthly price range of Tyler. It is apparent that when Tyler's dividend yield moves above the overvalue yield line or below the undervalue yield line, a reversal in the price trend takes place. Again, these undervalued and overvalued points for Tyler (2.2 percent and 4.5 percent dividend yields) are established by nothing more than studying a chart of historic dividend yields and noting the points where the stock normally reverses direction.

FIGURE 4.1 Dividend-Yield Chart

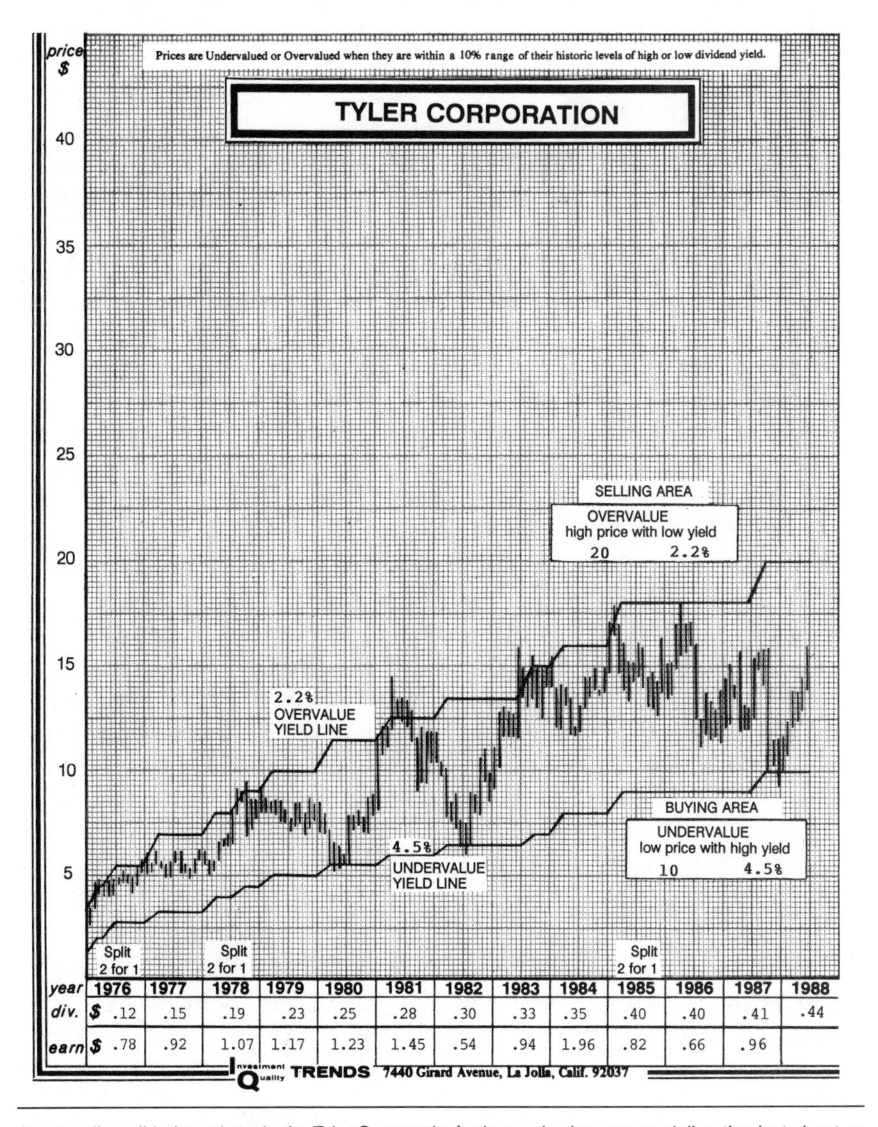

A generally well-behaved stock, the Tyler Corporation's share price has reversed direction just about on cue. It is a good buy when the dividend yield is 4.5 percent. Indications are that the share price is about to rise. To maximize total return, Tyler should be sold when its dividend yield declines to 2.2 percent. At that point, Tyler's price will be historically high.

When a dividend is raised, the undervalue and overvalue price limits are raised automatically so they will continue to reflect the historically established yield percentages. Or, if the price of the stock falls, the yield will move higher, indicating that the stock is still undervalued.

UNDERLYING LOGIC

These cycles establish themselves for good reasons. It works much like the old supply-and-demand theory taught in Economics 101. When a stock has declined in price to where the dividend yield is historically and attractively high, knowledgeable, long-term investors with large amounts of capital are motivated to buy. This accumulative buying halts the decline, stabilizes the price and begins to reverse the trend. An apparent reversal in the price of a stock then attracts other investors, and the price begins to rise.

As a rising trend continues, less sophisticated investors are attracted to the stock, while at the same time, investors who purchased the stock at undervalued prices become more and more inclined to secure their profits by initiating a sale. By the time the price reaches its historic level of overvalue, the yield is not alluring enough to attract a sufficient number of new buyers.

So, as more and more previous buyers secure their profits, the price begins to decline. A declining price trend alerts other stockholders to the possibility that their stock has fallen into investment disfavor. They become concerned, they sell, and the price continues to move downward until a historically high dividend yield again attracts enough new investors to halt the decline. There, at undervalue, the long-term investment cycle appears all over again.

INDIVIDUALITY IS IMPORTANT

Most important, each stock has its own distinctive high and low yield characteristics and must be evaluated individually. Some stocks yield 4.0 percent at undervalue and 2.0 percent at overvalue. Other stocks may bring 6.0 percent at undervalue and 2.5 percent or 3.0 percent at overvalue.

For example, Abbott Laboratories yields 3.5 percent at undervalue and 1.4 percent at overvalue. Pitney Bowes yields 5.0 percent at undervalue and 1.5 percent at overvalue. General Electric (see appendix) has established its profile of value between yield extremes of 5.0 percent at undervalue and 2.0 percent at overvalue. (See figures 4.2 and 4.3.)

This process, as explained earlier, measures total return. Therefore, a high-growth company with a rapidly rising share price can pay a low dividend and still offer appreciation in terms of total return. Slow-growth companies, such as utilities and those in mature industries, must pay a higher dividend in order to compete.

A FIVE-YEAR CYCLE

The average length of time required for a stock to rise from undervalue to overvalue is three years. Some stocks complete the journey in less time. Other stocks, especially those with frequent dividend increases that lift the prices at undervalue and overvalue, have a long upward climb; they may be held longer before a sale at overvalue is necessary.

The downhill run is a little faster. Typically, the transit from overvalue to undervalue takes two years. Hence, the time required to complete the full cycle averages about five years.

IMPRESSIVE ACHIEVEMENTS

Investors who buy shares when they are at the undervalued stage of the cycle and sell when they reach their historic overvalued level accomplish three objectives. They:

1. minimize downside risk in the stock market,
2. maximize upside potential for capital gains and
3. maximize growth of dividend income by buying maximum dividends at the lowest price possible.

As Baron de Rothschild once advised an investor, the secret to success in the stock market is to "buy cheap and sell dear." Determining the cycles of dividend-yield characteristic to each blue-chip stock is the key to knowing when a stock *is* "dear" or "cheap."

BULL AND BEAR CYCLES

Benjamin Graham, the respected proponent of investment on the basis of value, noted that a classic definition of a shrewd investor is one who bought in a bear market when everyone else was selling and one who

FIGURE 4.2 Dividend-Yield Chart

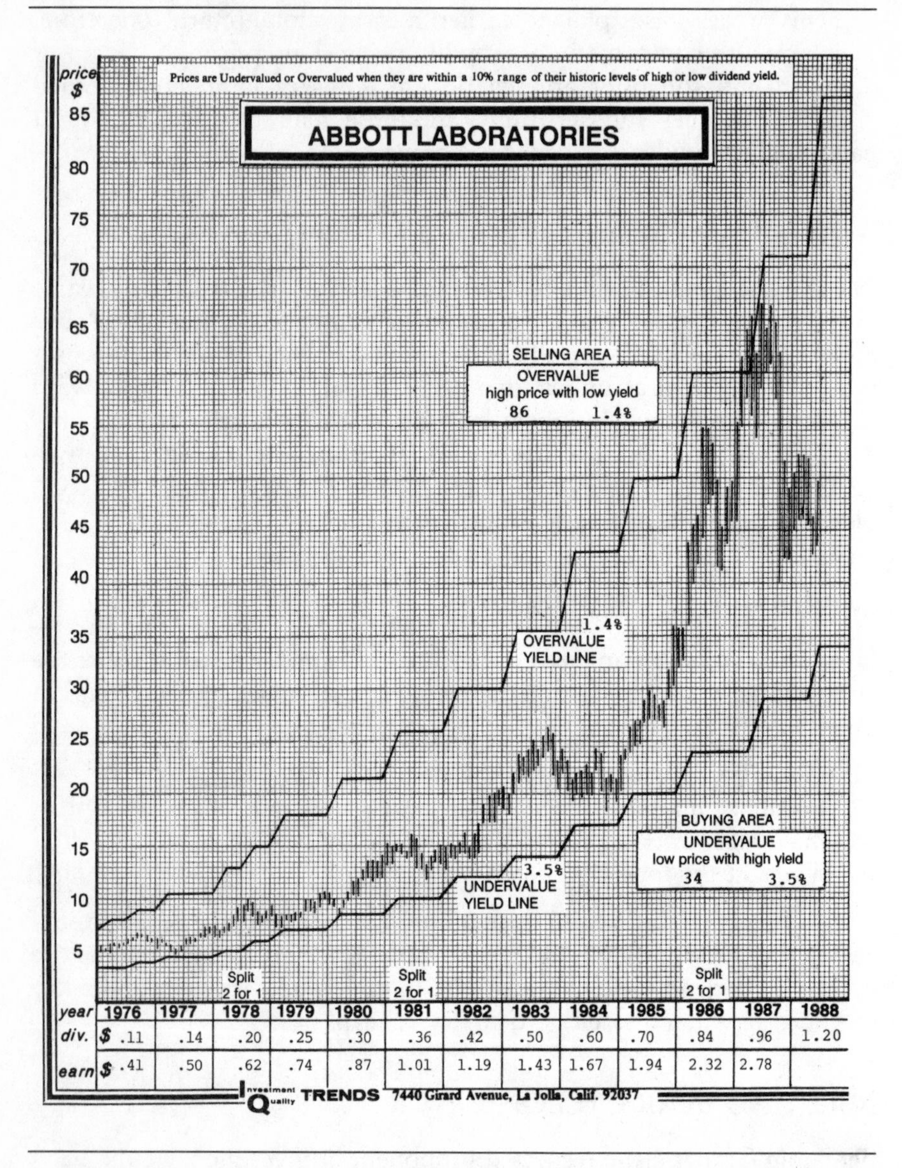

These two well-known companies show how different the dividend yield profiles for individual stocks can be. Their individuality reflects, among other factors, the diverse industries in which they operate, the maturity of the companies and various management philosophies.

FIGURE 4.3 Dividend-Yield Chart

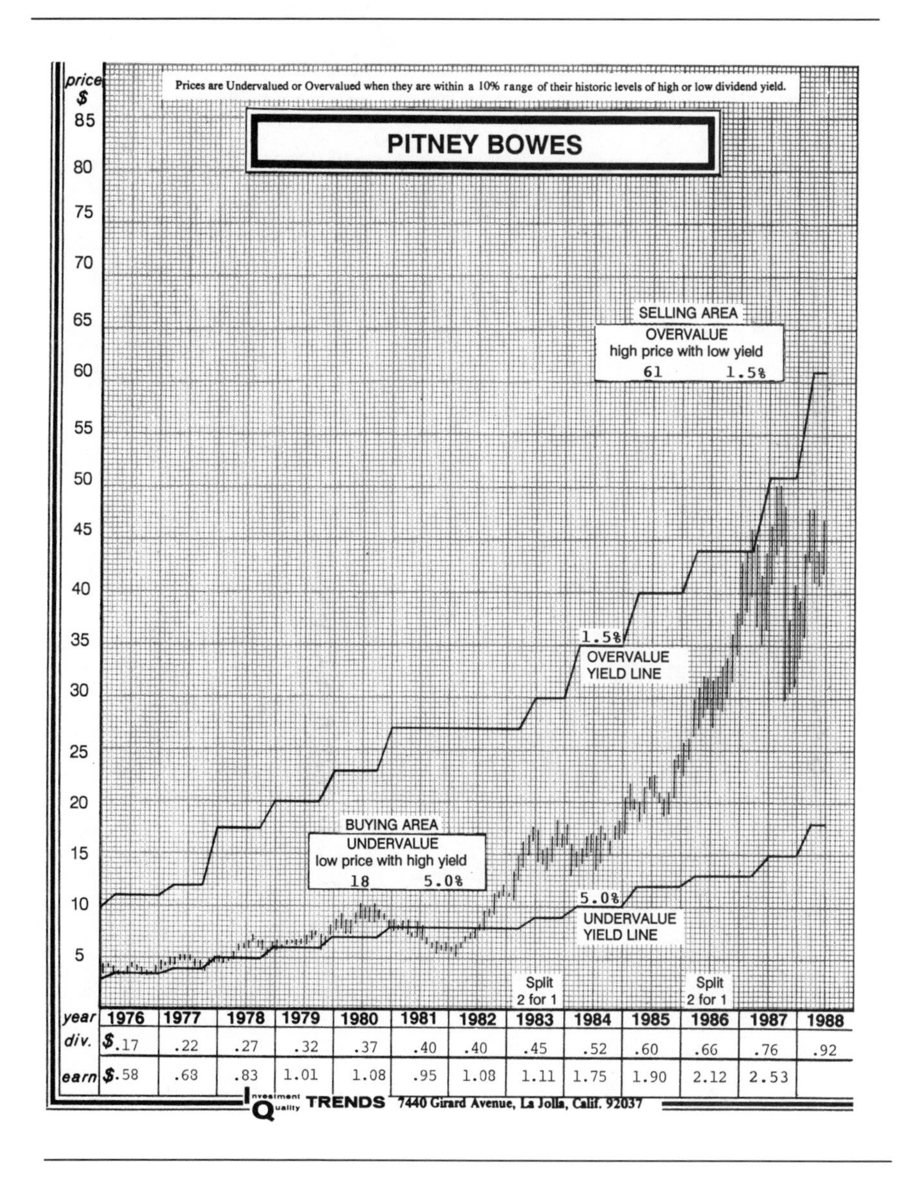

year	1976	1977	1978	1979	1980	1981	1982	1983	1984	1985	1986	1987	1988
div.	$.17	.22	.27	.32	.37	.40	.40	.45	.52	.60	.66	.76	.92
earn	$.58	.68	.83	1.01	1.08	.95	1.08	1.11	1.75	1.90	2.12	2.53	

FIGURE 4.4 Dividend-Yield Profile for the DJIA, 1947 to 1988

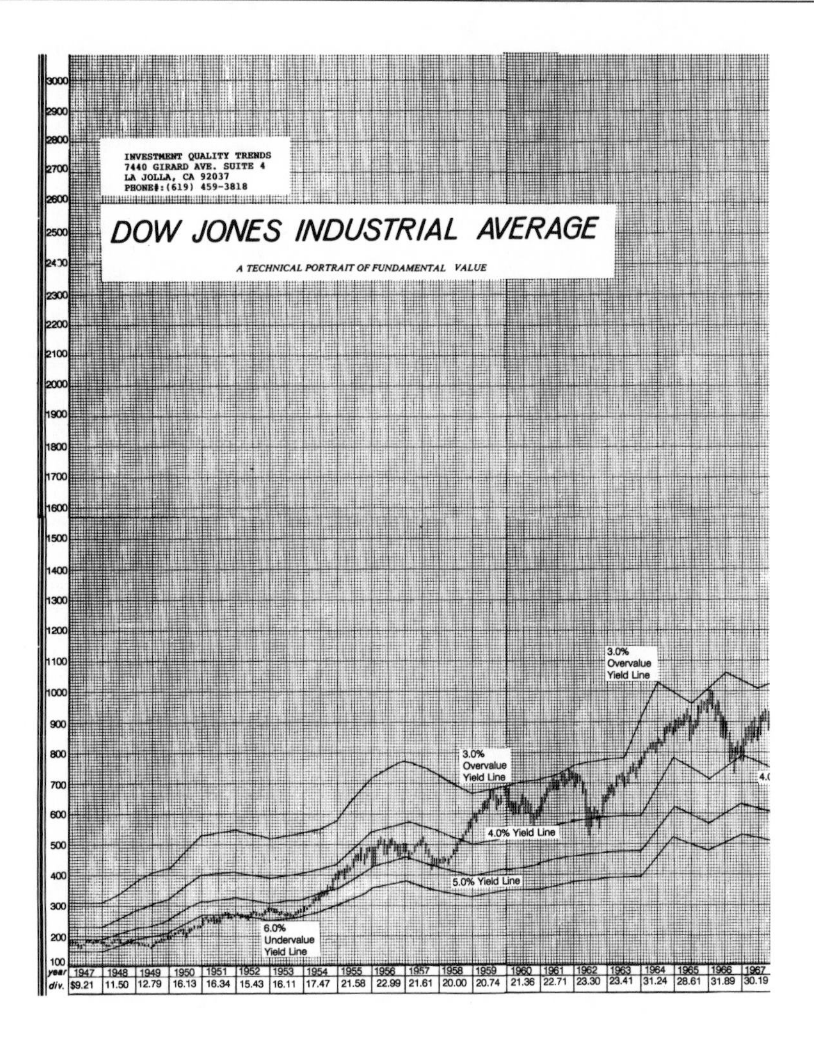

FIGURE 4.4 (concluded)

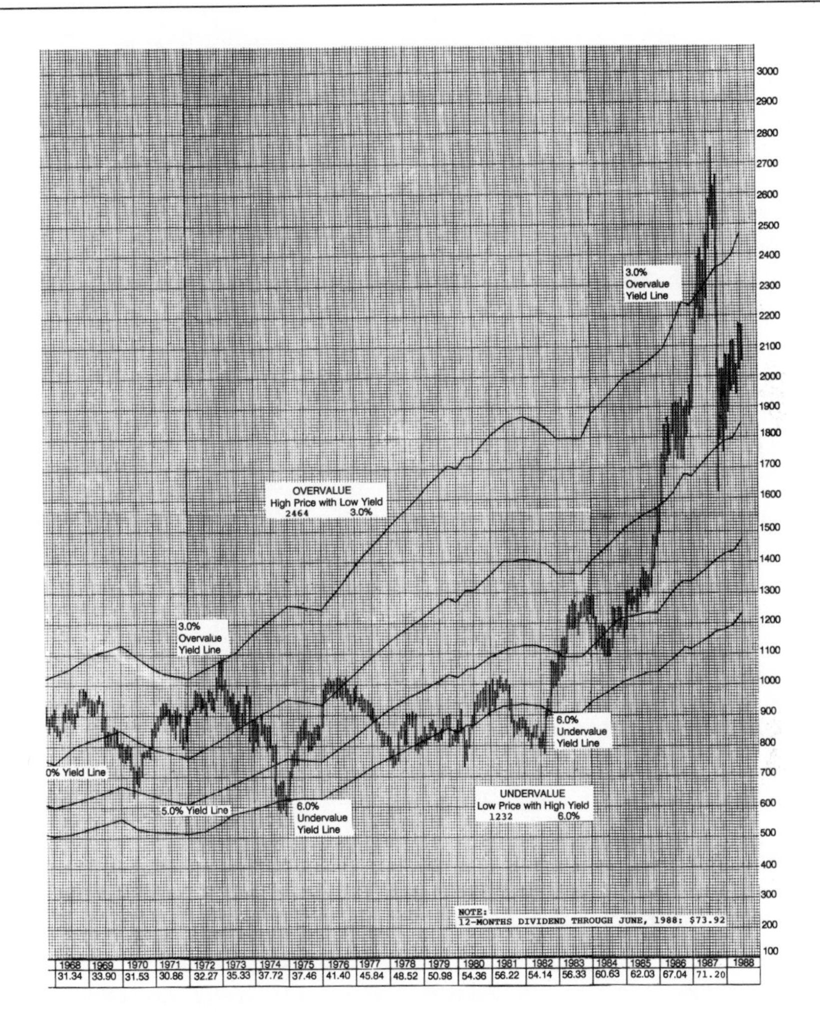

Through wars and peace, through inflationary periods, through expansion and recession, the Dow Jones Industrial Average fluctuates in a remarkably predictable pattern. The market the Dow represents is overvalued at a dividend yield below three percent, and undervalued at a dividend yield above six percent.

sold in a bull market when everyone else was buying. A solid contrarian philosophy, it sounds simple enough. But even the author had tongue in cheek when he wrote those words.

While the stock market reflects generally recognizable patterns, and bull and bear markets run from an average of four to seven years, the deviations from normal patterns are frequent enough to make it difficult for most observers to know exactly where the market is at any given time. If it is a bull market, is it a young bull with far to go, or is it near the end of its life? If it is a bear market, is it still falling or near the bottom?

The bull market that reached such a dramatic climax in late 1987 actually started in 1974—that's 13 years of growth! Even though the long-term trend was skyward during those years, investors may have been confused by several corrections that may have seemed like the beginning of a bear market.

The last bear market was eight years long, starting in 1966 and ending in 1974.

Economists usually agree only in retrospect as to when the true market roofs and floors have been established. However, when applied to the DJIA, the dividend-yield theory has given strong and reliable signals at these junctures.

DOW JONES GUIDELINES

Just as parameters of value can be established for individual stocks, so, too, good buying and selling areas can be established for the Dow Jones Industrial Average. The chart of the DJIA in figure 4.4 is a technical portrait of fundamental value, expressed by the dividend yield, extending back over the past 40 years. The top line of the chart shows when, in terms of dividend yield, the Dow and, hence, the market it represents are overvalued. The bottom line indicates a Dow level at which the market in general is undervalued.

It is evident that the Industrial Average has offered historically good value when the yield on the composite dividend rose to six percent, as it did in 1949 to 1953, in 1974 and from 1978 to 1982. In those years, the market offered good buying opportunities. They proved to be the times to load up on blue-chip stocks. The yield in 1982, just prior to the start of the final and strongest leg of the most recent bull market, was 6.9 percent.

The DJIA chart also shows that whenever the average yield of the Dow reaches three percent, to the top line on the chart, a rising trend has been reversed. This happened in 1959, 1961, 1966, 1968 and 1973—all of those years proved to be major tops in the market.

BEWARE THE IDES OF MARCH

In March of 1987, the composite dividend for the Dow Jones Industrial Average was $67.04 per share. When the price of the Dow then rose to 2235, the yield became three percent, and the market became overvalued. From then on, there was severe risk of a market reversal.

The bull market peaked on August 25, 1987, when the Dow Jones Industrial Average peaked at a price of 2722.42. The dividend yield at the end of the day hit an amazing low of 2.6 percent, making the DJIA more extremely overvalued than it ever had been in its 91-year history. (See figure 4.5.)

For the most part, the swings in the stock market indicators, whether one follows the Dow or the S&P 500 or some other composite index, do not represent the master key as to when and in what to invest. There are always some rising stocks in a bear market and some falling stocks in a bull market. The indices merely take the temperature of the market; market cycles can tell investors little about the selection of individual purchases.

LIMITED SELECTION AT BOTTOM, PLENTY AT TOP

Even so, as expected, at the bottom of a descending market are more undervalued stocks from which to choose, and at the top of an ascending market fewer undervalued shares are available for investment.

DISCOVERING A NEW INDICATOR

Based on that observation, in tracking a select universe of blue chips, yet another cyclical indicator emerges. The stocks we monitor are grouped together in categories of undervalued, overvalued, rising trends (where the price has risen at least ten percent from its undervalued base) and declining trends (where the price has declined at least ten percent from its overvalued peak). We regularly calculate how many stocks are in each category and what percent that number is of the total. Each category has been tracked for at least 25 years. This important indicator is called, "I.Q. Trends' Blue-Chip Trend Verifier." (See figure 4.5.)

When those figures are charted and compared with highs and lows on the Dow Industrials, it becomes clear that whenever the percentage of stocks in the undervalued category rises to between 73 percent and 80 percent of the total, the DJIA is at a low in its cycle, where many good buying opportunities are presented.

Conversely, when the percentage of undervalued stocks falls to 17 percent or less, the market is overvalued and vulnerable to a major decline.

In 1973, at the top of that bull market, 17 percent of the blue chips tracked were undervalued. In 1968, just before the market started a major decline, 12 percent of the stocks were categorized as undervalued. At the top in 1973, 32 percent of the stocks were listed in the overvalued category.

Jumping ahead to the spring of 1987, stocks in the undervalued category fell to only 12 percent of the total, the same reading found at the top of the market in 1968, and a lower percentage than in 1973. Thirty-three percent of our blue-chip stocks were in the overvalued category at that time, virtually the same reading found in earlier turnaround years.

In September 1987, when the market had already peaked but still hadn't taken its major plunge, 143 stocks on the tracking list were overvalued. That represented 41 percent of the total, the largest number and percentage of overvalued stocks ever to be listed in the 21-year history of the "Investment Quality Trends" newsletter. Until then, the high was 37 percent recorded in 1973 just prior to a major decline.

The DJIA was stretched to extreme levels of overvalue. Based on those cyclical trends, subscribers who had not already done so were advised to sell their overvalued stocks in market rallies. That admonition turned out to be timely. The market shock in October 1987 brought with it a new worry: was the booming economy going to turn downward as well?

VALUE STILL PREVAILS

While sensitivity to ups and downs in the economy and the overall stock market can help somewhat in achieving long-term investment goals, it is a mistake to become preoccupied with those cycles that are not directly related to the underlying quality and value of a company's shares.

FIGURE 4.5 The Trend Verifier Chart

Mid-August 1987

350 SELECT BLUE CHIPS—SUMMARY

Undervalued stocks	47 (13%)	Rising trend stocks	122 (35%)
Overvalued stocks	139 (40%)	Declining trend stocks	42 (12%)

By late summer 1987, *Investment Quality Trends Newsletter* reported that the percentage of stocks that were overvalued, in terms of dividend yield, was the highest in the newsletter's 21-year history.

"The most realistic distinction between the investor and the speculator," wrote Benjamin Graham in *The Intelligent Investor,* "is found in their attitude toward stock market movements. The speculator's primary interest lies in anticipating and profiting from market fluctuations. The investor's primary interest lies in acquiring and holding suitable securities at suitable prices."

Undervalued Stocks

"Genius is nothing but a greater aptitude for patience."

GEORGES LOUIS LECLERC DE BUFFON

It is an ill-kept investment secret that for every stock, there is a propitious time to buy and a prudent time to sell. If dividend income and investment growth are to be maximized, timing is all-important. Unless stocks are purchased when they are undervalued or in rising trends, stockholders may experience the painful realization that their investment capital has diminished, not grown. Regardless of glamorous growth labels or pie-in-the-sky income reports, growth of investment capital can be achieved only through strict adherence to value.

The surest way to spot a stock that is a good value—undervalued and ripe for purchase—is to track the dividend yield on the blue chips that may be investment targets. This tough-minded loyalty to established guidelines is important, because the possibility always exists of becoming caught up in the emotionalism of an exciting market or infatuated with charismatic company leadership. After all, investors are only human.

A STATISTICAL APPROACH

The approach to value through dividend yield is technical in the sense that it focuses on supply and demand as a factor in establishing share price and the change in price. It also plucks the best from fundamental analysis, in that it respectfully heeds the financial solidarity of the underlying company.

The dividend-yield theory identifies the cycles of undervalue and overvalue in terms of dividend yield, where, over the years, investors have been motivated to buy and sell their stock holdings. In that regard, it technically measures the sentiment and habit patterns of investors, as they view each individual stock.

But the approach is not coldly statistical. It is rooted in the most basic of all investment fundamentals—the dividend, representing, as it does, the current cash return a stockholder can realize on investment capital.

Technical: the charting of dividend yield
Fundamental: application to blue-chip stocks, as defined in this book

Stockholders have established these levels of undervalue and overvalue unconsciously. It has happened naturally and automatically, based on the evaluations of thousands of attentive investors.

SETTING PERIMETERS OF VALUE

Each stock has its own profile of undervalue and overvalue in terms of dividend yield, and each must be studied individually. Any investor can establish the dividend-yield profile of any stock paying a dividend. This is done by computing the dividend yield over a decade or longer (25 years is preferred) and charting the ups and downs on a grid, with the months and years running horizontally and the prices running vertically.

The historic high and low dividend-yield points—or "turning points"—can be seen on the stock's chart. It will become apparent that the stock in question turns in the vicinity of the same dividend yield each cycle. By averaging the turning points, the boundaries of bottom and top are defined.

Example: Company Alpha (a fictitious firm) reversed and began to climb at a 4.5 percent dividend yield in 1980, at a 4.4 yield in 1981 and at a 4.7 yield in 1984. In 1978 the stock reached a two percent dividend yield, indicating its top price for that cycle. In 1983 it went to 1.7 percent dividend yield, then in 1986 it hit two percent again, and traded above and below that yield for more than a year. This simple analysis shows that Company Alpha is likely to reverse a declining trend at about a 4.5 percent dividend yield, and apt to reverse a climbing trend at two percent. Remember, dividend yield is figured using both price and dividend, so the price of the stock at those junctures will vary, depending on the dollar amount of the dividend.

On the charts presented in this book, a solid line has been set at the historic dividend-yield points, creating an undervalue and overvalue line. While depicted as solid on the charts, the lines are actually somewhat fuzzy, as will be discussed in the pages ahead.

Let's consider a real-life example. By examining the chart for Allied-Signal Corporation (tracked from 1975 through March 1988) in figure 5.1, the cycles become clear.

Alied-Signal, the chart reveals, represents good value when the dividend yield is at seven percent. The stock is overvalued when the price rises and the yield falls to 3.5 percent. During the October 19, 1987 crash, Allied-Signal declined to a price of twenty-six. Based on the annual dividend of $1.80, the yield was seven percent and the stock was historically undervalued, as shown in the following equation.

Dividend		Price		Yield
$1.80	÷	$26	=	7.0%

A seven percent yield also identified good value in 1978, 1982 and in 1984.

One of the largest non-oil mergers in history took place in 1985 when Allied Corporation (founded in 1920 as Allied Chemical and Dye Corporation) merged with the Signal Companies (a blue-chip conglomerate with annual sales of six billion dollars). The merger set off a series of dramatic changes that altered the company's portfolio of businesses and secured its position as a powerful advanced technology company with more than one-half its operations serving the aerospace and electronics industries. Allied, it will be remembered, acquired Bendix Corporation (aviation and aerospace) in a widely publicized takeover in 1983. Today, the company is divided into three segments: aerospace, automotive and engineered materials. In each segment, Allied has a leadership position.

FIGURE 5.1 Dividend-Yield Chart

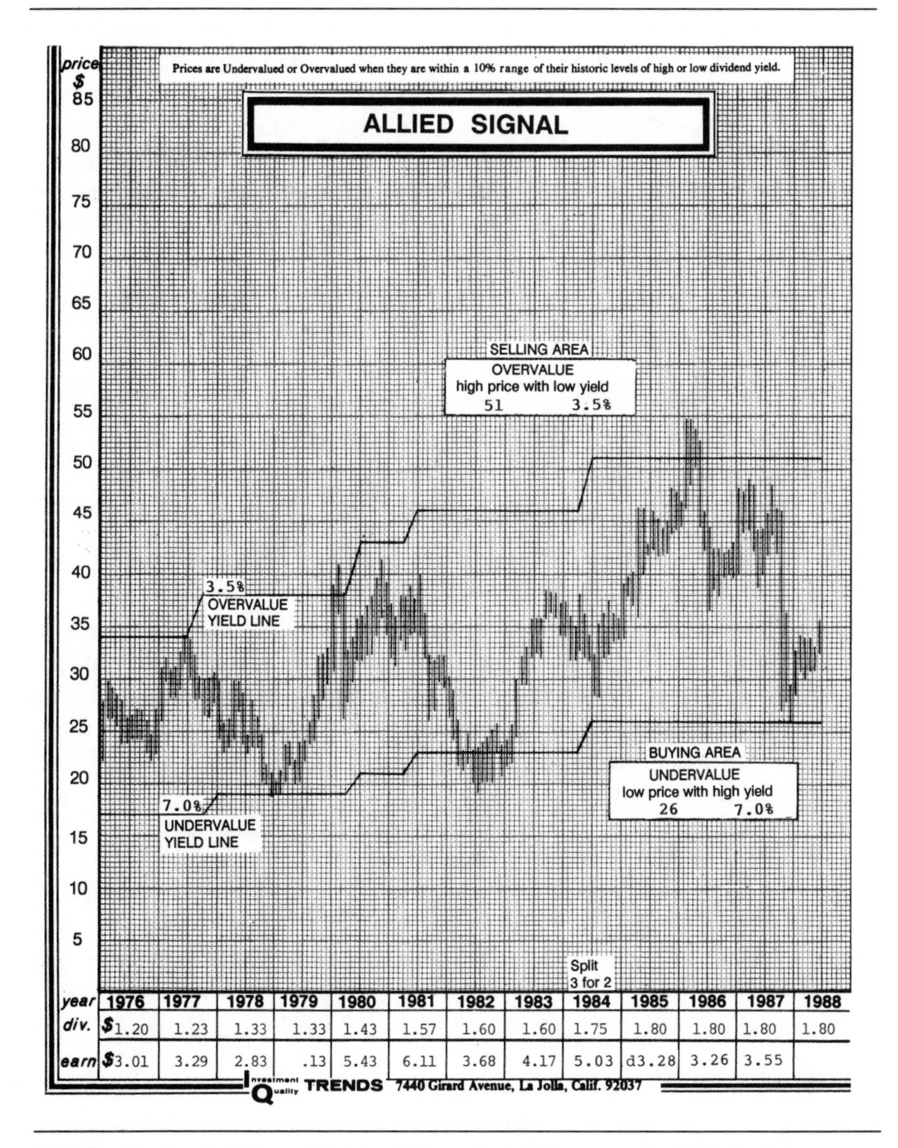

Allied-Signal generally fluctuates between yield extremes of 3.5 percent at overvalue and 7.0 percent at undervalue. Whenever this stock is priced to yield 7.0 percent, a profitable buying opportunity is at hand. When the price rises and the yield declines to 3.5 percent, a sale should be considered to preserve capital and profits. Like most companies, Allied-Signal does not rise or fall in a straight line.

For the past two years, Allied-Signal has been honing its market strategies and restructuring its operations. Several divisions have been sold and existing operations have been tightened. The company now is concentrating its resources on its strongest businesses which offer the highest returns. It is interesting to note that despite the fact that many changes have taken place in the form and composition of this company, the yields at overvalue and undervalue for its stock have not changed. A seven percent dividend yield continues to mark an area of good investment value. A yield of 3.5 percent identifies an area in which the stock should be sold.

KEEPING TRACK

The dividend-yield theory requires a certain amount of record-keeping. At the very least, an investor needs to know the undervalue and overvalue perimeters of the stocks that are of interest. After that, it is a matter of keeping track of the stock as it progresses through its cycles, making certain that the company does not slip quietly out of the kingdom of blue-chip stocks. When dividends are increased, the yield should be refigured to avoid selling too soon.

We have analyzed more than 350 blue chips in the manner employed with Allied-Signal. In order to keep tabs on their movement, the stocks are grouped into categories of undervalue, overvalue, rising trends and declining trends. Current prices, dividends, yields, earnings and other information are charted for each one.

Figure 5.2 shows the undervalued category and how the information related to quality and value is arranged. With this system, it can be determined at a glance which bargain stocks fit a particular investment goal. For example, a stock such as American Medical International, which has a "G" code (for rapid growth) and an "x" code (current price below undervalue), can be expected to have more upside or growth potential than the Bank of Boston (see figure 13.2), which had already entered its rising phase at this time. (AMI's dividend-yield chart is shown in figure 5.3.)

The listing of stocks in the undervalued category reflects conditions as they existed on March 1, 1987. But the stock market is alive and ever changing. Within six months the stocks in this illustration had shifted, painting a different, progressing picture. Because markets, industries and individual stocks exist in a dynamic world, vigilance must be maintained on the stocks one owns or is considering purchasing.

FIGURE 5.2 Undervalued Category

BUYING AREA:
Each stock has declined in price to produce its own distinctive high dividend yield. A further dip in price is minimized, since unreasonably higher dividend yield then would result.

STOCK		Change in Category	Current Price		Current Ind Ann Div	Current Div Yield	Potential Pts. Up	Potential % Up	TO Overvalue High Price	Overvalue Low Yield	S&P Qual Rank	Earn Last 12 Mos (Up or Down)	Price/Earns Ratio	Blue-Chip Status
AMERICAN ELEC. POWER			30		2.26	7.6%	60	201%	90	2.5%	A–	2.62U	11	6
AMER. MEDICAL INTL.	G	x	19	=	0.72	3.8%	29	153%	48	1.5%	A–	Deficit	0	5
ATLANTIC CITY ELEC.			38	=	2.62	6.9%	52	138%	90	2.9%	A–	3.50	11	5
AZP GROUP		x	31	=	2.72	8.8%	87	281%	118	2.3%	A–	3.04D	10	6
BAKER INTERNATIONAL		x	16	★	0.46	2.9%	42	259%	58	0.8%	A–	Deficit	0	6
BAXTER TRAVENOL	G		25	★	0.44	1.8%	24	96%	49	0.9%	A	1.70U	15	6
CAROLINA POWER-LT.			40	★	2.76	7.0%	70	176%	110	2.5%	A–	3.96	10	6
CENTERIOR ENERGY		x	24	=	2.56	10.7%	64	268%	88	2.9%	–	3.04	8	5
CHEMICAL NY CORP.		r	47	★	2.72	5.8%	44	93%	91	3.0%	A+	7.47U	6	6
CINCINNATI GAS-ELEC.		x	28		2.16	7.8%	44	157%	72	3.0%	–	3.38	8	4
COLUMBIA GAS			49	=	3.18	6.5%	35	71%	84	3.8%	A–	1.82U	27	6
COMMONWEALTH EDISON			38		3.00	7.9%	45	119%	83	3.6%	A	4.69U	8	5
DETROIT EDISON		x	19		1.68	8.9%	32	168%	51	3.3%	A–	2.58U	7	5
DOMINION RESOURCES		R	46	=	2.96	6.5%	95	206%	141	2.1%	A–	4.10U	11	6
DPL INC.		r	28	=	2.00	7.2%	29	104%	57	3.5%	B+	3.05U	9	5
FIRST CHICAGO CORP.		x	32	★	1.50	4.7%	43	134%	75	2.0%	B+	4.70U	7	5
HALLIBURTON			31		1.00	3.3%	36	115%	67	1.5%	B+	Deficit	0	5
HOSPITAL CORP. OF AMER.	G	New	34	★	0.72	2.2%	69	203%	103	0.7%	A+	2.08D	16	5
HUMANA INC.	G	x	23	=	0.76	3.4%	31	136%	54	1.4%	A–	0.40D	58	5
IDAHO POWER		x	26	=	1.80	7.0%	34	131%	60	3.0%	A–	2.00U	13	6
ILLINOIS POWER		x	30		2.64	8.9%	45	151%	75	3.5%	A–	3.98U	8	6
IMPERIAL OIL			42	=	1.60	3.9%	28	66%	70	2.3%	B+	1.74D	24	5
INTERSTATE POWER		r	28	=	1.96	7.1%	28	100%	56	3.5%	A–	2.05D	14	5
IPALCO ENTERPRISES		R	26	=	1.52	5.9%	22	83%	48	3.2%	A–	3.27	8	6
LOUISVILLE GAS-ELEC.		x	39	=	2.60	6.7%	65	167%	104	2.5%	B+	3.26	12	5
MANUFTRS HANOVER		r	47	=	3.28	7.0%	37	79%	84	3.9%	A	7.99	6	6
NALCO CHEMICAL	G		33		1.20	3.7%	27	82%	60	2.0%	A	1.62D	20	6
NY STATE ELEC.-GAS		x	30	=	2.64	8.9%	53	175%	83	3.2%	A	3.86U	8	6
NIAGARA MOHAWK POWER		x	17	=	2.08	12.3%	(NOTE: Dividend in Danger)					2.71D	6	6
OHIO EDISON		x	22	★	1.96	9.0%	39	178%	61	3.2%	B+	2.47	9	5
PACIFIC GAS-ELEC.			27	=	1.92	7.2%	37	137%	64	3.0%	A	2.60	10	6
PANHANDLE EASTERN			31		2.00	6.5%	(NOTE: Dividend in Danger)					Deficit	0	6
PHILADELPHIA ELEC.			24	=	2.20	9.2%	43	178%	67	3.3%	A–	2.60	9	5
PUBLIC SERVICE COLO.		x	22	=	2.00	9.1%	(NOTE: Dividend in Danger)					0.13D	0	5
ROCHESTER GAS-ELEC.		x	25	=	2.20	8.9%	56	226%	81	2.7%	A	3.33	8	5
SCHLUMBERGER	G		37	=	1.20	3.3%	55	149%	92	1.3%	A	Deficit	0	6
SHELL TRANSP.-TRADING	G	R	64	★	2.97	4.7%	71	111%	135	2.2%	A	5.87U	11	5
SONAT INC.		x	28	=	2.14	7.7%	58	206%	86	2.5%	A	3.17U	9	6
STANDARD OIL COMPANY			Below-Average S&P quality; stock will be replaced.											
TEXACO		R	34		3.00	8.9%	33	96%	67	4.5%	B+	3.01D	11	5
TEXAS UTILITIES			35	★	2.80	8.1%	65	186%	100	2.8%	A+	4.45U	8	6
UTAH POWER-LIGHT		x	29		2.32	8.1%	46	158%	75	3.1%	A–	2.26	13	6
VALLEY NATL. CORP.		x	40	=	1.44	3.7%	71	177%	111	1.3%	A–	4.97U	8	6

FOOTNOTE LEGEND

) A dividend increase appears imminent.
= The dividend has been increased within 12 months.
★ The most recent dividend was raised.
G Rapid growth stock with 10% compounded annual dividend growth rate.
x Current price is below undervalue, or above overvalue.

Change in Category:
Capital letter identifies a change, since the last issue.
Lowercase letter identifies a change within the past two months.
All initials in this column designate the former category.
U—Undervalued O—Overvalued R—Rising D—Declining

FIGURE 5.3 Dividend-Yield Chart

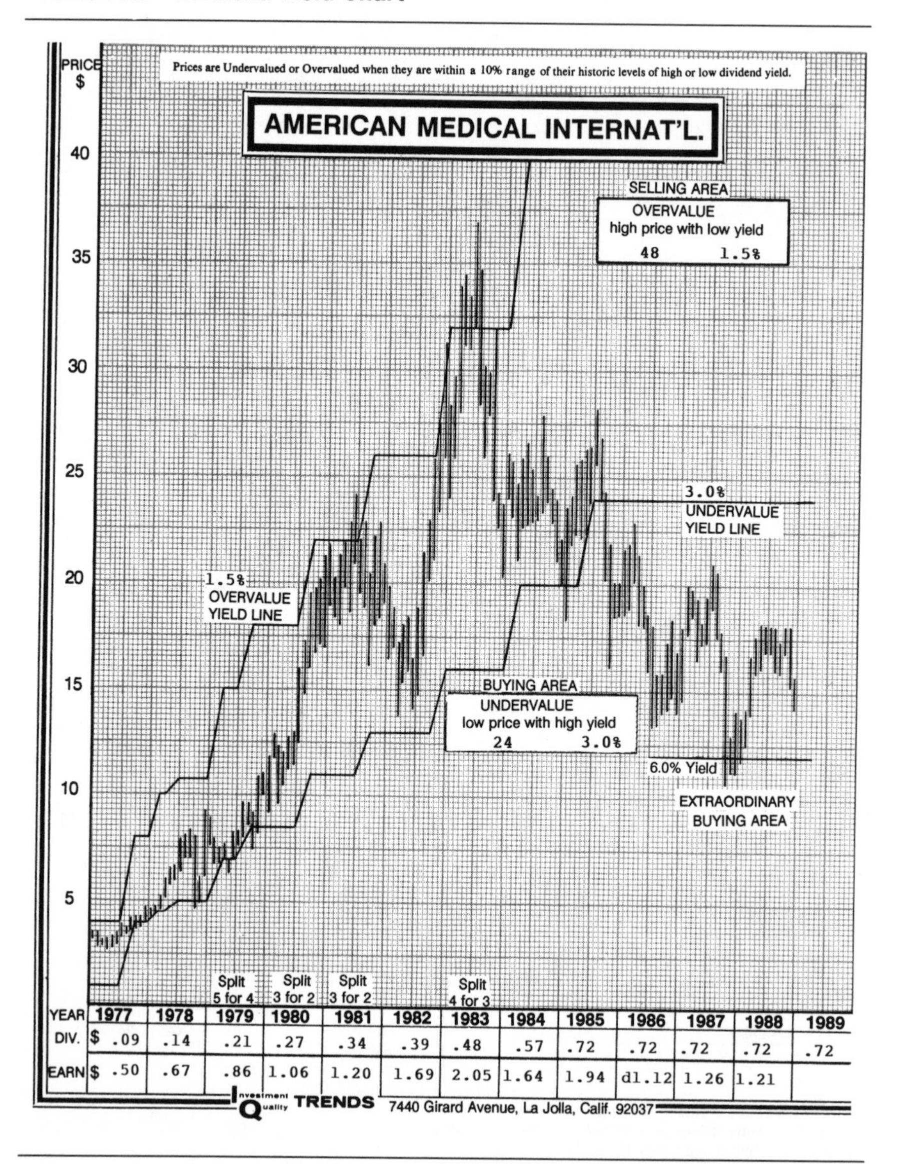

American Medical International is a stock that moves quickly when it moves. As this chart indicates, AMI became highly undervalued in 1985. Its history implies that the company was likely to move rapidly from this level of undervalue, offering the potential for quick, high profits for investors.

TROUBLED TIMES, TROUBLED COMPANIES

If the Dow Jones Industrial Average is at a cyclical summit and most stocks on the exchanges are high-priced, many stocks that are undervalued are cheap because they have problems. Not all of them are desirable buys. But once stocks have been screened very carefully for the bluest of blue chips, even troubled companies or companies experiencing unusually rocky times can be considered good buys.

Companies that do conform to the six blue-chip criteria outlined in chapter 3 have proven themselves winners and survivors. Their undervalued state offers investors an opportunity to buy at low prices and hold them until they've worked out their problems. They then can be sold at a handsome profit.

Cincinnati Gas & Electric is a case in point. (See figure 5.4.) In 1983, the utility was caught in a maze of legal entanglements over the construction of its Zimmer Nuclear Power Station. Costs had soared due to construction delays, and it looked as if the cash dividend, which had been paid without interruption since 1853, might be lowered or even canceled.

The stock declined to yield more than 21 percent. The price/earnings ratio was four to one, and the price was 35 percent below book value.

Four years later, Cincinnati Gas & Electric had made a complete turnaround. Zimmer's nuclear function was scrapped, and it was converted to coal generation. Lawsuits were settled, and in 1987 the company celebrated its 150th anniversary.

Between 1984 and 1986 the price of Cincinnati's stock rose by 200 percent. And the dividend that seemed in danger was increased. During those two years, stockholders received a 21.6 percent annual dividend.

Looking back, it seems obvious that Cincinnati would have been a good buy. But that's hindsight. At the time the company was experiencing such painful problems, the value wasn't so clear. Investors seeking high dividend income would have wanted to weigh the risk against the income stream that was available to them.

Another classic example of an undervalued blue-chip stock early in 1988 is Chase Manhattan, one of the oldest and largest banks in the nation. (See figure 5.5.)

Big money-center banks, those operating in world financial capitals and responsible for massive deposits and loans, were in disfavor at that

FIGURE 5.4 Dividend-Yield Chart

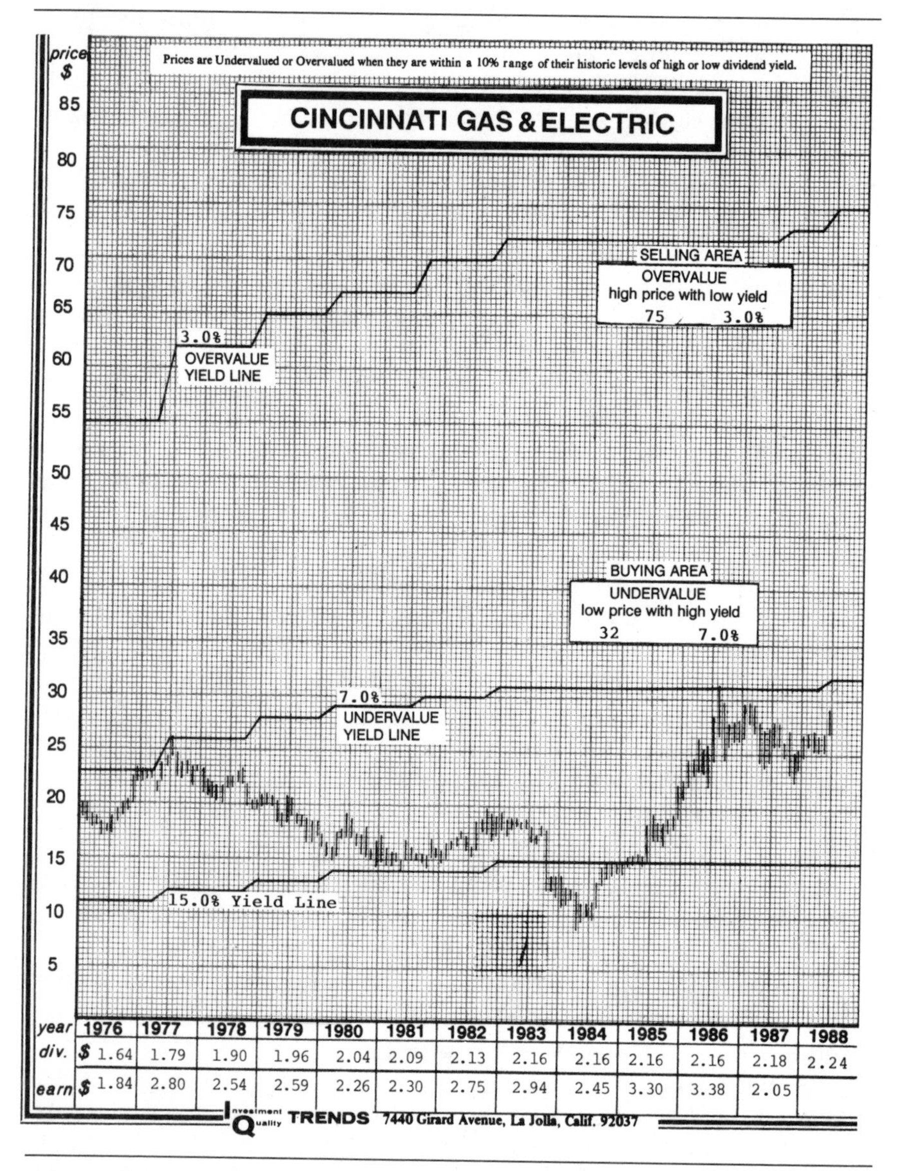

When a stock declines well below undervalue, as Cincinnati Gas & Electric did in 1984, a serious problem usually exists. The purchase of such a stock may bring higher risk for the investor, but a higher return is also offered. Investors must weigh the benefits of risk versus reward.

FIGURE 5.5 Dividend-Yield Chart

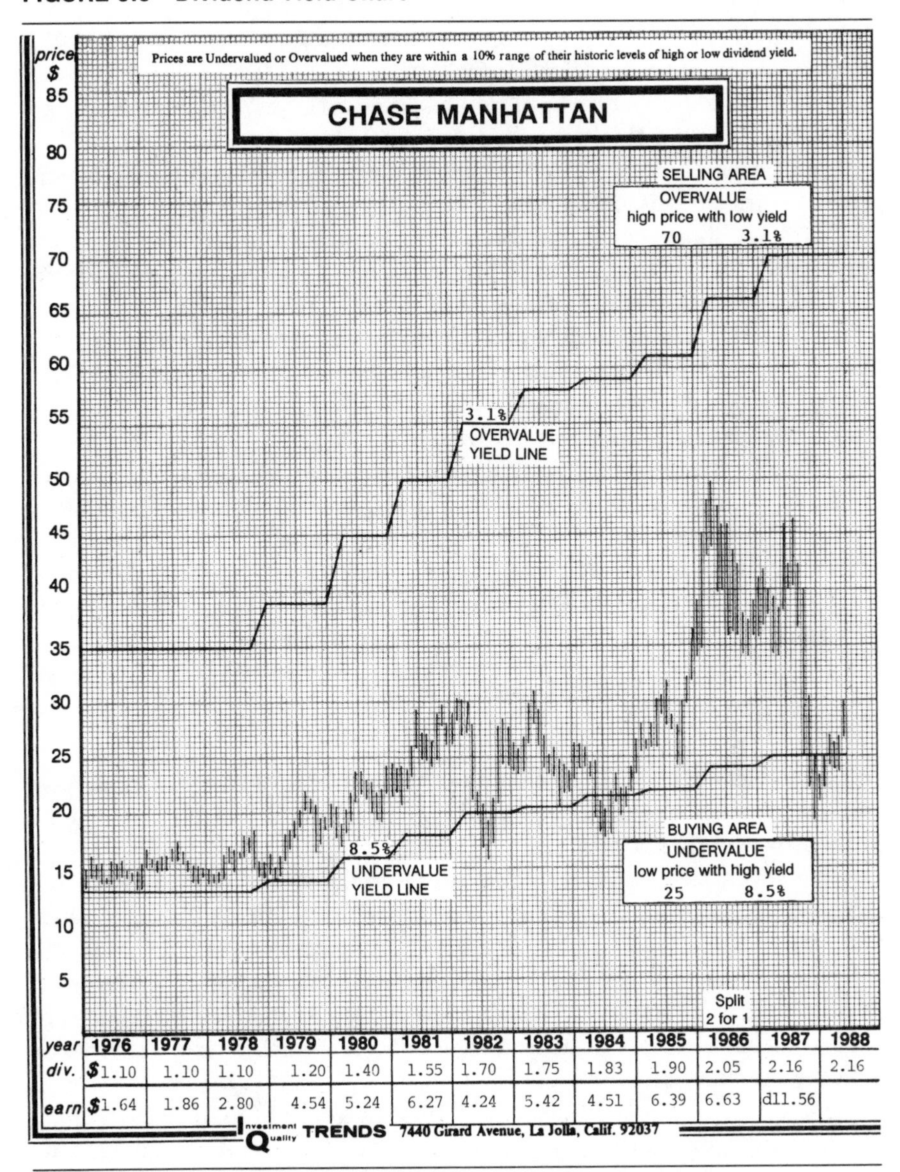

Though big banks were getting a lot of negative publicity over doubtful Third World loans, if an investor had faith in its ability to survive and again prosper, Chase Manhattan would have been a good buy for a long time. The New York bank had paid dividends without fail for 137 years.

time because of a series of problems, not the least of which were troubled loans to less-developed countries. Chase Manhattan had loaned $8.7 billion to LDCs, representing 8.8 percent of its total assets. In 1987, Chase set out to protect itself from the possible losses on these loans by adding $1.6 billion to its loan loss reserves, bringing them up to a total of $2 billion for a thicker cushion of safety.

Yet uncertainty over loans to Mexico and Central and South American countries frightened investors and detracted them from Chase Manhattan. Its share price fell below the undervalued line, offering a dividend yield of ten percent. The stock would have been a good buy even at a dividend yield of 8.5 percent.

Though book value declined in 1987 because of the addition to loan loss reserves, it still amounted to $38.70 per share, which was 77 percent above the price of the stock at the time. Or to turn that around, the stock was priced 44 percent below book value.

Despite the potential problems, Chase is so big, so well-managed and so important to the international banking community that it seemed highly unlikely that the company posed a serious risk to investors. Dividends, paid each year since 1848, had averaged 40 percent of earnings. Yielding ten percent on a dividend that appeared to be safe, Chase Manhattan represented a tempting purchase.

ARE THE NUMBERS ABSOLUTE?

When stocks such as Chase Manhattan or the other examples cited have declined to undervalue, the possibility of further slippage in the stock's price is reduced to a minimum.

However, the prices designating undervalued and overvalued levels are neither exact nor inviolate. These share prices reflect the historic repetitive limits of high yield at depressed undervalue levels and low yield at inflated overvalue levels. The specific prices mark areas of extremes in yield that a long-term investor can use to help in identifying degrees of value. Yields at undervalue and overvalue are calculated on dividends paid as far back as possible.

Many times prices violate the limits by a few points. A stock may even move an extraordinary distance beyond the confines of undervalue or overvalue. Nothing restricts price movement within *precise* frontiers, as all investors know. Logical and psychological factors motivate people to buy and sell in sufficient numbers to move prices, sometimes to speculative extremes.

However, in the vast majority of instances, overvalue and undervalue designations come within ten percent of the high or low in a major price move. Therefore, the dividend-yield theory considers prices to be undervalued or overvalued when they are within the ten percent range of their historic levels of high or low dividend yield.

AN OPPORTUNITY TO DIVERSIFY

While good values can be found at virtually any phase of the stock market cycle, more undervalued stocks can be found at the end of a bear market or during a major correction in a bull market. Because the selection of undervalued stocks is likely to be large, it is at this time that investors have an exceptional opportunity to diversify their holdings.

Especially at the lowest ebb of a bull market, many undervalued shares also will be selling near or below book value. For example, when the market was making a major correction and was at a low in the summer of 1984, among our 350 blue chips, 138, or nearly 40 percent of the total, were priced either below or very close to their book value figures.

Virtually every utility and bank stock on the list was priced below its net asset value. These have been interest-sensitive stocks, and the country was just coming out of a phase during which interest rates had been astronomically high.

Also on the undervalued list were liberal selections of oil stocks and other natural resources companies such as paper, rubber and mineral concerns. Chemical stocks and retail stores were prevalent. Incredibly, office equipment stocks, represented on the list by Burroughs, Sperry and Xerox, were priced below book value.

THE BREAKOUT

It cannot be determined precisely when a stock purchased at undervalue will begin to rise in price. But it is clear that these stocks are bargains, and that high-quality stocks that have proved their worth over the years command universal attention.

Even if the timing of a purchase is not exactly in step with the general market trend, stocks purchased at undervalue tend to hold their value and price. This is true even in a bear market. Sooner or later these undervalued stocks attract the interest of savvy investors. Eventually the industry cycle or business conditions that caused a decline are improved, interest is rekindled, and undervalued stocks move upward to provide excellent long-term capital gains.

Rising Trends

"We must take the current when it serves, or lose our ventures."

WILLIAM SHAKESPEARE (*JULIUS CAESAR*)

A Roman philosopher once observed that more people worship the rising than the setting sun. The same is true with stocks, except that it's a lot easier to tell when the sun is about to come up than when a stock is about to go up. Finding and buying a stock that is undervalued takes diligence and courage. Having done so, and then seeing that stock's price break over that undervalue horizon and start climbing, is what makes an investor feel that it's a bright new day.

CONTRARIANS SNAP TO ATTENTION

When the turnaround does come, either in the market as a whole or with an individual stock, events generally have been at their darkest hour.

It is at this point that true contrarians are buying. According to a contrarian, if the general public is certain that the stock market is a bad place to be, that it's stuck at the bottom and may never rebound, then it's time to dive into the market. Likewise, the contrarian believes that if investors have lost faith in the shares of a particular corporation and it appears hopelessly out of favor, then that's the time to buy.

This, reasons the contrarian, is because when the masses predict decline, they have already sold out. All the sellers are out of the market (or out of an individual stock), and now there is nowhere to go but up. Conversely, when the majority feel the market is going up, they are fully vested. They have no more purchasing power, which means the market has peaked and has nowhere to go but down.

The contrarians make some strong points, but contrarianism is an incomplete philosophy. To their basic concept, it is necessary to add a commitment to quality and an analysis of value by way of dividend yield. This approach provides the specific information needed to buy or sell at the correct time.

That time always does come for our dividend-paying blue chips, because stocks of quality and substance that have reliable histories command a formidable investor following. Those powerful investment dollars eventually recognize that a stock is fundamentally undervalued. Investment dollars then flow to that stock, and a rising trend is under way.

PATIENCE PRECEDES PROFITS

As pointed out earlier, it isn't always possible to tell exactly when a market will move up, or the very day a specific stock will take off.

As the charts in this book show, share prices will bob up and down, even at the undervalued level of their cycle. As long as these movements are minor, as long as they don't extend above the undervalue channel line in the stock portrait, they are of no real significance.

TEN PERCENT ABOVE UNDERVALUE

When a stock has risen ten percent above its historic level of undervalue, it can be considered a rising star. Procter & Gamble is a perfect example of a stock progressing upward through its normal undervalue-overvalue cycle. In 1982, as shown in the appendix, it launched a takeoff. Undervalued at a five percent dividend yield, Procter & Gamble is overvalued when the yield reaches a low of 1.5 percent.

First in the hearts of the washing-machine set, the company is the largest manufacturer internationally of soaps, detergents and other cleaning products. It also produces and markets food lines (Citrus Hill orange juice, Folger coffee and many more), cold remedies (NyQuil, Vicks VapoRub) and grooming products (Prell, Scope, Secret, to name a few). Procter & Gamble is America's largest advertiser.

At previous overvalued levels, Procter & Gamble sold at $180 per share. At undervalue, it bottomed at $54 per share. So even if the stock was purchased early in its rising trend, the potential existed for the share to more than double in price.

SHORT-TERM GAINS POSSIBLE

When the general market is in ascent, stocks that are in rising trends offer especially good opportunities for short-term profits. A rising-trend stock in a rising-trend market is more likely to reach overvalue in a briefer period of time than a stock that is undervalued. The rising-trend stock has a rocket booster behind it: the force of the entire stock market.

Although the dividend yield of a rising-trend stock is not as high as when that stock was undervalued, and the total appreciation potential to overvalue is not as great, the price movement usually is more rapid. The investor who is willing to risk the possibility of a return to undervalue may, in fact, achieve handsome short-term profits when purchasing a stock that is in a rising trend.

TIMING

It is important at this time to keep in mind that a move from undervalue to overvalue generally takes many months, if not years. Along the way, occasional setbacks to undervalue may occur, but this situation also presents its own special opportunity.

We have found that timing can be improved somewhat if investment selections are made from undervalued stocks that were recent arrivals to that category, if their descent to undervalue occurred during a general market decline. This is even more valid among stocks that had fallen back into the undervalued category from the rising-trends category. When the overall market begins to improve, such stocks are likely to resume their rising trends quickly.

For example, assume that a particular company had been in a rising trend, but general market conditions reversed that progress and returned the stock to below ten percent of its undervalued price. When the market improves, the company is likely to take off faster than other similarly undervalued stocks. So for investors hoping for a rapid start and quicker gains, such a company represents a good buy.

K-Mart Corporation rose above its undervalue line in 1982 and began a rising trend. Though figure 6.1 shows two setbacks to undervalue, they were short-lived. Ultimately, the path of K-Mart's dividend yield continued higher.

The reason for K-Mart's dividend-yield pattern can be easily understood. Following a period of very rapid expansion in the 1970s, the discount retailer took time out in the 1980s to consolidate its resources, upgrade merchandise, remodel its stores and otherwise revitalize operations. As proof that the time and money were well spent, fiscal year 1987 earnings moved smartly upward, climbing more than 20 percent to a record high.

A GROWTH STOCK

K-Mart could be considered a growth stock, as are many stocks during their rising trends. The collection of rising-trend stocks in figure 6.2 presents fundamental information as of March 1987 on blue chips that had lifted out of the undervalue area and were accelerating.

A "G" following a company's name in figure 6.2 indicates that the stock was in a phase of rapid growth, with a ten percent compounded annual dividend growth rate. Traditionally, growth stocks outperform other slower stocks, but they do present a somewhat greater risk. They may, for example, be more volatile, or more vulnerable to economic or external events. Even so, through careful attention to blue-chip qualifications, much of the risk has been buffered in the growth stocks presented in the chart.

At the time K-Mart's chart was completed (February 1988), a dividend increase was expected. This move by company management, at this time in the dividend-yield cycle, would likely have a strong impact on K-Mart's fundamental value and the direction of its share price.

DIVIDEND INCREASES BOOST THE CLIMBER

If during a stock's rising trend, the company also increases dividends, this positive phase of the stock price cycle is granted an extended life. One of the nation's most commanding corporate personalities, General

FIGURE 6.1 Dividend-Yield Chart

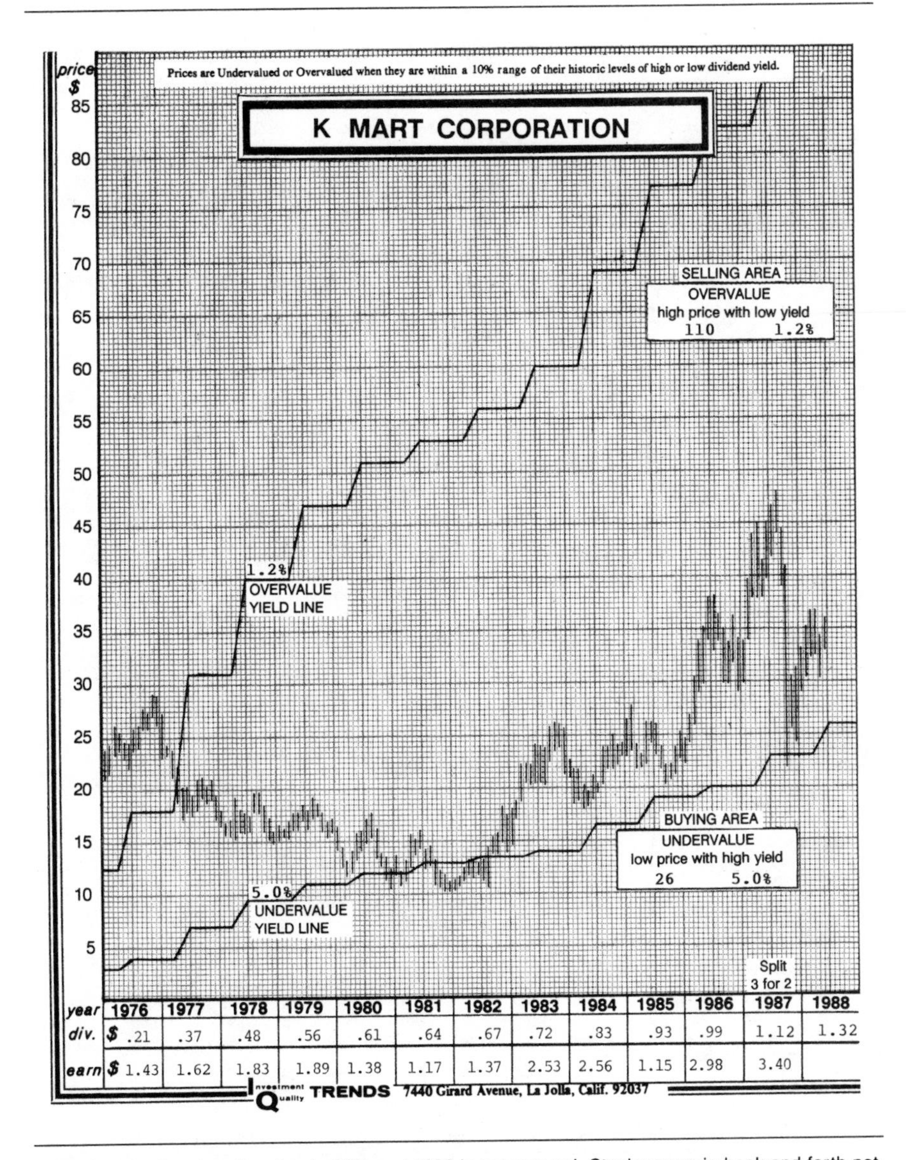

K-Mart's behavior at undervalue in 1981 and 1982 is not unusual. Stocks move in back-and-forth patterns, and often will hit undervalue, make a start up and then fall back to undervalue. K-Mart's price finally gained power because of positive financial results at the company. Steadily increasing dividends indicated management's faith that growth problems could be solved.

FIGURE 6.2 Rising-Trends Category

STOCK	Change in Category		Current Price		Current Ind Ann Div	Current Div Yield	Potential Pts. Up	Potential % Up	TO Overvalue High Price	Overvalue Low Yield	S&P Qual Rank	Earn Last 12 Mos (Up or Down)	Price/ Earns Ratio	Blue-Chip Status
ALCO STANDARD CORP.	G		47	=	1.28	2.8%	17	36%	64	2.0%	A+	2.72U	17	5
ALLEGHENY POWER			47	=	2.92	6.3%	44	94%	91	3.2%	A	4.03	12	6
AMOCO CORP.	G		73	=	3.30	4.6%	37	51%	110	3.0%	A	2.91D	25	6
HEILEMAN (G) BREWING	G		28	=	0.52	1.9%	24	86%	52	1.0%	A+	1.83U	15	5
HELMERICH & PAYNE	G		25	=	0.36	1.5%	47	188%	72	0.5%	B	0.42	60	5
HERCULES CORP.			63	=	1.76	2.8%	25	40%	88	2.0%	B+	4.02U	16	5
HOLIDAY CORP.	G		80		Dividend undeclared due to planned recapitalization.									
HONEYWELL			69	=	2.00	2.9%	(NOTE: Dividend in Danger)					Deficit	0	6
HOUGHTON MIFFLIN	G		31	=	0.58	1.9%	8	25%	39	1.5%	A–	1.61	19	5
HOUSEHOLD INTL.			55	=	1.86	3.4%	30	54%	85	2.2%	B+	4.48U	12	5
HOUSTON INDUSTRIES	G		38	=	2.80	7.4%	74	195%	112	2.5%	A	3.81D	10	6
HUBBELL INC. CL B	G		34	=	0.84	2.5%	8	24%	42	2.0%	A+	2.12U	16	6
INGERSOLL-RAND			77	=	2.60	3.4%	16	21%	93	2.8%	B+	4.48U	17	5
INTERCO, INC.			43	=	1.60	3.8%	21	49%	64	2.5%	A–	3.03U	14	6
IBM	G	u	143	=	4.40	3.1%	77	54%	220	2.0%	A+	7.81D	18	6
K-MART	G		58	=	1.48	2.6%	65	113%	123	1.2%	B+	2.33U	25	5
KERR MCGEE	G		31	=	1.10	3.6%	(NOTE: Dividend in Danger)					Deficit	0	5
LILLY (ELI)	G		90	★	2.00	2.3%	92	102%	182	1.1%	A+	4.01U	22	6
LINCOLN NATIONAL			50	★	2.16	4.4%	44	88%	94	2.3%	A–	4.35	11	6
LUBRIZOL CORP.	G	u	38	=	1.20	3.2%	22	58%	60	2.0%	B+	1.92U	20	5
LUCKY STORES	G		29		Dividend undeclared due to buyback.						A–	4.47	6	6
MARSH MCCLENNAN CO.	G		67	=	1.90	2.9%	45	67%	112	1.7%	A	3.30U	20	6
MASCO CORP.	G		35	=	0.36	1.1%	55	157%	90	0.4%	A	1.45U	24	6
MCDONNELL DOUGLAS	G		78	★	2.32	3.0%	51	65%	129	1.8%	A+	6.86D	11	6
MCGRAW HILL			71	★	1.68	2.4%	82	115%	153	1.1%	A	3.04U	23	6
MELVILLE CORP.	G		70	★	1.76	2.6%	65	93%	135	1.3%	A+	4.40U	16	6
MERCK	G		148	=	2.20	1.5%	35	24%	183	1.2%	A+	4.85U	31	6
MINNESOTA MINING	G		127	★	3.72	3.0%	183	144%	310	1.2%	A	6.80U	19	6
MOBIL CORP.	G		43	=	2.20	5.2%	18	42%	61	3.6%	B+	3.44	13	5
MOORE CORP., LTD.			24	)	0.72	3.1%	31	131%	55	1.3%	A–	1.48D	16	6
MOTOROLA, INC.	G		47	=	0.64	1.4%	81	172%	128	0.5%	A–	1.53U	31	6
MURPHY OIL CORP.	G		29		1.00	3.5%	(NOTE: Dividend in Danger)					Deficit	0	5
NATIONAL FUEL GAS			41	=	2.28	5.6%	22	54%	63	3.6%	A+	3.43D	12	5
NATIONAL MED. ENTERP.	G		26	=	0.60	2.4%	20	78%	46	1.3%	A	1.09	24	5
NBD BANCORP		u	35	=	1.20	3.5%	13	37%	48	2.5%	A	3.87U	9	5
NEW ENGLAND ELEC. SYS.			31	★	2.00	6.5%	19	61%	50	4.0%	A+	3.20U	10	6
NORTHERN STATES POWER			33	=	1.90	5.8%	21	65%	54	3.5%	A	3.09	11	6
NORTHROP CORP.			44	)	1.20	2.8%	(NOTE: Dividend in Danger)					0.89D	49	6
NORTON COMPANY			46		2.00	4.4%	(NOTE: Dividend in Danger)					Deficit	0	6
NORWEST CORP.	G		42		1.80	4.3%	30	71%	72	2.5%	A–	3.64U	12	6
OKLAHOMA GAS ELEC.			35	★	2.18	6.3%	38	108%	73	3.0%	A–	2.75U	13	6
PACIFIC LIGHTING			54	=	3.48	6.5%	38	70%	92	3.8%	A	1.34	40	5

These stocks have lifted out of the undervalued category, and show promise of future growth. They should be held in a portfolio until they near the overvalue area. At that point, they should be evaluated and tracked carefully. It soon will be time to convert paper profits into real money.

Mills, demonstrated this principle in the pattern of its dividend yield during most of this decade.

General Mills hovered at its undervalued yield for almost two years in the early 1980s. As figure 6.3 illustrates, the company then began an orderly march toward higher ground. That climbing path has continued for more than six years, and at the time this chart was completed in 1987, General Mills still was not overvalued.

Paced by frequent generous dividend increases starting in 1980, the stock had advanced more than 400 percent when the chart was completed, and it was still progressing. A great deal of headroom remained before the stock could be considered overvalued.

With more than $5 billion in sales and $222 million in earnings, the food company decided to tighten operations by selling some of its subsidiaries. As a result, it closed out 1987 with record financial results.

At this phase in the company's cycle, a period of price consolidation may move the stock sideways for awhile, but the downside risk was not considered to be great. Despite the down-trend market at the end of 1987, a stock with a dividend-yield pattern and corporate history like General Mills's was still an excellent purchase at that time, if made during normal price declines.

DIVIDEND INCREASES ARE KEY INDICATORS

The serious investor knows that among the many signposts that point to corporate and investment growth, a rising dividend trend is perhaps the most significant.

First as an indication of corporate growth and profitability, then as a measure of investment value and finally as protective insurance against a market reversal and the loss of investment capital, all investors should heartily rejoice when the dividend is raised. Every increase boosts the original yield on an investment and offers a measure of investment security. A stock that has been purchased at undervalue is less likely to return to its original purchase price with each successive dividend increase.

THE PATTERN IS IMPORTANT

Investors should be more favorably impressed with the management of a company that has increased its dividend in each of many years, than

FIGURE 6.3 Dividend-Yield Chart

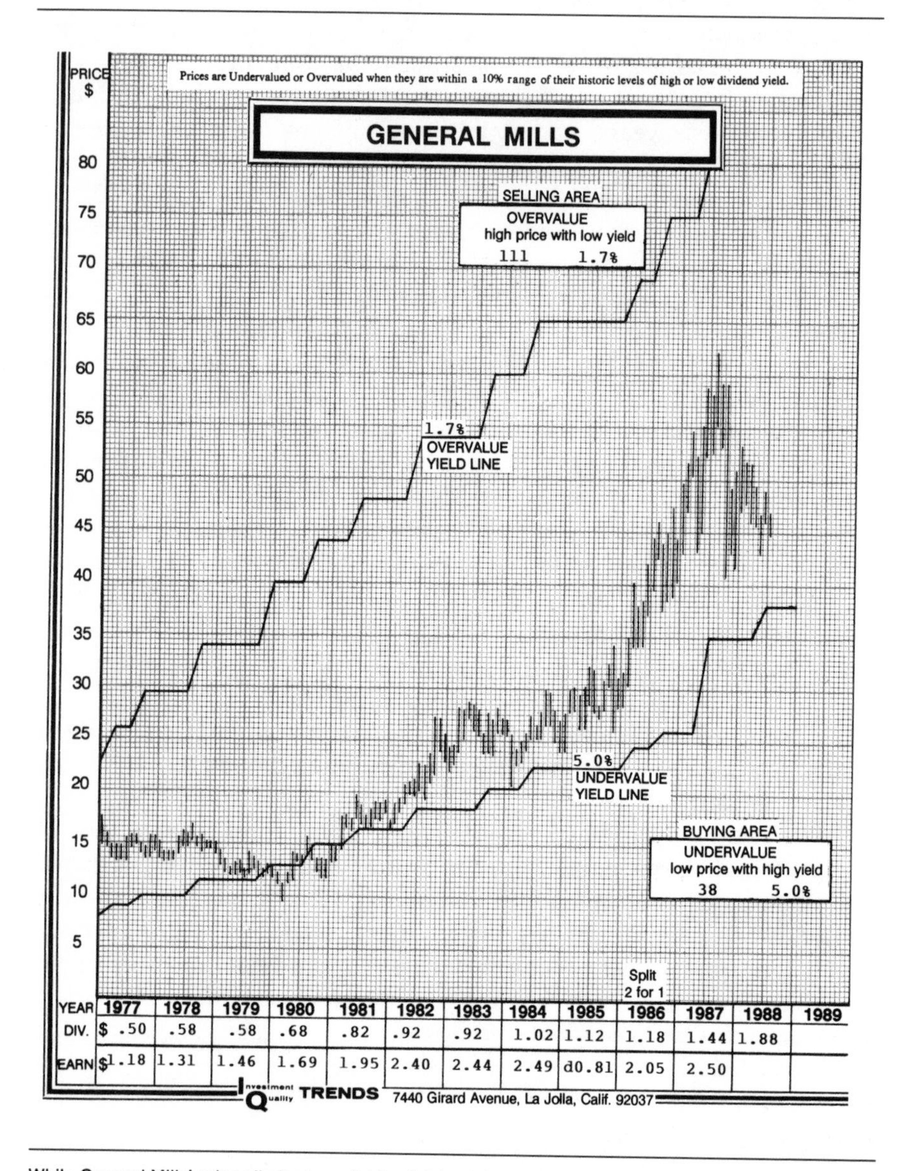

While General Mills' price climbed, so did its dividend. It was great value in 1980, and rising dividends made it a wise purchase several times later in the decade as well.

with a company that occasionally raises its dividend by a large amount, even though the end result after ten years or so may be the same percentage gain.

All companies experience good and bad years. Companies that regularly bolster their cash dividends, regardless of economic and financial vicissitudes, show strength and steadiness. These are the shares astute investors are watching and will find attractive either at undervalue or early in their rising trends. Later, as it becomes obvious that a company's share price is taking off, less analytical investors step in, pushing the price higher—eventually to its overvalued level.

RISKS

A rising trend means the race is on; investors receive maximum dividends for their investment, and profits are at the starting gate. Only a few risks are present at the beginning. A stock can float above and below the undervalue line before starting for the finish line. That is why a stock is still considered undervalued when it is proximate to its undervalue line.

Selecting for purchase a stock that has crossed over into the rising trend involves somewhat greater risks to investment capital than selecting a stock that is still undervalued. In a severely declining market, stocks that had just begun to rise may be caught in the tide of decline and swept back down to an undervalued price area. The state of the overall market exerts great influence. Therefore, in selecting a stock that already is in a rising trend, an investor always should weigh the potential for gain against the risk of a setback.

Commonwealth Edison is an example of a company that struggled out of an undervalued area, then slipped back, before again rebounding to its rising trend.

As figure 6.4 shows, the further Edison advanced along the rising-trend line, the less likely it was to slip below the 12 percent yield line, at which it was unquestionably undervalued and ripe for acquisition. The stock consolidated strength as it moved up, but then took a severe hit during the market decline in the fall of 1987. Fortunately though, even that market shock did not move it all the way back to its undervalue level.

Notice that Commonwealth Edison has three solid horizontal lines rather than two. The middle line is called the undervalued yield line,

FIGURE 6.4 Dividend-Yield Chart

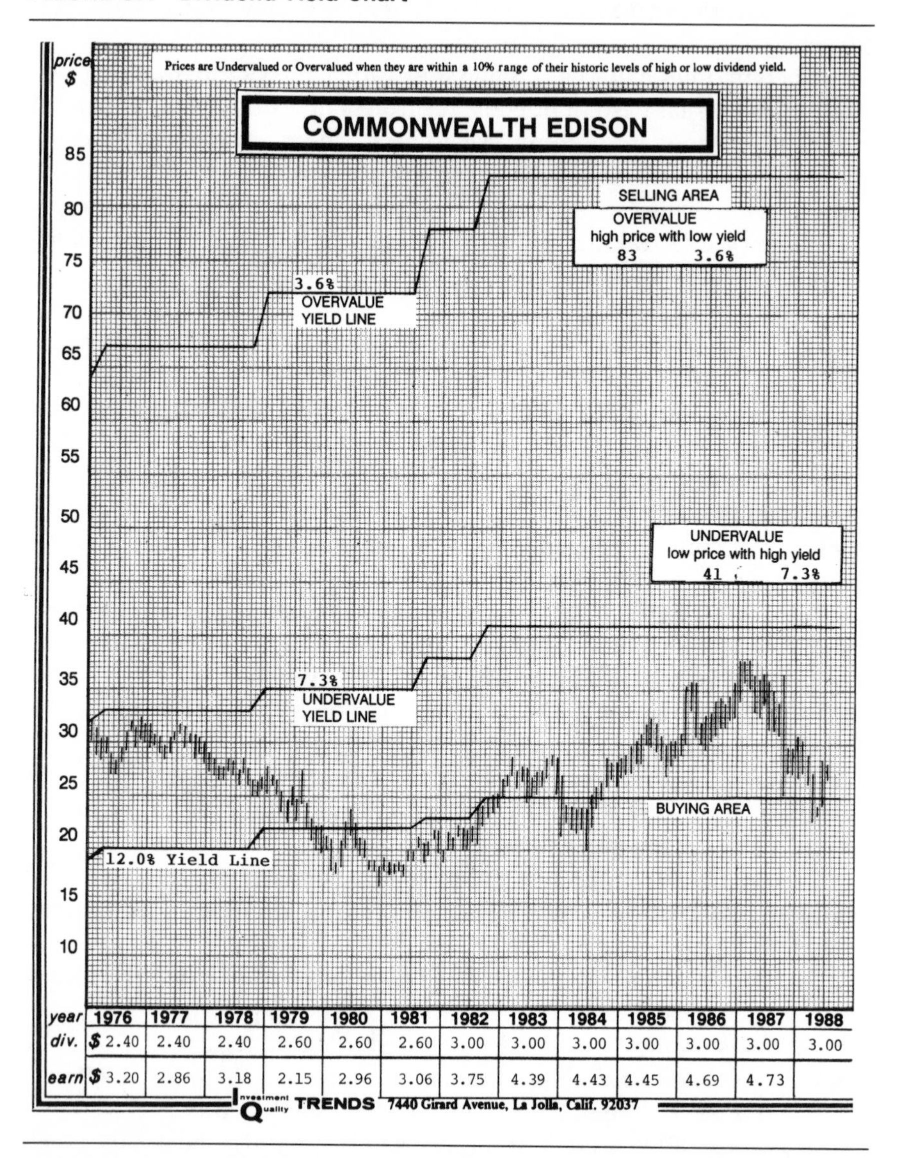

Like so many other utilities, Commonwealth Edison's share price was severely impacted by high interest rates. Its dividend yield changed drastically and it established a new pattern. As Commonwealth Edison dealt with many problems confronting utilities, its performance showed the vulnerability of stocks as they first accelerate out of the undervalued category.

and the space between the bottom line and the middle line is the buying area. This is a unique situation that exists among utilities, due to extremely high interest-rate climates in the 1970s and early 1980s. The special condition of and treatment regarding utilities is explained in chapter 12.

WATCH OUT FOR AN AGING CLIMBER

Though a stock may gain firmer footing as a rising trend advances, certainly a rising-trend stock that is close to an overvalued price area should not be considered for an original purchase. As rising stocks near the overvalued area, they require monitoring. An investor doesn't want to sell prematurely or hold a stock too long. Unless some pressing reason requires taking a profit, investors should be patient and not sell rising-trend stocks until they reach their overvalued phase.

KNOW WHEN THE PHASE IS OVER

Overvalue is not identified simply by a sharp rise, perhaps doubling the price of the stocks. Some stocks can rise 200 or 300 percent before they reach overvalue if dividend increases have kept pace with the rising price trend.

Overvalue for a particular stock is identified only by an historically low dividend yield that in the past has coincided with the top of a major price rise. Each stock has its own distinctive overvalue yield, and the stock remains in a rising trend until that point is attained.

7

The Overvalued Phase

"It is the mountaintop that the lightning strikes."

HORACE

When a stock market or a stock is charging like a bull, regularly reaching higher highs, talk of its vigor dominates the investment community. In fact, everyone everywhere is talking about it. A booming market makes news. Often, the economy also is doing well, and people see only a rosy future ahead.

When this glowing haze of happiness has lasted for a certain length of time, an amazing euphoria sometimes sets in. This phenomenon was first noticed at the turn of this century. The McKinley bull market was raging in 1901, and the general public (and many professional investors) began to think prices would go up forever. "Probably 1901 was the first of such speculative demonstrations in history," wrote Alexander Dana Noyes in his book *The Market Place,* "which based its ideas and conduct on the assumption that we were living in a New Era; that old rules and principles and precedent of finance were obsolete; that things could safely be done today which had been dangerous or impossible in the past. This illusion seized on the public mind in 1901 (in New York at any rate) quite as firmly as it did in 1929."

This kind of stock market euphoria has repeated over the years, and it was seen again in 1987. Many investors believed that foreign investors, lots of liquidity and myriad other factors would push the market even higher.

THE END OF THE DREAM

It generally isn't until some time after the top of a cycle has been reached that people realize that it has come and gone. The summit of the stock market is a happy time because it is a time to see plans, expectations and dreams become realities. An overvalued market phase is a time to reap profits. But it is a sobering time, too, because the top of a cycle means that the other side of the mountain—and a trail down—lies just ahead.

While only dedicated historians of the investment markets remember the bottoms of bear markets, every child in school learns about October 29, 1929. On that Black Tuesday, $50 billion was lost in the market in a single day—signaling the pinnacle of a magnificent bull market. That same historic event sounded a warning of the Great Depression of the 1930s.

Events sometimes unfold in this manner—great joy before great distress—for a very human reason.

GETTING ON THE BANDWAGON

While the bull market still seems strong, excitement and enthusiasm take over. Investors and prospective investors see large sums of money being made. Prices have been going up. Stock holdings are increasing in value. Many people begin to think that they should partake of the bounty. They often rush in too late, but in doing so, they perpetuate the rising market, pushing stock prices above their realistic value.

SPECULATION FEVER

When an individual stock rises, the same feeling of goodwill is likely to attach to it, even if the market as a whole is not overvalued. The company becomes a "glamour" stock, and many investors want to be associated with it. They buy without regard to fundamental value.

GREED IS A MOTIVE

Some observers see the motivation behind this kind of behavior as more than merely crowd psychology. "Greed takes over late in a bull market," said Charles Royce, president of New York–based Quest Advisory in an interview in *Financial World* magazine in May 1987, "and people reach for what hasn't been taken."

Not in every case does a bull market become explosively overheated before it cools off, but the possibility exists. Certainly that was the case in 1987.

RECENT HISTORY

In early September 1987, an analysis of dividend yield on the Dow Jones Industrial Average warned that the market had reached a top in the previous March. It was then that the DJIA first had hit a three percent dividend yield, signaling that it had become fundamentally overvalued. The Dow Industrial was priced at 2.7 times book value. It had a price/earnings ratio of 21 to 1, and the dividend yield was 2.6 percent. All things considered, the Dow Jones Industrial Average was more extremely overpriced than it ever had been in its 91-year history.

"Now, the Dow Jones Industrial Average has moved higher, above all historic levels of investment value, into uncharted waters," stated "Investment Quality Trends," in its September 1, 1987, issue, "and the percentage of overvalued stocks is at a new, record high. Neither we nor anyone else knows where the bull market will end. Most investors will not get out at the top, wherever it may be. They either will sell too early or stay too late. To buy in an undervalued area and to sell in an overvalued area is about the best that any investor can hope to do. Perhaps no one ever will fully master the market. As the saying goes. . . just when we think we have the key, someone changes the lock."

THEN COMES THE CORRECTION

The newsletter went on to advise readers that when the correction came, a modest ten percent adjustment was the least they could expect: "A more likely correction would be 30 percent from the top, returning the Dow Jones Industrial Average to a price of 1925."

As it turned out, a market decline had begun in August 1987, and it came abruptly to the public's attention on October 19 when the Dow plunged 508 points, an astounding 22 percent in a single day, closing at 1738.74. The entire market decline from August to October of 1987 amounted to 36 percent.

A runaway market, like a runaway train, continues in one direction until its supply of fuel (or money, in the case of stocks) is exhausted. Or, until it is derailed by an unexpected event.

A SALVATION IN DIVIDEND YIELD

Sticking loyally to the dividend yield theory, however, can insulate investors from being caught up in a stock market frenzy. By tracking the dividend yield of an individual stock, investors can know when that stock is overvalued and can anticipate a reversal to an undervalued level.

In the past, whenever the Dow Jones Industrial Average has reached a dividend yield of three percent, a trend reversal has occurred. Prices have declined. Dividend increases may provide reprieve, but generally, when the Dow moves toward the three percent area, it is a time for caution. (See figure 7.1.)

RED FLAG AT THREE PERCENT

Stock yields approached the three percent level in 1966, 1968 and 1973. All three were market tops, though the first two were intermediate tops, with 1973 the final top in the third stage of the market cycle. From the peak of the 1973 bull market to its bottom in 1974, stock prices dropped as much as 50 percent, bringing the dividend yield on the DJIA back to six percent.

DON'T ABANDON ALL HOPE

When the Dow Jones Industrial Average is overvalued, the entire stock market is placed in a perilous position.

However, investment decisions must be based on specific values for individual stocks. Each company has its own distinctive level of overvalue. Even in an aging bull market, not all stocks are overvalued. And among those that are, not all stocks are overvalued to the same extent.

FIGURE 7.1 Annual DJIA Dividends

ANNUAL DIVIDENDS AND PERIMETERS OF VALUE FOR THE DOW JONES INDUSTRIAL AVERAGE

Year	*Ann. Div.*	*% Increase*	*6% Undervalued Price*	*3% Overvalued Price*
1987	71.20	+ 6.2%	1187	2373
1986	67.04	+ 8.1%	1117	2235
1985	62.03	+ 2.3%	1034	2068
1984	60.63	+ 7.6%	1011	2021
1983	56.33	+ 4.0%	939	1878
1982	54.14	− 3.7%	902	1805
1981	56.22	+ 3.4%	937	1874
1980	54.36	+ 6.6%	906	1812
1979	50.98	+ 5.1%	850	1699
1978	48.52	+ 5.8%	809	1617
1977	45.84	+10.7%	764	1528
1976	41.40	+10.5%	690	1380
1975	37.46	− 0.7%	624	1249
1974	37.72	+ 6.8%	629	1257

The table reviews the annual composite dividends for the Dow Jones Industrial Average, stretching back to 1974, at the start of the bull market. It also shows the percent of dividend increase or decrease for each year, and the annual perimeters of undervalue and overvalue. The largest dividend increase was in 1977, when the payout jumped 10.7 percent, following a 10.5 percent boost in 1976. The worst year for dividends was 1982 (a recession year), when the payout for the Dow Jones Industrial Average declined 3.7 percent. We expect the dividends of U.S. blue chips with multinational operations to increase this year along with stronger-than-expected earnings gains from overseas orders and currency translations.

By charting the dividend yield on a stock, and observing at which yield that stock has historically reversed its course, it is possible to determine the dividend yield at which it is overvalued. When a specific stock's price rises to the upper channel line on the dividend-yield charts shown in this book, the yield is reaching a level at which, in essence, an investor is paying too much for the dividend that will be received. The stock has reached its historical overvalue phase. (See figure 7.2.)

The cyclical chart of EG&G, Inc., in figure 7.3 illustrates two complete fluctuations from undervalue to overvalue. EG&G, a high-technology engineering organization that had its origins at the Massachusetts Institute of Technology, moves between a fairly narrow range of top and bottom prices, which makes its full cycles somewhat shorter than those of a great many other stocks.

FIGURE 7.2 Overvalued Stocks

STOCK	Change in Category		Current Price		Current Ind Ann Div	Current Div Yield	Potential Pts. Up	Potential % Up	TO Overvalue High Price	Overvalue Low Yield	S&P Qual Rank	Last 12 Mos (Up or Down)	Price/ Earns Ratio	Blue-Chip Status
ALBERTSON S INC.	G	x	28	=	0.48	1.8%	18	66%	10	5.0%	A+	1.72U	16	5
AMERICAN CYANAMID		x	44	=	1.05	2.4%	28	63%	16	6.5%	A–	3.02U	15	6
AMERICAN STORES	G	x	56	)	0.84	1.6%	35	63%	21	4.0%	A	4.45U	13	6
BALL CORP.	G		29	=	0.96	3.4%	14	49%	15	6.5%	A+	2.80U	10	6
BORDEN		d	50	=	1.28	2.6%	32	63%	18	7.0%	A+	3.62U	14	6
BROWNING-FERRIS	G	x	25	★	0.48	2.0%	16	65%	9	5.5%	A+	1.23U	20	6
CBS, INC.		x	158	)	3.00	1.9%	108	68%	50	6.0%	A–	17.46U	9	6
CLOROX CO.			28	=	0.88	3.2%	17	61%	11	8.0%	A+	2.25U	12	5
CONAGRA INC.	G	x	27	=	0.67	2.5%	17	63%	10	6.7%	A+	1.84U	15	6
CONSOL. FREIGHTWAYS	G		27	=	0.90	3.4%	14	52%	13	7.0%	A–	1.93D	14	6
COOPER TIRE & RUBBER		d	31	★	0.52	1.7%	25	79%	7	8.0%	A–	2.83U	11	5
DEXTER CORP.	G	d	23	=	0.60	2.7%	11	48%	12	5.0%	A–	1.62U	14	6
DREYFUS CORP.	G	x	28	=	0.48	1.8%	21	74%	7	6.5%	A	2.21U	13	5
ETHYL CORP.	G	x	20	★	0.44	2.3%	13	63%	7	6.0%	A	1.57U	13	6
GERBER PRODUCTS		x	40		1.32	3.4%	25	63%	15	9.0%	A–	1.41	28	5
GILLETTE		d	37	★	0.86	2.4%	25	67%	12	7.0%	A	0.51U	73	6
GRAINGER (W.W.)	G	x	53	=	0.80	1.6%	30	57%	23	3.5%	A	3.02U	18	5
GULF + WESTERN INC.	G	x	71	=	1.20	1.7%	51	72%	20	6.0%	B+	5.76U	12	5
HANNAFORD BROS.	G	x	36	★	0.64	1.8%	26	73%	10	6.5%	A	2.60U	14	5
HERSHEY FOODS		x	27	=	0.62	2.3%	18	66%	9	6.8%	A+	1.60U	17	6
HILTON HOTELS	G	x	78		1.80	2.4%	48	62%	30	6.0%	A–	5.59U	14	6
IC INDUSTRIES			31	=	0.88	2.9%	21	68%	10	9.0%	B+	2.23U	14	5
INGERSOL-RAND		d	34		1.04	3.1%	17	49%	17	6.0%	B+	2.17U	16	5
KELLOGG	G		51	★	1.52	3.0%	26	50%	25	6.0%	A+	3.10U	16	6
KIMBERLY CLARK	G		51	=	1.44	2.9%	28	54%	23	6.2%	A+	3.73U	14	6
KRAFT INC.	G	d	53	=	1.88	3.6%	26	49%	27	7.0%	A	3.60U	15	5
LUCKY STORES	G	x	29		0.50	1.8%	22	76%	7	7.2%	A–	6.50U	4	6
MARTIN MARIETTA		x	45	=	1.10	2.5%	33	73%	12	9.0%	A–	4.25U	11	6
MCDONALD'S CORP.	G	D	45	=	0.50	1.2%	20	44%	25	2.0%	A+	3.14U	14	5
MCKESSON CORP.			27	=	1.28	4.8%	13	47%	14	9.0%	A	2.07	13	5
MEDTRONIC INC.	G		87	=	1.04	1.2%	51	59%	36	2.9%	A–	5.72U	15	5
MORTON-THIOKOL			40	=	0.84	2.1%	26	65%	14	6.0%	A	2.92U	14	6
OLIN CORP.	G	D	42	=	1.60	3.9%	19	46%	23	7.0%	B+	3.38	12	5
PETRIE STORES	G	d	19		0.20	1.1%	16	84%	3	6.6%	B+	1.41D	13	5
ROCKWELL INTERNATIONAL			18	=	0.66	3.7%	10	53%	8	7.8%	A+	2.45U	7	6
ROHM AND HAAS	G		30	=	0.92	3.1%	15	49%	15	6.0%	A	2.85U	11	5
RUBBERMAID INC.	G	d	24	=	0.36	1.6%	16	67%	8	4.5%	A	1.15U	21	6
SCOTT PAPER		x	68	★	1.48	2.2%	45	67%	23	6.5%	A–	6.11U	11	6
SEAGRAM CO. LTD.			53	=	1.10	2.1%	26	48%	28	4.0%	A	5.18U	10	6
SNAP-ON-TOOLS CORP.	G	d	37	=	0.76	2.1%	21	57%	16	4.8%	A	2.13U	17	6
SQUARE D			52	★	1.92	3.7%	28	54%	24	8.0%	B+	3.82	14	5
STERLING DRUG		r	89	=	1.52	1.8%	61	69%	28	5.5%	A+	3.42U	26	6

Each stock has reached its own distinctive high price with low dividend yield. Unless dividends are raised, it may be anticipated that overpriced stocks will decline toward undervalue. It is important to recognize the potential downside risk that exists at the overvalue level. Selling here preserves profits and capital.

Incidentally, its chart reveals that EG&G was still a bargain at a time when most of the market was overvalued. With sound finances and total debt of only seven percent of capitalization, it can be a good buy even in chancy economic conditions.

A more languid pattern is demonstrated by Quaker Oats, figure 7.4. A recent journey from undervalue to overvalue took more than a decade, with several setbacks along the way.

NO ONE RINGS A BELL AT THE TOP

As with other phases, it isn't easy to call the exact moment of a market top or to predict precisely when an individual stock has reached its turnaround mark. As previously noted, the fact that a stock is overvalued *should* stop speculators from buying and driving prices beyond their value limits, but it sometimes does not.

MAKE USE OF MARKET VOLATILITY

In fact, a market at the apex is characterized by increased volatility for that very reason. There is a classic tug-of-war between two opposing groups of investors. One group (the bulls) is convinced that either foreign or institutional or some other capital will move stock prices substantially higher. So, when stocks decline, bullish investors buy, giving the market support at critical price levels.

The other group (the bears) recognizes that the bull market is historically mature and statistically overvalued. So, when the market rises, bears sell into strength, thereby creating technical resistance to an extended upward movement.

Even though a reason for the volatility exists, the hectic movement can trigger investor motion sickness.

GET A GRIP ON YOUR NERVES

Because history shows that irrational behavior often occurs at the overvalue range of the stock market, investors need to remain calm at this time. The situation calls for prudence and patience, not panic.

The DJIA can linger in the overvalued territory for an excruciatingly long time. This can be a stressful stretch for investors. Nothing is more

FIGURE 7.3 Dividend-Yield Chart

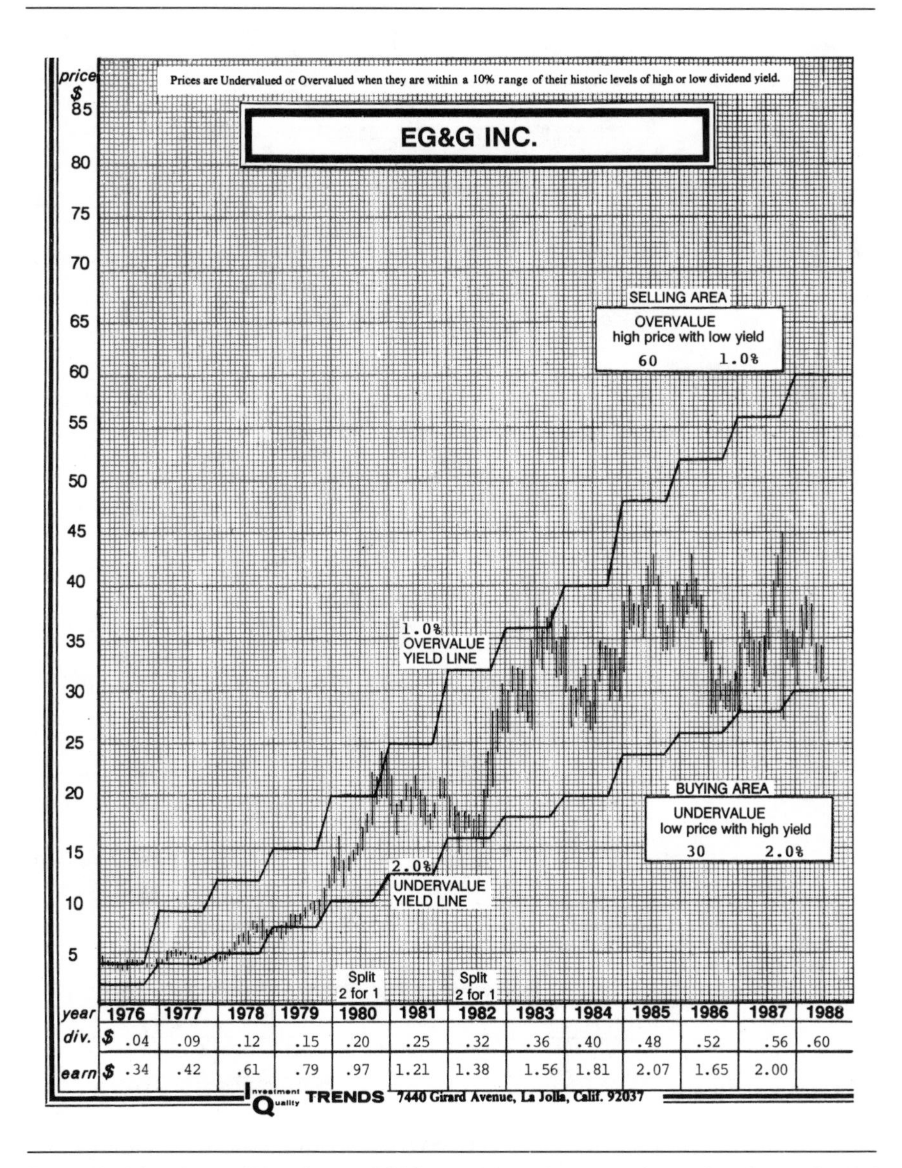

Even with dividends steadily on the rise, EG&G moved through two complete cycles of overvalue and undervalue between 1980 and 1987. A third cycle was aborted by the October 1987 crash, but EG&G quickly began a rebound.

FIGURE 7.4 Dividend-Yield Chart

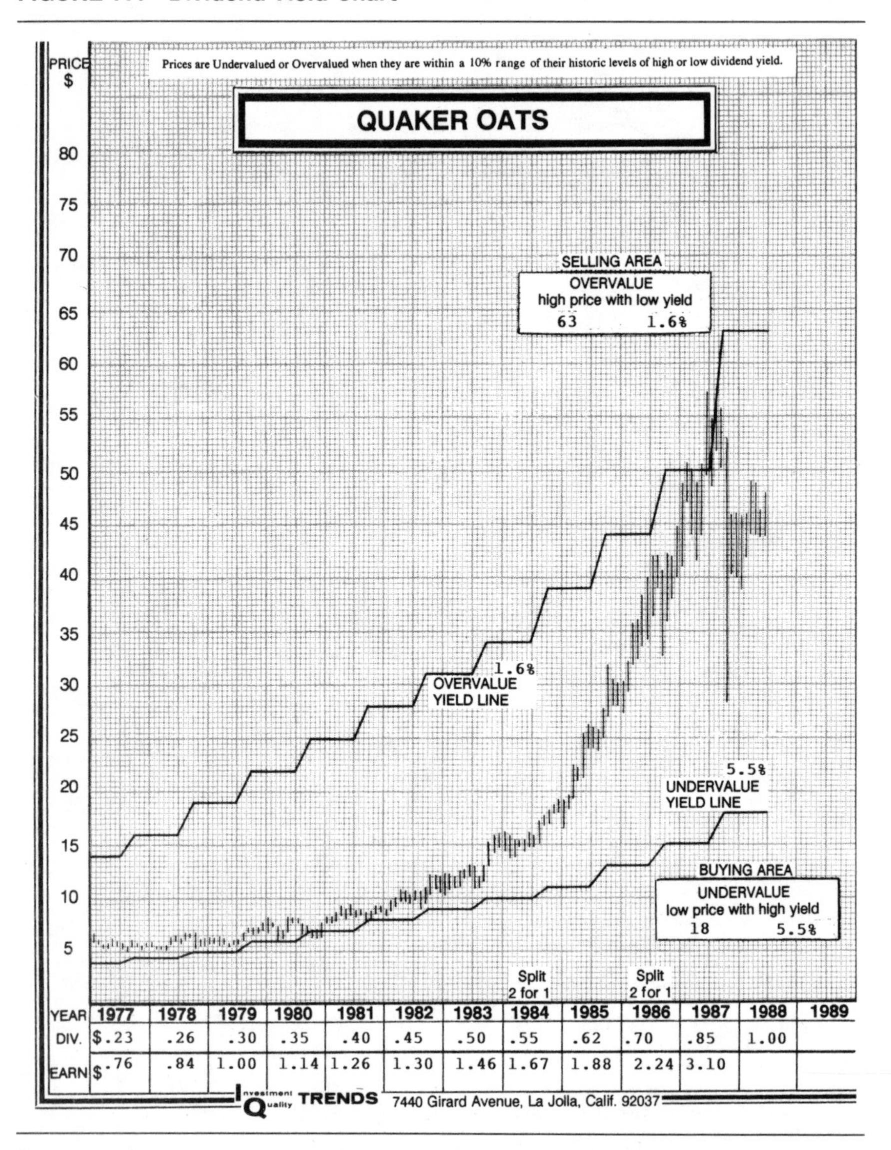

YEAR	1977	1978	1979	1980	1981	1982	1983	1984	1985	1986	1987	1988	1989
DIV.	$.23	.26	.30	.35	.40	.45	.50	.55	.62	.70	.85	1.00	
EARN	$.76	.84	1.00	1.14	1.26	1.30	1.46	1.67	1.88	2.24	3.10		

Quaker may have come out with quick oats, but its stock took its time to move to overvalue during the early 80's. It offered an exceptionally high dividend yield for a half-dozen years. Yet, dividends and earnings continually improved.

difficult than turning one's back on an exciting market. Attention is on the action and the high-flying stocks. Enthusiasm and optimism run wild.

CALCULATE DOWNSIDE RISK

Successful investing depends on the ability to recognize the potential downside risk that exists at the overvalue level. During this time, scrupulous attention should be paid to high quality and good value. This is no time to throw caution to the wind.

Investors are advised to absolutely avoid buying any overvalued stocks during such a period, regardless of their attractive fundamentals. Nothing is basically wrong with overvalued blue-chip companies; their stock is simply trading at too high a price and is vulnerable to heavy profit-taking.

CLEAN THE GARAGE, HAVE A SALE

When the DJIA is yielding 3.0 percent or less, it is the time to examine portfolios for stocks that need to be sold. Specifically, these would be the stocks with dividend yields that are within ten percent of overvalue. Profits can be collected and tucked away for better buys later.

BUT DON'T RUSH

If somehow a stock in the declining trend was not sold earlier, it should be sold now into market rallies. It will take a while for the market to unwind; bull markets do not turn on a dime. More than one opportunity will present itself to sell stocks that already have peaked at overvalue and now are in primary downtrends.

LEAVING THE STOCKS YOU LOVE

Stocks in a declining trend may not be an investor's worst problem. Newly overvalued stocks still hold considerable charm. When a share price is still rising, many investors cannot bring themselves to sell, even when they realize that a stock is overvalued. But it is better to miss a little of the upswing than to lose a lot when the turn comes.

Probably the best protection against a significant loss in the case of a market's sudden decline is to place a stop-loss order at ten percent under the price of any stocks in which one has substantial profits.

While this gives some peace of mind concerning stocks that are beyond the halfway mark in the rising category, it is an especially wise tactic for overvalued stocks to which investors have become emotionally attached and that they do not have the heart to sell, even when they are at the top. The stop-loss order would prevent devastating losses if the market turns tail with a vengeance, as it has been known to do occasionally. Stocks are automatically sold when a stop-loss price is reached.

"Puts" also can be an effective defense against such a price decline. A put option is a contract that grants the right to sell at a specified price a specific number of shares by a certain date. However, the time constraints on the investor using puts, which do not exist when using a stop-loss order, make them less advantageous. In either case, the risk of a small financial loss can be viewed as insurance against a large loss.

MARGIN IS DANGEROUS

Probably the great lesson of the 1929 crash is that buying on margin (or on borrowed money) in a mature bull market is folly. The uncertainty and volatility of that particular phase of the market causes thoughtful investors to limit their risk and limit their exposure to debt financing. In a big market decline margin calls are virtually guaranteed. When the bill comes due, it could be shockingly high.

For the same reasons, overvalued stocks should be sold at this phase to preserve profits and capital. Squeezing out a few more dollars of profits is seldom worth the risk.

KEEP SOMETHING IN RESERVE

The capital from selling overvalued shares can be reinvested in undervalued stocks or kept in liquid money accounts until a larger number of good values are available from which to make new selections. While at least 50 percent of available investment funds should be out of the market at the top, it isn't necessary to get out of the market completely.

DIVIDEND TRENDS HOLD TRUE

Even in a bear market, stocks that are undervalued or in the rising-trend categories need not be abandoned—especially stocks of companies with long histories of frequent dividend increases.

IS REPRIEVE POSSIBLE?

Unless dividends are raised, it is certain that sooner or later, overpriced stocks will decline in value and price. Usually at this stage, additional upside potential created by the possibility of a dividend increase does not justify the considerable downside risk of holding an overvalued stock.

But if dividends are raised, particularly when strong earnings are available to support those increases, a stock can spend a longer-than-usual time in the overvalue phase. As the American Business Products chart in figure 7.5 indicates, when dividends are raised, undervalued and overvalued prices also rise, extending the upside potentials and reducing the downside risk.

ABP reached overvalue in 1983, but dividend increases lifted the price and held them aloft for some time. The stock had additional support in that though it was initially overpriced, the Dow Jones Industrial Average, and therefore the market in general, had not reached overvalue.

As long as they're not overvalued, companies that have scored at least a ten percent compound annual dividend growth rate over the past decade can be held in a portfolio, even when the DJIA is overvalued. Such records are proof of good management and indicate that dividend growth is likely to continue in the future. These stocks can be held, even through a bear market, for uninterrupted income, growth of dividends and future capital gains.

TURN TO TOTAL RETURN

When a market is at maturity, a steady stream of dividend income takes on added importance. It implies that there will be a somewhat predictable return, even in a turbulent market. When a stock has a history of steadily increasing dividends, the growing dividend yield can compensate for possible declines in a stock price, and often total return on an investment can be maintained at its usual level.

FIGURE 7.5 Dividend-Yield Chart

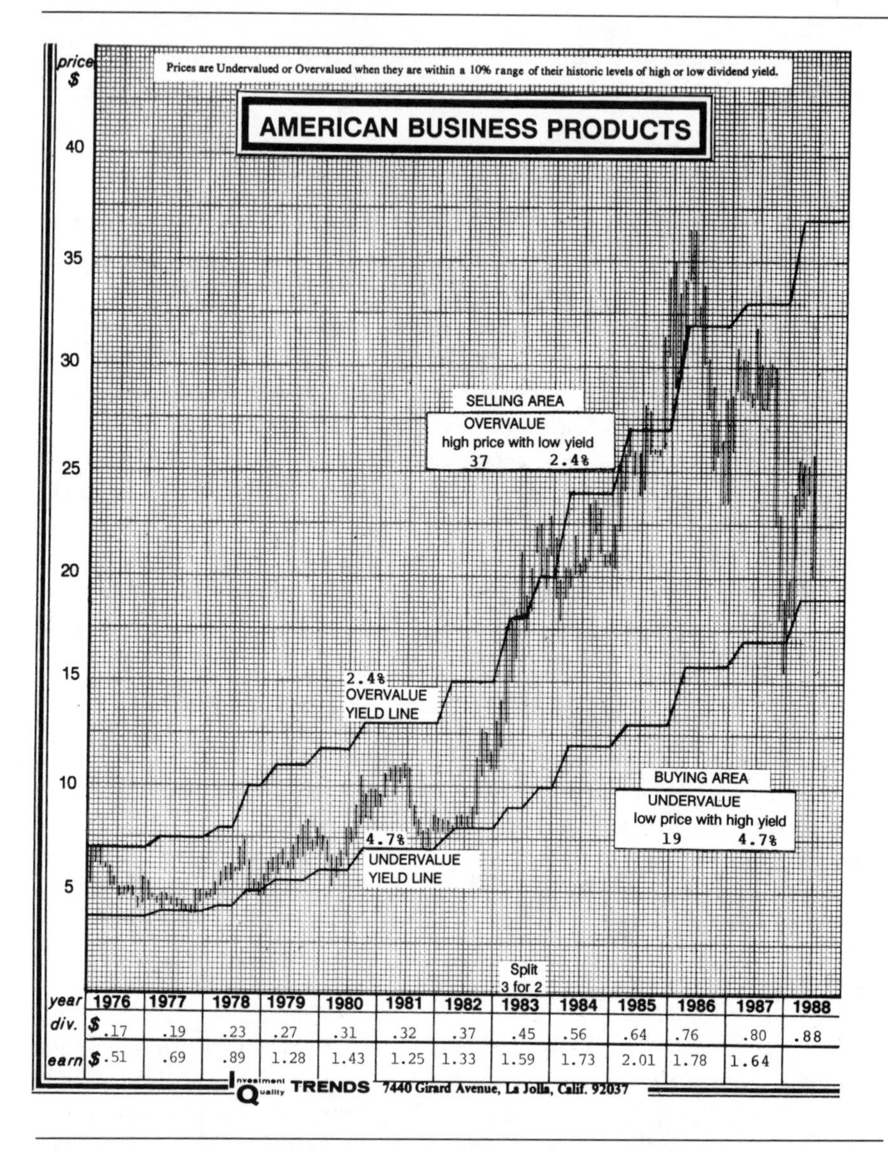

Investors who bought American Business Products in late 1977 and early 1978 were delighted by the rising stock price and the increasing dividend, but would have been foolish to sell before late 1983 or early 1984. Because of the dividend increases, the stock was undervalued until then. The price continued to move higher, but the risk of a reversal grew greater.

At the overvalued phase of the stock market, it is essential for investors to monitor the total return of their holdings. Total return, again, refers to capital gains (appreciation of share price) plus dividends. The dividend-yield theory shows that those stocks with increasing dividends are most likely to have increasing share price as well.

Figure 7.2 shows overvalued blue-chip stocks tracked in February of 1988. The shares with a rapid rate of dividend increases are designated by the letter "G" following the name. The other fundamental information on the chart allows close observation of a stock's status at this hazardous time in its cycle.

ON THE DEFENSIVE

Certain stocks traditionally provide defenses against an impending bull market. These are discussed in more detail in the next chapter.

Utilities with their high dividend yields are relatively safe, even in extended market declines. This is not to say, however, that they (or any stocks) are impervious to down pressure in a bear market. In addition, companies that manufacture drugs and disposable consumer products such as toothpaste, facial tissue and soap are thought to be defensive positions for troubled times. People always buy them. Food and tobacco stocks also have held up well in the past, for the same reason. However, even with these traditionally defensive stocks, it is essential to study dividend yields and avoid stocks that are overvalued or in a declining trend.

TIME PURCHASES CAREFULLY

Even for defensive undervalued or rising-trend stocks, it makes sense to wait for a temporary market decline to make purchases. These downticks present opportunities to fish for bargains. Because of the volatility at the top of markets, the temporary declines are sometimes frequent and rather deep.

PATIENCE PAYS OFF

Usually, at this stage of the market, investors should be thinking in terms of what to sell, rather than what to buy. The best bargains will come later; the market will always be there. It is wise to make certain that your capital will be there, as well. "You should not try to be a hero in today's markets," advised one broker when the stock market was overvalued and undergoing extreme volatility just before the 1987 breakdown. "Don't try to make an extra buck. Just be happy to keep the buck that you have already earned."

The Declining Trend

"Serene, I fold my hands and wait. . . ."

—JOHN BURROUGHS

"One of the French Rothschilds was asked the familiar question: 'How did all the members of your family manage to amass such a vast fortune?' The old baron smiled faintly and answered, 'By always selling too soon.' "

This story is told in *The Book of Business Anecdotes* by Peter Hay. The Rothschilds, it seems, developed the talent for getting out before a market declined. This alone was enough to make them very wealthy.

THE ROAD BACK DOWN

In the stock market, almost nothing is so dreaded and feared as a declining stock or a tumbling market. However, as alarmed as investors may be at regressing prices and gloomy news from Wall Street, these events do not come without warning. And while these are distressing times, they are as important as the booming years.

"It is my strong belief," William J. Lippman, president of L. F. Rothschild Managed Trust and chairman of the committee that sets policy for several mutual funds, wrote in a 1987 article for *Financial Strategies* magazine, "that one of the keys to building capital is preserving it during down periods in the market. This can be more important than outperforming the market on the upside."

Lippman recommended what he described as a "rising dividend approach," explaining, "The fact that a company can consistently raise its dividend provides a cushion during down markets also. To some degree, it insulates that company's stock against sharply declining prices. In a falling market, a company which pays a reasonable dividend is better protected than one with little or no dividend."

The dividend creates a price floor for any dividend-paying stock, he explained, because as the stock declines, its dividend yield increases, and more investors are attracted to it. Assuming that the fundamentals are sound, buying support is created.

Lippman recalled that during 1974 and 1975, many stocks suffered steep declines. "Exxon Corporation was a stock I followed and which I purchased when it dropped to $28," he said. "Exxon's dividend at that time was $2.80. At that point, the stock ended its decline. Why? It is my contention that people suddenly realized that the stock was paying a ten percent yield and said, 'This dividend is secure. It has always been paid. The company will probably raise the dividend again next year. At ten percent we will take a chance on the stock even in a bad market.' "

But even with the dividend cushion, as Lippman implies, declining markets can be perilous. No insurance can cover every risk. So in a declining market, even the best blue-chip stocks require attention.

AN OVERVALUED DOW

The first step in tending a portfolio is to recognize when the market is actually in a decline. The declining trend will begin at somewhere near the 3.0 dividend yield on the Dow, but the style with which it makes its entrance is unpredictable. It can slip in quietly, or dash in with great hoopla. Even if the reversal is abrupt, catching some investors unaware, it should not throw the unprepared investor into despair. Typically, stockholders get a second chance to sell in a declining market.

LANDINGS ON THE STAIRCASE

If history is a gauge, the retreating DJIA should find support again in the 4.0 percent yield area. This is an area from which a strong rally is likely to start, perhaps even a reversal of a bear market. It is in such a rally that overvalued stocks that through some oversight are remaining in a portfolio absolutely should be sold.

An example of this support level occurred in the second half of 1987. From its intraday high price of 2747 in August, the DJIA began to slip. At the close of the market on October 19, 1987, the dividend yield rose from 2.6 percent to 4.0 percent. That represented the first downside objective of a new bear market. As could be expected, the market rallied after Black Monday, giving investors an opportunity to recoup losses. In the more fortunate cases, the rally provided the chance to maximize profits.

SOME RALLIES ARE LENGTHY

Profitable rallies in a bear market can last for months, and sometimes even years. During these revivals, the DJIA occasionally returns to overvalue—the 3.0 percent yield value.

The bear market that started in 1966 did not produce a 6.0 percent yield on the DJIA until 1974, eight years later. During those eight years, two profitable rallies lasted between two and three years each. One advanced the price of the Dow by more than 30 percent; the other, by more than 60 percent.

AN UNEVEN IMPACT

Stocks that are marching out of step with the market in general, especially those independent-thinking renegades that are at the bottom when the market is at the top, could linger at the bottom somewhat longer. Stocks in their rising trends may face setbacks.

The down-market danger for an individual stock is demonstrated by the chart for Travelers Corporation in figure 8.1. Travelers was progressing nicely to overvalue in its typical "three steps forward, one step back" pattern when it was subverted by the bull market of late 1987.

Notice the more orderly decline beginning late in 1976. That trend took several years to reach the point where Travelers represented a good buy. The 1987 major market correction sent the company back in short order, though in these circumstances, a stock generally returns to its normal pattern with little time lost.

The impact of that dark Monday in October sent the insurance company's stock tumbling all the way to undervalue. Back at its undervalued level, the upside potential of Travelers exceeded 100 percent, and the downside risk was practically nonexistent.

The chart of Fort Howard Corporation (figure 8.2), a major producer and seller of papers and paper products, also illustrates the different, and sometimes unpredictable, characteristics of a declining trend. The journey back down the chart for Fort Howard was sudden and slippery in 1987, much different from its earlier pattern.

The volatility in these charts compares a generally orderly market with one that is highly overheated and consequently quite reactive.

DURATION OF A BEAR MARKET

A bear market historically can last from a minimum of two months up to nearly a decade. But those are extreme conditions. Under ordinary circumstances, a two-year decline can be expected.

DOWN, DOWN, DOWN

When following the path it most frequently has taken, a bear market has three down legs, separated by two intermediate rising trends, which offer chances again to take profits. The length of time for each of these stages varies, but the process can be studied in more detail by reviewing the historic chart of the DJIA dividend yield in chapter 4 (figure 4.4).

- As pointed out earlier, the first down leg can be expected to halt at the 4.0 percent yield area.
- After a period of revival, the second leg is likely to carry the DJIA even lower to a 5.0 percent yield.
- Hitting bottom: The third down leg is the most devastating of all to stockholders who have not prepared for it. In this final phase, the DJIA dividend yield generally declines to the 6.0 percent mark. On rare but gloomy occasions it has descended as low as 7.0 percent.

Again, to comprehend more fully the behavior of bear market trends, study the long-term Dow Jones Industrial Average chart in chapter 4.

FIGURE 8.1 Dividend-Yield Chart

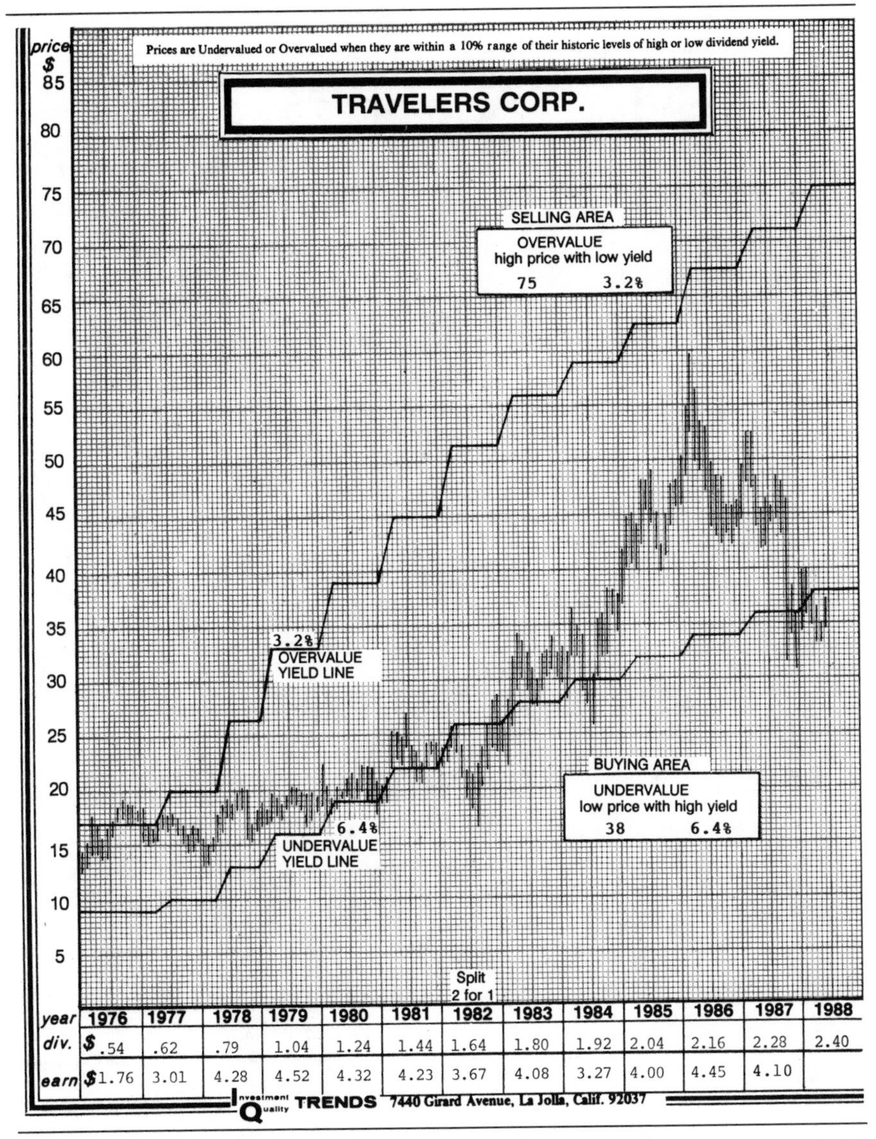

Travelers was too close to overvalue to withstand the shock of October 19, 1987. The stock tumbled all the way to undervalue. However, investors should remember that the 1987 crash was an extraordinary event. Seldom is a stock market so highly overvalued.

FIGURE 8.2 Dividend-Yield Chart

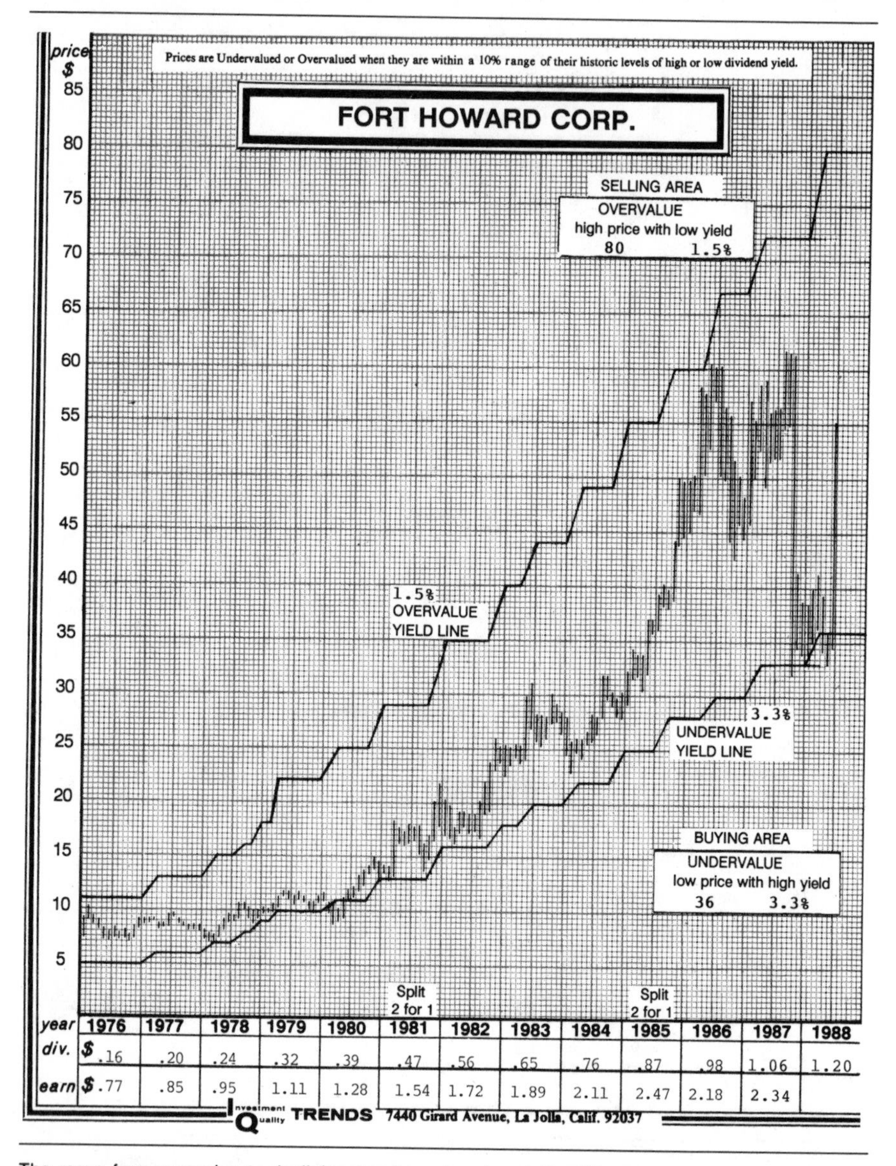

The move from overvalue to declining trend can be abrupt. For this reason, all overvalued stocks should be sold. Proceeds should be reinvested in undervalued stocks, or held in an interest-bearing account until a desirable stock becomes undervalued and can be purchased.

The Panhandle Eastern chart, figure 8.3, is a profile of what the three-step decline looks like in an individual stock. Panhandle reached overvalue in 1981 and, in three progressively lower levels, touched undervalue in late 1982. The stock's price was given support along the way by dividend increases.

The sudden drop in the dividend yield in 1986 came when Panhandle Eastern, a Texas natural gas and pipeline holding company, spun off Anadarko Petroleum Corporation to shareholders.

Panhandle's chart illustrates a historic pattern of undervalue and overvalue between yield perimeters of undervalue at 7.4 percent and overvalue at 3.3 percent. Although the price dropped below undevalue in 1982 when the nature of the pipeline industry began to change, it reestablished its undervalue base at 7.4 percent in 1983, 1984, 1985 and 1986. After the distribution of Anadarko to shareholders, Panhandle again rallied above the 7.4 percent yield line, where it remained until the October 1987 meltdown, when it again dipped briefly below undervalue.

SOUNDING THE DEPTHS

The rally points of the first two down legs of a declining trend also mark moments when markets can recover if the bear turns out to be timid. A revival occurs at these landings if there is a concrete surge in dividends, one backed by sales and earnings. In that case, the downturn may represent nothing more than a major correction in an ongoing bull market.

In the bear markets of 1960, 1962 and 1967, declines were curtailed and redirected when the dividend for the DJIA produced a 4.0 percent yield. The 1970 bear market was arrested in the 5.0 percent yield area.

In a fully mature bear market, the DJIA slides all the way to the six percent yield line. Until the market either confirms its upward path or declines below previously achieved low points though, some uncertainty exists as to the timing of the reversal.

THE COMFORT OF CONFIRMATION

Fortunately for investors' peace of mind, several methods of confirming a true bear market are available. One is the venerable Dow Theory, which states that a major trend in the stock market must be confirmed

FIGURE 8.3 Dividend-Yield Chart

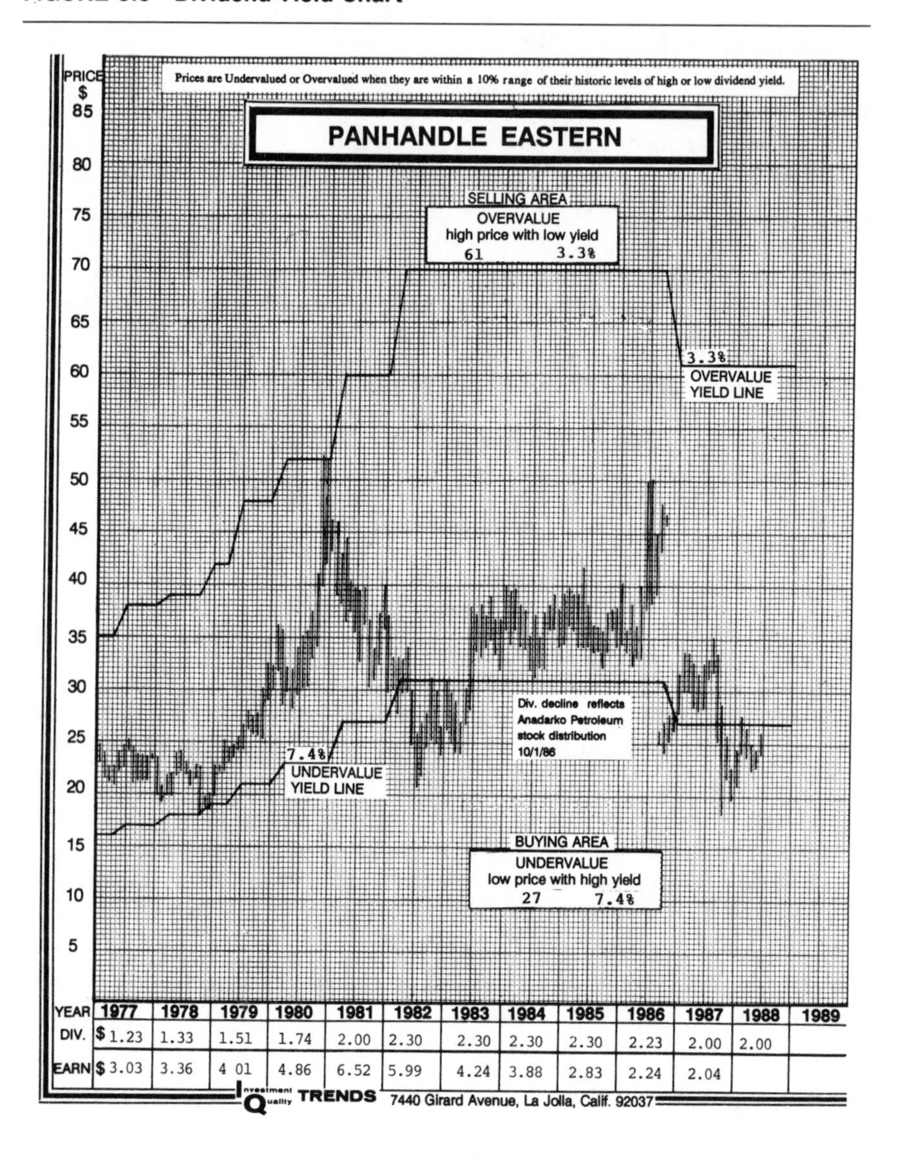

Panhandle Eastern's stock declined in the classic three-step pattern, a configuration that is often exhibited by the Dow Jones Industrial Average as well.

by similar movements in both the Dow Jones Industrial Average and the Dow Jones Transportation Average. A significant trend is not verified, according to the theory, until both indexes reach new highs or new lows. If they fail to do so, the market will fall back to its previous trading range. While helpful, the Dow Theory has not proved itself to be 100 percent reliable. It should be used as one more confirmation for the information provided by the dividend-yield theory.

Another compass for the direction of the market is a measurement of the increasing number of stocks that regress from overvalued into the declining trend, as measured by their individual dividend yields. The chart of declining-trend stocks, figure 8.4, is a sampling of shares that were declining in value as of mid-February 1987. By mid-February of the following year, the number of stocks in that category had doubled.

BEAR MARKET CONFIGURATION

What can be expected of stocks in a bear market? Stock prices, of course, trend down. But they don't follow a smooth and direct path. Yet in a bear market, prices do reach lower highs on every rise, and fall to lower lows on each decline. As the bear market approaches maturity, an increasing number of blue-chip companies will fall into the undervalued category, where patient, long-term investors can buy for current income and future capital gains.

INVESTMENT STRATEGY

The strategy in a declining market falls into two phases. Early in the game is the taking of profits; and later on, preparing to angle for bargains at the bottom.

While the trend is still new, investors are compelled to focus on selling those stocks that become overvalued or that have slipped into declines. Since not all stocks reach these stages in unison, some months could be required to weed a portfolio of overvalued and declining-trend shares.

Any vulnerable rising-trend stocks, such as those that do not have regular dividend increases or that are very near the top of their rising trend, can also be sold. If they are not sold, this is the time to consider a stop-loss order or some other measure to protect gains.

FIGURE 8.4 Declining-Trends Category

STOCK	Change in Category		Current Price		Current Ind Ann Div	Current Div Yield	Potential Pts. Down	Potential % Down	TO Undervalue Low Price	TO Undervalue High Yield	S&P Qual Rank	Earn Last 12 Mos (Up or Down)	Price/ Earns Ratio	Blue-Chip Status
ALLIED-SIGNAL CORP.			45	=	1.80	4.1%	19	43%	26	7.0%	B+	3.26	14	5
AMERICAN EXPRESS	G		68	★	1.44	2.2%	32	47%	36	4.0%	A	5.55U	12	6
AMERICAN GENERAL	G	O	40	★	1.25	3.2%	21	52%	19	6.5%	A	4.47U	9	6
AMERICAN GREETINGS	G		28	=	0.66	2.4%	10	35%	18	3.6%	A+	2.12D	13	6
AMERICAN HOME PROD.	G		81	★	3.34	4.2%	25	31%	56	6.0%	A+	5.18U	16	6
AMES DEPT. STORES	G		24		0.10	0.5%	22	90%	3	4.0%	A+	1.12	21	5
AMETEK, INC.			32	=	1.00	3.2%	17	53%	15	6.7%	A	1.66U	19	5
ANGELICA CORP.	G		26	★	0.64	2.5%	15	59%	11	6.0%	A	1.72D	15	5
BANKERS TRUST NY			48	★	1.66	3.5%	18	37%	30	5.5%	A	6.01U	8	6
BLOCK (H & R)	G	O	52	=	1.48	2.9%	31	59%	21	7.0%	A	2.41U	22	6
BROWN GROUP	G		39	★	1.50	3.9%	18	45%	21	7.0%	A–	2.17D	18	6
BURLINGTON NORTHERN			65	=	2.00	3.1%	(NOTE: Dividend in Danger)					Deficit	0	6
CHUBB CORP.	G		65	★	1.68	2.6%	39	60%	26	6.5%	B+	7.05U	9	5
CORNING GLASS WORKS	G		57	=	1.40	2.5%	22	39%	35	4.0%	B+	4.04U	14	5
DELUXE CHECK PRINT.	G		37	★	0.72	2.0%	21	57%	16	4.5%	A+	1.42U	26	6
DIEBOLD, INC.	G		54	★	1.20	2.3%	24	44%	30	4.0%	A	2.66	20	6
ECHLIN INC.	G	O	22	=	0.50	2.3%	12	53%	10	4.8%	A–	1.15U	19	6
FLEMING COMPANY			40	=	1.00	2.6%	24	60%	16	6.2%	A+	1.80D	22	5
FORT HOWARD PAPER	G		51	★	1.08	2.2%	18	36%	33	3.3%	A+	2.18D	23	6
FOSTER-WHEELER	G		18	)	0.44	2.5%	11	61%	7	6.3%	B+	0.70D	26	5
GORDON JEWELRY CL A	G		19	=	0.52	2.8%	7	38%	12	4.4%	B+	1.17	16	5
HARCOURT-BRACE			34	=	0.40	1.2%	27	80%	7	6.0%	A–	1.93U	18	5
HARTMARX CORP.			28	=	0.92	3.3%	14	49%	14	6.5%	A+	1.20D	23	6
HEWLETT-PACKARD			53	=	0.22	0.5%	31	58%	22	1.0%	A+	2.02U	26	5
INTL. MULTIFOODS			26	=	1.18	4.6%	11	41%	15	7.7%	A–	1.50D	17	5
KIDDE INC.	G		33	)	1.20	3.7%	13	39%	20	6.0%	A–	1.12D	29	5
LOMAS & NETTLETON FIN.	G		32	★	1.12	3.6%	14	44%	18	6.2%	A+	2.12	15	5
MCA, INC.	G		42	=	0.68	1.7%	25	60%	17	4.0%	B+	2.02	21	4
MELLON BANK CORP.			54	=	2.76	5.2%	17	32%	37	7.5%	A+	6.20	9	6
MEREDITH CORP.	G		32	)	0.50	1.6%	21	64%	11	4.4%	A+	1.63D	20	6
MORGAN, J. P.	G		45	★	1.36	3.1%	18	40%	27	5.0%	A+	2.37D	19	6
NATIONAL SERV. INDUS.	G		23	★	0.64	2.8%	13	57%	10	6.5%	A+	1.47U	16	6
NCR CORP.	G		59	★	1.00	1.7%	41	69%	18	5.5%	A	3.42U	17	6
PHILIP MORRIS	G		85	★	3.00	3.6%	35	41%	50	6.0%	A+	6.20U	14	6
PILLSBURY	G		40	★	1.00	2.6%	19	47%	21	4.7%	A+	2.40	17	6
PITNEY BOWES		O	40	★	0.76	1.9%	25	62%	15	5.0%	A	2.12U	19	6
SHAKLEE CORP.	G		24		0.72	3.1%	12	50%	12	6.0%	A–	1.08	22	5
SOUTHLAND CORP.	G		53	=	1.12	2.2%	28	53%	25	4.5%	A+	4.39U	12	6
STRIDE RITE			31	★	0.88	2.9%	20	65%	11	8.0%	A–	2.25U	14	5
SYNTEX CORP.	G		70	=	1.60	2.3%	(NOTE: Dividend in Danger)					0.19	0	5

These stocks are moving DOWN toward the undervalue area. The investor holding these declining stocks should expect shrinking prices until a turnaround takes place, usually in the undervalue area. The investor looking for investment opportunities should avoid these stocks until their declining trends are concluded.

Fort Howard Corporation, the paper and paper products company mentioned earlier (figure 8.2), is another illustration of how vulnerable rising-trend stocks nearing overvalue can be. A move to overvalue was completely aborted in the fall of 1987 when the market turned on its heel and fled to lower levels. The beginning of the rising trend for Fort Howard, however, suggests that its recovery and a repeat move to overvalue could be quite rapid.

A similar pattern is demonstrated by Air Products & Chemicals in figure 8.5. This major international supplier of medical gases and related equipment ordinarily took at least a year to move from overvalue to undervalue. But in the 1987 market shock, it also plunged. However, the upward reaction was also just as abrupt and steep.

PROSPERING IN A DULL MARKET

While it is obvious that no smart investor buys a stock when it is still on the downward trail, it is not true that money cannot be made or stock cannot be bought in a declining stock market. These are techniques, however, for investors who are able to handle some level of risk. For those who demand preservation of capital, it is best to take a more cautious route.

A BEAR MARKET BUYER

Even in a bear market, undervalued stocks can be found. It's just that there are fewer of them, making it ever more difficult to match purchases to a balanced and diversified portfolio. The greatest safety can be found in the defensive stocks mentioned in the previous chapter and discussed in greater detail later on.

SELLING SHORT

When the bull market has ended and the bear market is in full view, very aggressive investors may want to "short" some of the stocks that remain overvalued. The short selling of a security can be utilized to take advantage of an expected decline in a share's price. In this procedure, an investor borrows stock certificates (usually from his or her broker's firm)

FIGURE 8.5 Dividend-Yield Chart

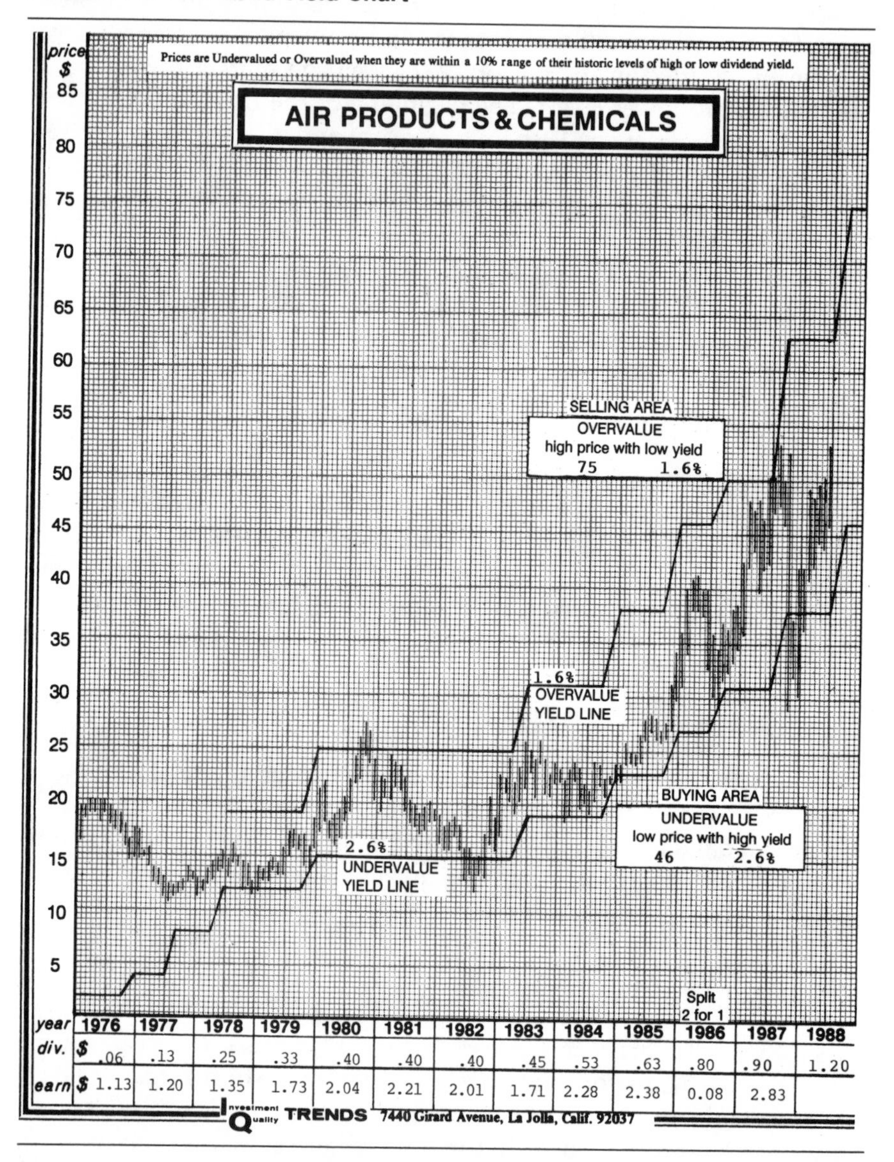

year	1976	1977	1978	1979	1980	1981	1982	1983	1984	1985	1986	1987	1988
div. $	.06	.13	.25	.33	.40	.40	.40	.45	.53	.63	.80	.90	1.20
earn $	1.13	1.20	1.35	1.73	2.04	2.21	2.01	1.71	2.28	2.38	0.08	2.83	

Stocks nearing overvalue should be carefully tracked. Air Products & Chemicals became vulnerable to a decline as it neared overvalue. Poor 1986 earnings contributed to the stock's sensitivity. Earnings recovered, but a market crash sent the stock quickly to undervalue in late 1987.

for delivery at the time of the short sale. If the seller can buy the borrowed stock later at a lower price, a profit is taken; if the price rises, however, a loss results.

For example, an investor who anticipates a decline in the price of Benjamin Corporation (a fictitious company), which is grossly overvalued at $60 per share, may instruct the broker to short perhaps 100 shares of Benjamin when the stock trades at $50. The broker lends the investor 100 shares either from the brokerage's own inventory or from the margin account of another customer. The investor now has a short position, holding but not owning Benjamin. At some point the investor must buy the shares to repay the broker. If the stock falls to $20, the investor can then buy the shares, repay the broker the $2,000 owed and claim a profit of $3,000.

Short selling can work in any market with an overvalued stock, but it is more likely to result in profit when used with an overvalued stock in a declining market. To further enhance chances of a profit, investors should select a stock without a record of frequent dividend increases.

TERROR TAKES OVER

It has been said that the market's driving forces are love, greed and fear. Love prevailed in the rising market; greed stepped in when the market was at the top. Later, in a declining market, many investors are gripped in the fist of fear.

But information, not a churning stomach, should be a guide for selling. Stock sales should be as judiciously planned as the purchases that are just ahead. The respected investor Warren Buffett once said that "the market, like the Lord, helps those who help themselves. But, unlike the Lord, the market does not forgive those who know not what they do."

PLANNING FUTURE PURCHASES

It should take more than falling prices at this stage to make investors pick up the telephone and instruct their broker to buy. Good value is not identified merely by a steep decline from a previously high price. A stock may depreciate 50 percent or more and still not be undervalued by historical standards. Or it may decline only moderately and be historically undervalued due to substantial increases in the dividend.

STUDY THE FUNDAMENTALS

Price is an absolute; value is relative. Therefore, price always must be related to other significant investment factors to determine value in an appropriate and valid manner. A noteworthy reduction in price, however, should alert investors to the possibility that a stock has become fundamentally undervalued.

BUYING AT THE BOTTOM

One should not be disturbed by the fact that a stock that has reached undervalue may ebb down even further before it reverses and climbs. Exact bottoms, like precise tops, have a certain illusive quality. But at a stock's historic undervalue level, it does not have much lower down to go. It is a good buy; the best an investor can hope for is to buy in the undervalued range. It is self-defeating to worry about the few dollars lower a stock might drop, or does drop, after a purchase.

A FIRE SALE ON WALL STREET

There is never a bad time to buy good value in the market. But some times are better than other times. At the bottom of a declining market, investors can have a heyday.

A declining market is difficult for some investors to wait out. They get restless. They hate to hold money temporarily in low-yielding liquid accounts. It is far better, however, to accept a relatively low rate of return in the money market for a short while than to lose one's capital in the stock market forever. It would also be a pity to miss out on the chance to buy wonderful values at low prices.

Investors who time their purchases to significant yields on the Dow Jones Industrial Average have a wide and diverse selection of undervalued choices from which to select when the bottom arrives. Those purchases also have the best opportunities for long-term growth of capital and growth of dividend income.

When the market finally reaches its nadir, general pessimism will prevail. Just as it isn't easy to be the only naysayer when the investment world is ecstatic with growth, it is not easy to be the only optimist in a disgruntled crowd. But this is the time at which the enlightened investor becomes alert.

Louis Rukeyser tells about the infamous day in 1929 when the stock market crashed. His father happened to meet Bernard Baruch on the street. "This is a terrible day in the stock market," said Mr. Rukeyser. "Not for buyers," answered Mr. Baruch.

BUILD A BETTER PORTFOLIO

At a low point in the market, it is best to accumulate as much cash as possible for the many excellent buying opportunities that will become available. So many good buys will be offered that it could be difficult to pick the best. So one should buy a variety of stocks. This is the time to strengthen a portfolio by diversification and to, once more, patiently and with complacent certainty, await a rising trend. Investors who consistently take home profits understand this principle well.

"Most people get interested in stocks when everyone else is," Warren Buffett was quoted in a 1985 *Newsweek* article as telling an estate-building seminar. "The time to get interested is when no one else is. You can't buy what is popular and do well."

9

The Dow and Its Cousin Indexes

"Order and simplification are the first steps toward the mastery of a subject."

—THOMAS MANN

The Dow Jones Industrial Average, created nearly a century ago to gauge the direction of the New York Stock Exchange, has become something of a national oracle. Politicians look to it for confirmation of worth. Both presidents Lyndon Johnson and Ronald Reagan saw it as a measure of their success—though with differing results.

Devotees turn to the Dow for mystical signs, omens of events. If the month of January ends on an up note, say certain high priests of the market, so will that entire year. The all-knowing DJIA maintains mysterious relationships with other elements of the American society. For example, if the Dow's favorite baseball team wins the World Series, the market will rise in celebration. Otherwise, it broods and lashes back at investors with a poor market performance. And obviously the god of Dow Industrials has an eye for the ladies. Supposedly if hemlines go higher, so does the market; if hemlines gravitate toward the ankles, the DJIA is displeased.

If Americans seem to need a little silliness and superstition to lighten the workday, they're not the only ones. In Japan, *gosugi soba* is a slang term that describes the bouyant prices on the Tokyo Stock Exchange on the first business day of the New Year. The New Year is a felicitous time, and no matter what the realities may be, it would not do to have a slumping market. So buyers and sellers usually conspire to give the market a boost when it reopens for business after the New Year holiday.

This book devotes a great deal of attention to the Dow Jones Industrial Average. The Dow frequently has been used as a gauge of the market and as a predictor of future investment climates, though no magical qualities have been attributed to it. In fact, as a gauge of stock market activities, the Dow has its critics. So it's important to ask the question: Does the Dow Jones Industrial Average really matter to most investors? After all, one buys individual stocks, with their own specific characteristics and measures of value; what difference does an index, which certain experts say doesn't reflect the market anyway, make? Wouldn't it be more accurate and contemporary to use the Standard & Poor's 500 or some other broad measure of stock market activity?

AN AUGUST INDICATOR

Despite its critics and criticism, the DJIA has provided a reasonably accurate indication of general market trends since 1897. Whatever inaccuracies the DJIA may be accorded, the wide acceptance it has enjoyed for so long a period of time by generations of investors underscores its importance and attests to its service as a measure of the market.

THINK PERCENTAGES

To use the Dow Jones averages as the tool they were intended to be, additional information is helpful. This oldest and most widely studied of market indicators is quoted in points, not in dollars. And as the DJIA levels rise ever higher, the average should be regarded with percentages in mind, rather than real numbers. After all, when the Dow was at 1000, a 100-point drop (or ten percent) was infinitely more meaningful than was a 100-point loss (or 3.7 percent) when the index reached 2700.

"The DJIA is calculated by adding the closing prices of the component stocks and using a divisor that is adjusted for splits and stock dividends equal to ten percent or more of the market value of an issue as well as for substitutions and mergers," according to Barron's *Dictionary of Finance and Investment Terms.*

The Dow Industrial is not adjusted for inflation, so its long-term direction is always upward. However, when dividends are included for a total return and adjusted for inflation, the direction still is a genuine upward slope.

THE DOW UNIVERSE

The DJIA comprises 30 companies, not all of them industrial, which represent between 15 and 20 percent of the market value of the New York Stock Exchange stocks. No stocks from the American Stock Exchange or the over-the-counter markets are included in the DJIA; nor are low-capitalization stocks or small companies.

All of the Dow Industrial stocks, along with recent fundamental information on them, are included in the chart in figure 9.1. At the back of this book, dividend-yield profiles for each DJIA stock are also represented.

A BLUE-CHIP INDICATOR

While the stocks included in the DJIA may not closely parallel all of the companies trading on all of the stock markets, they do provide a generally reliable reflection of the stocks that meet the blue-chip standards outlined in this book.

Even so, not all of the 30 stocks included in the Dow Industrials meet our blue-chip criteria. At the start of 1988, eight of the 30 fell below our minimum Standard & Poor's stock ranking. Three of the 30 were not paying dividends.

THE DOW REFLECTS THE U.S. INDUSTRIAL CORE

Nevertheless, the DJIA stocks are among the largest, oldest and most reliable companies in the United States. They represent diverse industries; they have an enormous investor base; and a great deal of research information is available on them. When something happens to one of these stocks, or a change occurs in the industries in which they operate, investors far and wide react. Their buying and selling is reflected in share price, and therefore in the Dow itself.

Likewise, the dividend yield of each stock in the average creates a market trend. The dividend yield and growth of the yield, like the index

FIGURE 9.1 Dow Jones Industrial Stocks

12-MO. HI-LO	D.J.I.A. STOCKS	RECENT PRICE	ANN. DIV.	DIV. YIELD	P/E RATIO	UNDERVALUE PRICE/YIELD		OVERVALUE PRICE/YIELD		BOOK VALUE	12-MO. ERNGS.	S&P QUAL.	TICK. SYMB.
65–34	ALCOA	47	1.20	2.6%	19	24	5.0%	48	2.5%	39	2.52	B–	AA
49–26	ALLIED-SIGNAL	33	1.80	5.5%	9	26	7.0%	51	3.5%	10	3.90	B+	ALD
41–21	AMER. EXPRESS	27	.76	2.8%	23	19	4.0%	42	1.8%	13	1.20	A–	AXP
36–23	AT&T	29	1.20	4.2%	15	15	8.0%	34	3.5%	13	1.88	A–	T
23– 7	BETH. STEEL	23	–	–	15	DIVIDEND OMITTED				12	1.48	C	BS
54–34	BOEING	50	1.40	2.8%	16	23	6.0%	93	1.5%	31	3.10	B+	BA
65–32	CHEVRON	45	2.40	5.3%	15	34	7.0%	73	3.3%	45	2.94	A	CHV
53–29	COCA-COLA	40	1.20	3.0%	16	24	5.0%	48	2.5%	3	2.43	A+	KO
131–75	DU PONT	87	3.40	3.9%	12	65	5.2%	126	2.7%	51	7.39	B+	DD
71–40	EASTMAN KODAK	42	1.80	4.3%	12	36	5.0%	138	1.3%	18	3.52	A–	EK
51–33	EXXON	44	2.00	4.5%	13	24	8.5%	53	3.8%	23	3.43	A	XON
66–39	GEN. ELECTRIC	44	1.40	3.2%	19	28	5.0%	70	2.0%	25	3.20	A+	GE
94–50	GEN. MOTORS	72	5.00	6.9%	7	83	6.0%	167	3.0%	56	10.06	B	GM
77–35	GOODYEAR	66	1.60	2.4%	5	20	8.0%	67	2.4%	31	12.73	A–	GT
176–100	IBM	114	4.40	3.9%	13	110	4.0%	220	2.0%	63	8.72	A+	IBM
58–27	INTER. PAPER	44	1.20	2.7%	12	22	5.5%	48	2.7%	34	3.68	B+	IP
61–31	MCDONALD'S	47	.50	1.1%	15	25	2.0%	50	1.0%	18	3.14	A+	MCD
223–144	MERCK	160	3.84	2.4%	24	110	3.5%	320	1.2%	18	6.68	A+	MRK
84–45	MMM	64	2.12	3.3%	14	35	6.0%	177	1.2%	20	4.02	A	MMM
9– 4	NAVISTAR INTL.	6	–	–	13	DIVIDEND OMITTED				d5	.60	C	NAV
125–77	PHILIP MORRIS	94	3.60	3.8%	12	60	6.0%	129	2.8%	7	7.75	A+	MO
54–22	PRIMERICA	31	1.60	5.2%	9	17	9.2%	40	4.0%	18	3.05	B+	PA
104–60	PROCTER&GAMBLE	82	2.80	3.4%	29	56	5.0%	187	1.5%	24	2.76	A+	PG
60–30	SEARS, ROEBUCK	38	2.00	5.3%	9	29	7.0%	167	1.2%	33	4.35	B+	S
48–27	TEXACO	45	–	–	–	DIVIDEND OMITTED				57	DEF.	D	TX
33–16	UNION CARBIDE	25	1.50	6.0%	14	21	7.0%	43	3.5%	7	1.76	B–	UK
61–30	UNITED TECH.	42	1.40	3.3%	9	19	7.5%	39	3.6%	27	4.52	A–	UTX
39–21	USX CORP.	32	1.20	3.8%	65	17	7.0%	34	3.5%	17	.49	B–	X
75–40	WESTINGHOUSE	52	1.72	3.3%	10	22	8.0%	52	3.3%	19	5.12	A+	WX
60–30	WOOLWORTH	48	1.32	2.8%	13	17	8.0%	53	2.5%	23	3.58	B+	Z

This fundamental information on the 30 stocks that are used to calculate the Dow Jones Industrial Average was compiled April 1, 1988.

itself, forecast coming events or, at the very least, investor expectations about coming events.

The Standard & Poor's 500, the Value Line Composite Index and the Wilshire 5000 Equity Index each comprise more stocks and therefore may more closely approximate what is happening generally in the markets. However, the Dow, because of its selectivity, suits our needs best.

THE FUTURE FORETOLD

The Dow Industrial Average, like other market indicators, continually discounts the future. It looks forward and reflects a consensus of expectations for the economy and for the stock market.

Historians contend that the stock market never writes off the same event twice. A recession of considerable magnitude was discounted in the August-to-October 1987 decline of 36 percent, when one trillion dollars was erased from equity values. If that recession should fail to appear, or if it should turn out to be less severe than originally anticipated, the market will have made the adjustment before the actual event.

At the time of the August–October 1987 decline, the Dow, based on its dividend yield, was overvalued to below the historic 3.0 percent yield at which a bull market ends. It fell to 2.6 percent, a major deviation for the DJIA dividend yield.

The aberrant behavior of the Dow in relation to its dividend yield practically guaranteed a substantial correction. Like on a bobsled ride, the effects of leaning too far in one direction must be compensated for by leaning far in the opposite direction.

At only one other time did a 3.0 percent dividend yield on the DJIA not reverse a rising-trend market. The record shows that in 1964, after reaching a 3.0 percent yield area, the Dow Industrials extended a rising trend by an additional 15 percent, while the composite dividend (derived from all three Dow indexes, as discussed later in this chapter) rose by 22 percent. When the Industrial Average finally peaked at the beginning of 1966, the dividend yield was still 3.0 percent. Except for that single, two-year period of rapidly rising dividends, a 3.0 percent yield on the DJIA has signaled the end of primary bull markets stretching back as far as 1929.

INVESTORS ON ALERT

As the values of the Dow stocks increase, so must dividends. Otherwise, investors are paying too high a price for the shares they buy.

Dividends were increased in 1987, but not by as much as they had been in earlier years. The dividend of the DJIA rose 6.2 percent in 1987, reflecting a $4.16 increase in the total payout of the 30 component companies. The increase fell short of the 8.1 percent growth of 1986. Moreover, dividend increases for the Dow Industrial stocks were not in keeping with earnings increases, indicating that corporate management for these companies had some misgivings about releasing cash or maintaining the dividend increases in the future.

The 6.2 percent dividend growth was disappointing in view of an estimated 29 percent gain in profits for 1987. Where did the profits go, if not to the shareholders? Some companies spent their cash on mergers and acquisitions, while others began paying off debt to improve the look of their balance sheets and perhaps to shore up defenses against an anticipated economic downturn.

Still, without tangible evidence that corporate executives saw a good year ahead, without assurance that they could provide improved values and higher returns for stockholders, the potential for sustainable stock market gains in that year and in 1988 became limited and uninspiring.

A RESPITE FOR THE MARKET

That the market would take a breather at this point was not surprising. Between 1984 and 1987, the DJIA had climbed 150 percent (from 1100 to 2747) without so much as a ten percent bout of profit-taking. A 150 percent surge over a period of three years amounts to a remarkable gain of 50 percent a year, and it is generally perceived that a 50 percent annual return on any investment is unsustainable.

As early as mid-September 1987, only nine of the Dow stocks were in the rising trend and appropriate for holding for future gains. Seventeen of the 30 were either overvalued or already in a declining trend.

"Unless dividends are raised," warned "Investment Quality Trends," "these stocks are likely to decline toward undervalue."

BEWARE OF ROUND NUMBERS

Another clue that the Dow could make a U-turn was the index's sailing past the 2000 mark virtually as if it weren't even there. Big round numbers in the Dow Industrials, in the past, had always presented price rise barriers.

The Industrial Average reached its first 1000 price milestone in 1966. That barrier was not decisively penetrated until 16 years later in 1982. During those 16 years were periods of rising and declining prices in which investors made (and lost) money.

The market did indeed reverse itself on October 19, 1987, with something of a pyrotechnic show, losing more than 1000 points before the DJIA settled down, well under the 2000 mark.

Blue chips tracked by "Investment Quality Trends" reacted in concert with the Dow Jones Industrial Average, with dividend yields adjusting in a predictable fashion. By the next day, October 20, 1987, the number of stocks in the undervalued category had risen from 49 (14 percent of the total 350 stocks tracked by the advisory) to 91 (26 percent). The number of stocks in the overvalued category had declined from 118 (34 percent) to 49 (14 percent).

This news-making turn of events naturally led to worries that a weakening economy would follow. All too often, a recession does follow the onset of a bear market. A study of previous markets shows that when an anticipated recession does arrive, the markets move smartly upward, reflecting the likelihood of lower interest rates and the outlook for an economic recovery somewhere down the road.

THE DJTA, THE DJUA AND THE COMPOSITE

Just as overvalue and undervalue levels can be established for the Industrial Average, so too can they be set for the Dow Jones Transportation and Utility averages. Figure 9.2 shows the undervalue and overvalue perimeters of the DJTA and the DJUA. Transportation stocks follow the industrials closely, overvalued at three percent and undervalued at six percent. The utilities, which are studied in chapter 12, are overvalued at a three percent dividend yield and undervalued at 12. Charts from 1977 and 1987, figures 9.3 and 9.4, are also included here so that a comparison of the market at different phases can be made.

The Dow Jones Composite is sometimes called the 65 Stock Average. It combines the Dow industrial, transportation and utility averages. While this index is a good barometer of market trends, it is too broadly based to be of significant use in the dividend-yield system.

THE DOW THEORY

As mentioned earlier, the Transportation Average, which includes 20 airline, railroad, trucking and similar companies, is useful as a verifier of DJIA trends. If the Industrial Average reaches a new high or falls to a new low, and the Transportation Average does the same, then a trend is thought to be confirmed.

The Utility Average is intended to act as a windsock for those who hold utility stocks. It tells which way the breeze is blowing. The DJUA is made up of 15 gas and electric companies, and can show the direction and magnitude of utility trends. It also can show how closely that industry group is aligning itself with the DJIA, or with industry as a

FIGURE 9.2 Measures of the Market—1988

Dividends for the Dow Jones Averages reflect the 12 months through March 1988.

Dow Jones Industrial Average	*Current*			*Potential to Overvalue*				*Potential to Undervalue*			
	Price	*Ann. Div*	*Yield*	*Pts. Up*	*% Up*	*High Price*	*Low Yield*	*Pts. Down*	*% Down*	*Low Price*	*High Yield*
	2048	$71.85	3.5%	347	17%	2395	3%	850	42%	1198	6%

Dow Jones Transportation Average	*Current*			*Potential to Overvalue*				*Potential to Undervalue*			
	Price	*Ann. Div*	*Yield*	*Pts. Up*	*% Up*	*High Price*	*Low Yield*	*Pts. Down*	*% Down*	*Low Price*	*High Yield*
	845	$51.26	6%	864	102%	1709	3%	—	—	854	6%

Dow Jones Utilities Average	*Current*			*Potential to Overvalue*				*Potential to Undervalue*			
	Price	*Ann. Div*	*Yield*	*Pts. Up*	*% Up*	*High Price*	*Low Yield*	*Pts. Down*	*% Down*	*Low Price*	*High Yield*
	170	$15.90	9.4%	360	212%	530	3%	37	22%	133	12%

Investment Quality Trends 7440 Girard Avenue, Suite #4, La Jolla, CA 92037

whole. Because of a unique set of conditions surrounding the utility industry, special consideration must be given to establishing value for utilities. Those factors are discussed at length in chapter 12.

BACK TO TOTAL RETURN

Though it is not an indicator that must be followed on a regular basis, a fascinating snapshot of long-term market trends is provided by the New York Stock Exchange Total Return Index, which has been compiled by the Institute for Econometric Research. This index demonstrates that despite impressive showings from time to time by collectibles, gold and other esoteric investments, when dividends are considered, stocks still are the most rewarding long-term financial investment around.

The index covers 20 years, and shows that even the market collapse in the fall of 1987 did not significantly change the overall outlook. See figure 9.5.

"If you had bought ten years before the August (1987) market peak," reported *Business Week* magazine in its issue of December 28,

FIGURE 9.3 Measures of the Market—1977

	Current			Potential to Overvalue				Potential to Undervalue			
Dow Jones Industrial Average	Price	Ann. Div	Yield	Pts. Up	% Up	High Price	Low Yield	Pts. Down	% Down	Low Price	High Yield
P/E Ratio: 10	927	$42.63	4.6%	494	53%	1421	3%	74	8%	853	5%

	Current			Potential to Overvalue				Potential to Undervalue			
Dow Jones Transportation Average	Price	Ann. Div	Yield	Pts. Up	% Up	High Price	Low Yield	Pts. Down	% Down	Low Price	High Yield
P/E Ratio: 8	233	$9.26	4%	76	33%	309	3%	79	34%	154	6%

	Current			Potential to Overvalue				Potential to Undervalue			
Dow Jones Utilities Average	Price	Ann. Div	Yield	Pts. Up	% Up	High Price	Low Yield	Pts. Down	% Down	Low Price	High Yield
P/E Ratio: 8	108	$7.67	7.1%	148	137%	256	3%	—	—	128	6%

FIGURE 9.4 Measures of the Market—1987

Dividends for the Dow Averages reflect the 12 months through June 1987

	Current			Potential to Overvalue				Potential to Undervalue			
Dow Jones Industrial Average	Price	Ann. Div	Yield	Pts. Up	% Up	High Price	Low Yield	Pts. Down	% Down	Low Price	High Yield
	2608	$69.36	2.7%	—	—	2312	3%	1452	56%	1156	6%

	Current			Potential to Overvalue				Potential to Undervalue			
Dow Jones Transportation Average	Price	Ann. Div	Yield	Pts. Up	% Up	High Price	Low Yield	Pts. Down	% Down	Low Price	High Yield
	1033	$15.99	1.5%	—	—	533	3%	767	74%	266	6%

	Current			Potential to Overvalue				Potential to Undervalue			
Dow Jones Utilities Average	Price	Ann. Div	Yield	Pts. Up	% Up	High Price	Low Yield	Pts. Down	% Down	Low Price	High Yield
	200	$15.76	7.9%	325	163%	525	3%	69	35%	131	12%

By comparing stock market fundamentals in 1977 to 1987, it becomes clear how much things can change, and how varied the markets can be.

FIGURE 9.5 New York Stock Exchange Total Return Index

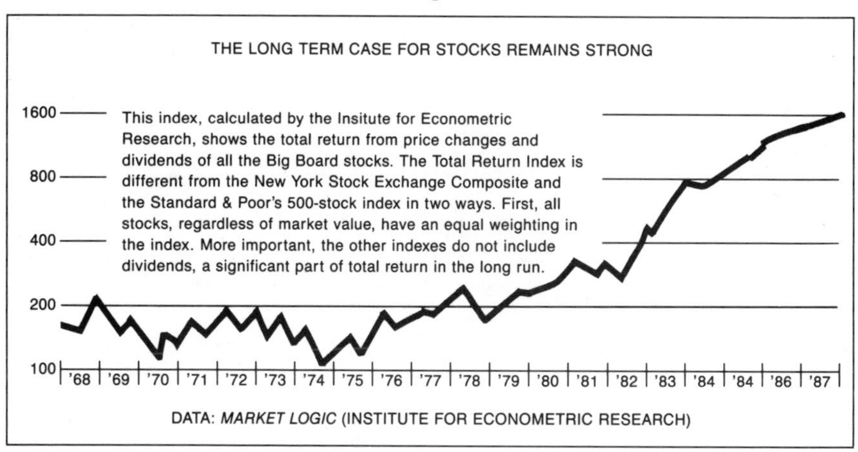

SOURCE: Business Week, December 28, 1987.

1987, "your total return as of August 25 would have been 666 percent. That means if you had put $1,000 into stocks in August 1977 and reinvested the dividends, your portfolio would have grown to $7,660. That's a compounded annual return of 22.6 percent."

Even investors who had not sold in time and had kept their stocks until after the crash on October 19 would still have seen their portfolios fatten their bank accounts with an annual return of 18 percent. And the partial market recovery after the crash improved even on that return.

Other averages confirm these figures. During the same period, the DJIA rose 212 percent for an annualized return of 12 percent, and the Standard & Poor's 500 stock index climbed 241 percent for an annualized return of 13 percent.

Yet the Total Return Index adds dividends into consideration, giving a clearer picture to those who utilize the dividend-yield theory in making investment decisions. The Total Return Index clearly shows that dividends help sustain higher profits.

As illuminating and fascinating as they are, the Dow and its cousins should not be the basis on which individual investment decisions are made. Stocks should be evaluated individually in terms of quality and value. The market indicators do, however, offer altitude readings, signposts and other helpful information along the way. They can assist in planning a portfolio, and they can help refine investors' understanding of how stocks will behave in the different economic and industry cycles.

SECTION

Planning a Profitable Portfolio

10

Planning a Portfolio

"Pessimism, when you get used to it, is just as agreeable as optimism."

ENOCH ARNOLD BENNETT

Benjamin Franklin may have been uncommonly suspicious when he warned in *Poor Richard's Almanac,* "Distrust and caution are the parents of security."

His admonition wasn't aimed at the contemporary investor, but the warning is worth heeding for several reasons:

- Nobody cares about your money as much as you do.
- No one understands your financial needs and your investment goals better than you do.
- Nobody else will be the careful steward that you can be.

So drive your own car, and don't be intimidated by the gadgets on the dashboard. They are there to help you, and aren't so complicated when you take a good look at them.

This does not mean that you can't get investment help and information from reliable outside sources. Reading the business press, seeking advice from an objective market analyst or subscribing to an investment advisory letter can be of enormous value. Investment sense is a wisdom that can be attained. In fact, investing is fun.

Successful investing requires not so much talent as discipline. People who are smart enough to accumulate capital generally are smart enough to manage it.

In the name of diversity, investors are wise to explore a variety of areas outside the stock market. A percentage of total investment capital can be allocated to bonds, real estate, gold and other non-stock market investments. But the main focus should be on blue-chip stocks. They provide the broadest and safest area in which wealth can be accumulated over a lifetime. As the chart in figure 10.1 comparing stocks with corporate bonds and government securities shows, in the long run, income-producing stocks yield the best return.

A TRUSTED PHILOSOPHY

The dividend-yield theory establishes a foundation for a lifetime of investing. It can be used to achieve the goals of the beginning investor, for young families, for families facing the college years with their children, and for people planning ahead for retirement. For those who are retired, an investment program utilizing the theory can provide a high level of safety and maximum income.

The dividend-yield concept is geared to the most basic of all investment fundamentals: getting a return on your investment dollar. In the real estate market, the return is rent, or the avoidance of paying rent. In the money market, the return is interest. In the stock market, as noted earlier, it is dividends, capital gains, or a combination of the two for total return.

The dividend-yield theory is not a short-term approach, though the method has some short-term applications. The most appealing characteristic of the dividend-yield theory is its valid, sensible, enduring approach to the stock market. The most successful portfolios are built on a diversified selection of blue-chip stocks, bought when they are bargains, and held until they become overvalued and can be sold for a profit.

INVESTMENT GOALS

The widespread notion that all investors are in the stock market for the same reason is not entirely true. While certainly no investor wants to see

FIGURE 10.1 Comparative Investment Performance

Comparative Investment Performance: Stocks versus Bonds: 1946 to Mid-1986
Total Investment Returns: Price Appreciation plus Income Reinvested

	Dow Jones Industrial Stocks			*Dow Jones Corporate Bonds*			*U.S. Treasury Bills*		
	Index	*Percent Return*		*Index*	*Percent Return*		*Index*	*Percent Return*	
Year	*Price*	*Year*	*Cumulative*	*Price*	*Year*	*Cumulative*	*Price*	*Year*	*Cumulative*
1946	100.00	...	...	100.00	...	...	100.00	...	...
1950	171.49	+26.4	+14.4	110.27	+ 4.25	+ 2.47	104.03	+ 1.23	+ 0.99
1955	467.38	+26.6	+18.7	123.00	+ 0.47	+ 2.33	112.60	+ 1.75	+ 1.33
1960	718.87	- 6.1	+15.1	129.00	+ 9.07	+ 1.84	129.54	+ 2.96	+ 1.87
1965	1340.27	+14.4	+14.6	157.58	+ 1.46	+ 2.42	151.55	+ 3.99	+ 2.21
1970	1398.68	+ 9.2	+11.6	199.05	+16.92	+ 2.91	199.13	+ 6.54	+ 2.91
1975	1746.02	+44.7	+10.4	284.24	+14.53	+ 3.67	265.34	+ 5.92	+ 3.42
1980	2594.32	+22.2	+10.0	340.23	- 5.04	+ 3.67	388.61	+11.74	+ 4.07
1981	2501.76	- 3.6	+ 9.6	344.13	+ 1.15	+ 3.57	443.52	+14.13	+ 4.35
1982	3179.88	+27.1	+10.1	476.52	+38.47	+ 4.43	491.59	+10.84	+ 4.52
1983	4005.56	+26.0	+10.5	517.88	+ 8.68	+ 4.55	534.89	+ 8.81	+ 4.64
1984	4057.86	+ 1.3	+10.2	598.33	+15.53	+ 4.82	587.07	+ 9.76	+ 4.77
1985	5419.15	+33.5	+10.8	759.54	+26.94	+ 5.34	631.81	+ 7.62	+ 4.84
(mid) 1986	6750.66	+47.5	+11.2	855.66	+24.23	+ 5.59	652.41	+ 6.95	+ 4.86

SOURCE: Wright Investors' Service, Bridgeport, CT 06604.

Stocks, when total return is considered, have consistently outperformed corporate bonds and U.S. Treasury bills.

the value of his or her holdings decline, many different and worthwhile considerations motivate investors to purchase common stocks.

Most investors, however, want assets that are relatively liquid, that is, assets that can be converted into cash. In addition to some degree of liquidity, the primary investment goals are:

- preservation of capital,
- income and
- growth (in terms of either share price or dividends).

Depending on the circumstances or stages of one's life, most investors will aim at one of these goals or, more likely, will fashion objectives of their own that turn out to be a combination of the three.

The following profiles of investors are offered to help readers think through investment goals. Not everyone will fit neatly into one of these stereotypes. Money is a personal subject, and each investor is entitled to his or her own unique attitude and approach.

THE INVESTOR WHO NEEDS TO PRESERVE CAPITAL

More than dividend income or capital gains, preservation of capital is likely to be foremost on the minds of the majority of investors. "It's one thing not to make as much money as I'd hoped to," explained an investor who had put all of her investable funds into a single, high-risk stock. "But to get out with less money than I went in with makes me angry and disgusted beyond belief. I've never felt so stupid."

To most, preservation of capital is a basic, unspoken goal. To some it is a well-verbalized, overriding concern. This type of investor includes those who are retired or who depend on an inheritance or a once-in-a-lifetime insurance settlement for lifelong income.

Anyone who is a caretaker of money for another person will feel a responsibility to preserve the original amount, or the capital, of the funds.

THE INVESTOR WHO NEEDS INCOME

Certain investors primarily are interested in earning the highest dividends possible for current income. Those who have no other source of income are included in this group. Retired investors who have their long-term obligations behind them generally seek the highest current yield available.

THE INVESTOR SEEKING GROWTH

To other stock market participants, capital gains may be the major consideration. Affluent investors may be attracted to low-yielding, high-growth stocks. Personal net worth will multiply, but the dividends won't necessarily put them in a higher tax bracket. Or, an investor in his or her peak earning years may want to defer current income in favor of capital gains, thus building net worth for the retirement years.

A younger investor who has many productive years ahead to recoup losses can take risks that an older investor would not assume. The young person may seek to accelerate growth in the early years, hoping to accumulate a bigger nest egg in order to maximize dividend yield in the later years. This investor also may opt for shares with a higher return that compensates for a somewhat elevated risk factor.

THE INVESTOR ON A SHOESTRING

An investor with a small cache of funds may be attracted to low-priced stocks that meet a unique financial situation. This person may aim for income or for growth, depending on age, family responsibilities or gambling spirit. But since it is more costly and difficult to buy odd-sized lots of stocks, the investor on a small budget will want to buy at least 100 shares (a round lot) of a lower-priced stock.

PERSONAL TOLERANCE FOR RISK

Where risk is involved, personality differences must be considered. Some people are chronic worriers. They fuss over each downtick; they agonize over every decline in the Dow Jones Industrial Average. They even worry when their stocks rise, for fear that they won't squeeze the last inch out of profits. For their own peace of mind and for the quietude of those around them, these investors should purchase low-volatility stocks—those that trade in a relatively narrow range without heart-stopping price swings.

The chart for Pacificorp in figure 10.2 reflects a stock that doesn't need to be bought or sold too often. The California utility was at its intermediate top, yielding 7.5 percent when the chart was compiled in March 1988. If this stock was bought at undervalue in 1980 and held until 1985, during that time investors would have received a yield on their investment that varied between 13 and 7.5 percent.

Through ups and downs, Pacificorp's chart pattern is relatively even. When it moved down, it went down in a gradual slope. Its upward trend is steady, and it holds its ground well. Even in the market shock of October 19, 1987, near the end of the chart, Pacificorp did not slip far. And it quickly adjusted close to its pre–October 19 level. This is not a stock that rattles the nerves.

Lest the chronic worriers be embarrassed by their higher states of anxiety, let it be noted that in July 1987, just before the market's rude awakening, this item appeared in "Investment Quality Trends":

"Most investors, by nature, are optimists, hoping for the best regardless of the circumstances," said the investment advisory. "But blind optimism can be very destructive. Investors who fail to heed the signs of danger set themselves up for inevitable losses of capital and profits. Decisions should be based on realistic standards of quality and value. More money is lost in the stock market by optimists than by realists."

While many shareholders were plummeted to earth when the market's hot-air balloon burst in the second half of 1987, others had taken the cautious route, using admirable self-discipline to get out of the market when the optimists were saying the Dow would go to 3000 or maybe even 4000.

Perhaps one should be thankful for the gamblers and speculators though. Even if they frequently get stung, they are responsible for driving the market and stocks higher than they reasonably should be. In doing this, they set the stage so that the conservative investor, the one tracking dividend yields, can take profits.

Since investors are neither financially, temperamentally nor objectively alike, only individuals can decide how much action or how much assurance is wanted from their investments.

RATES OF RETURN

In different economic climates, varying rates of return become possible. When interest rates were sky-high in the early 1980s, some fixed-income investors bought Treasury bills yielding in the high teens. At one point, banks' prime interest rates went as high as 21 percent. Then, when inflation and interest rates reverted to normal later in the decade, rather than being pleased at the improving economy, these same investors were frantic.

"Don't you think the government owes it to us senior citizens to make sure we get these returns?" asked one retiree. When he had come to rely on an 18 percent return on a government-guaranteed bond, it was not easy to adjust to eight percent.

Stock market investors can lose their perspective, too. During the rising phase of a bull market or the rising trend of a certain stock, some have seen their holdings double or triple in worth in a surprisingly short time. What a thrill! But it is important to remember that these bursts of price acceleration represent exceptional circumstances. It happens sometimes, but not all the time.

In deciding what a reasonable rate of return should be, it might be prudent to take a cue from an expert. Omaha's billionaire investor and

FIGURE 10.2 Dividend-Yield Chart

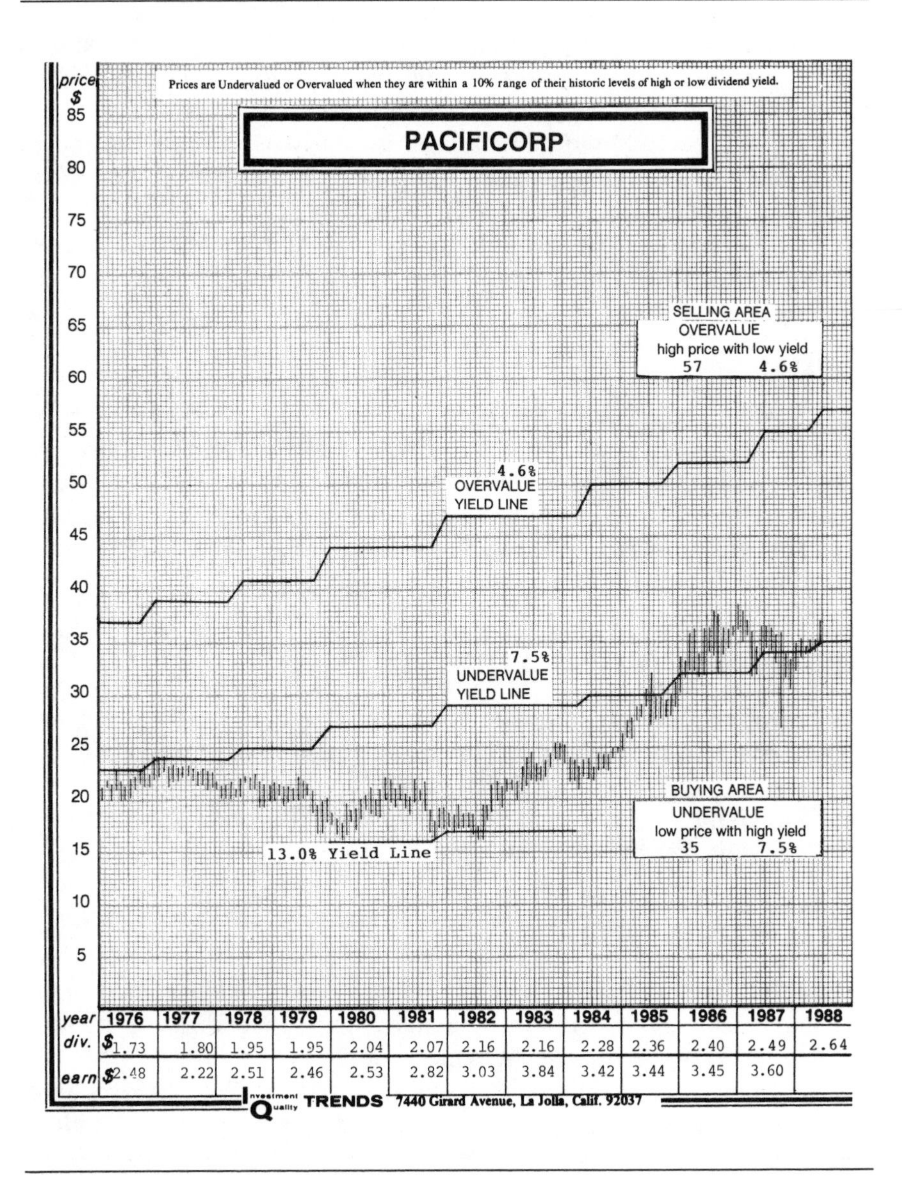

Pacificorp has shown price stability, making it a good selection for the investor made nervous by stocks exhibiting wide price swings.

chairman of Berkshire Hathaway Corporation, Warren Buffett, in one of his annual letters to investors, set a goal for his company to achieve an average annual 15 percent return on equity for a ten-year stretch. Obviously, in some years he would do better than 15 percent, and in other years he would do less well. But over the long haul, he would be satisfied with that respectable and realistic rate of return. Buffett's investors are loyal to him because he so frequently overshoots that mark, but at least he has the sense not to promise returns that an honest investment manager may not be able to sustain.

Some investors state virtually the same goal in another way. They aim at doubling their assets every five years.

PORTFOLIO TACTICS

So how does one go about investing in order to achieve the best returns as well as personal goals? Blue-chip stocks are available that satisfy every investment objective, from safety of capital to steady, dependable income to rapid growth. From banks and utilities, with their somewhat regulated environments, to freewheeling high-technology companies to everything in between, the choices are abundant.

ACHIEVING CONSERVATIVE GOALS

Conservative investors, those with preservation of capital in mind, will cling to the blue-chip criteria outlined in chapter 3. Extra safety also can be found in defensive stocks. The defensive issues, described in some detail in chapter 11, won't be champions in all economic phases, but they will survive the best over time.

MAXIMIZING INCOME

Investors who seek income will try to nail down a higher yield on an original stock purchase. But if these investors also pay diligent attention to value, they get a bonus: dividend growth.

As previously mentioned, stocks that reward their holders with growth of dividend income are twice blessed. Not only does a dividend increase raise the percentage of yield on previously invested capital and return more dollars to the investor, but it also pushes the stock price higher.

SCHEDULING MONTHLY DIVIDENDS

Investors who would like to collect dividend checks monthly in order to make income planning simpler can structure their stock portfolios so that they receive checks each month. "The concept is simple," explained Daniel Horgan in a 1988 *USA Today* article. "Most stocks pay dividends four times a year. The payment date varies by firm. By picking a basket of stocks based on their dividend schedules, you can get a dividend check in the mail every month—even if you hold as few as three stocks."

For example, General Electric pays dividends in January, April, July and October. J. C. Penney pays in February, May, August and November. RJR Nabisco pays in March, June, September and December. "So," he explained, "if you hold those three stocks, you'll get a check from one of them every month of the year."

Figure 10.3 shows the months in which certain companies mail dividend checks. Similar information on any stock can be obtained from a company's annual report or from its investor relations department.

Warning! Don't be tempted to stray from quality and value in purchasing shares, just to schedule dividend payments. Buy blue-chip stocks when they are undervalued in relation to their dividend yield. With no fewer than 350 blue chips from which to choose, time and patience will allow the construction of a portfolio with monthly dividend payments. It takes a little homework, but it may be worth the effort.

GOING FOR GROWTH

Investors who are not obliged to consider their investments as a major source of income will explore the market for stocks of corporations that appear to be growing at a rate that is higher than its industry average. *Barron's*, *Forbes* and other financial publications often group stocks along industry lines and provide comparative information for companies within a given industry. By examining these analyses (which frequently are published early in the year), investors can get an idea of how a stock compares with its siblings.

More daring investors will be willing to forego a high current return in exchange for more rapid dividend growth and better-than-average appreciation of capital. This less conservative route is of course somewhat more perilous. It requires added attention to the status and health

FIGURE 10.3 Dividend Payment Schedule

Companies with Dividends Paid in January, April, July and October

Eastman Kodak
General Electric
General Signal
Heinz
J.P. Morgan
Northern States Power

Companies with Dividends Paid in February, May, August and November

Betz Laboratories
Bristol-Myers
Citicorp
Colgate-Palmolive
Humana
Marsh & McLennan
Pacific Enterprises
J.C. Penney

Companies With Dividends Paid in March, June, September and December

Allied-Signal
American Brands
American Home Products
Amoco
Atlantic Richfield
Dennison Manufacturing
Du Pont
Exxon
IBM
Norfolk Southern
RJR Nabisco

Selecting stocks that pay dividends in different months allows investors to arrange income that is spread throughout the year.

of stocks held in a portfolio, but it can result in a total return of more generous dimensions.

The mix varies from time to time, but among the 350 blue-chip stocks tracked in "Investment Quality Trends," usually more than half are rapid-growth stocks with a compound annual dividend growth rate of at least ten percent.

American Business Products, figure 7.5 in chapter 7, illustrates a blue-chip, dividend-paying stock with consistent growth patterns. For more than a century, the company has been a leading supplier of business equipment, forms and envelopes. Dividends have grown at an average annual rate of 16 percent.

The chart shows that if American Business Products had been purchased at undervalue in 1982 and sold at overvalue in 1983, the gain would have been an impressive 125 percent. If the stock had been held past its overvalue point, extra gains may have been possible. But beware of riptides. The chart shows exactly how fast and far an overvalued stock can fall. In mid-1986 American Business Products was trading in the overvalue area, where it had been for about a year. It started an orderly price decline, then took a plunge. By January 1988, it was selling below its price of five years earlier. However, it again had outstanding potential for growth.

Some of the other high-quality stocks that also have offered opportunities for good growth over extended periods of time are American Express, R. R. Donnelley, Kellogg, Rohm and Haas and SmithKline Beckman.

The same criteria that apply to all other blue chips are used for growth stocks. However, an examination of the fundamentals, of the company's history or of the economy often shows that these stocks have skated closer than others to violating the blue-chip guidelines. If utilities, they may have greater nuclear exposure; if they are industrials, they could be operating in a rapidly changing environment. Frequently a study of a high-growth stock reveals a heightened element of risk.

THE SAFETY NET OF DIVERSIFICATION

Regardless of objectives, risk tolerance and other personal factors, a sturdy, safe and elastic portfolio for long-term investors is built on three legs: diversification, quality and value. Earlier chapters devoted much attention to quality (blue chips represent the cream of the crop) and value (dividend yield takes ascendency over earnings and book value), so most of this section discusses how to spread the risk in a portfolio by introducing variety and balance.

Personal investment objectives not withstanding, all prudent portfolios are constructed the same way. Only the stock choices will differ. The investor begins with a list of undervalued blue-chip stocks. Such a list can be developed according to the criteria of good quality discussed in chapter 3 and the identification of good value, described in chapters 2 and 4.

Selections from the undervalued blue-chip list should be made, based on individual investment objectives and the amount of money one has to invest. The level of diversification an investor will be able to achieve will depend, in large part, on the resources available for investment.

IDEAL PORTFOLIO SIZE

If the investment nest egg is relatively small, say $10,000, that money should be divided into a minimum of three equal parts. The most conservative investors would want a minimum of five stocks in a small portfolio. Each of those parts should be invested in a separate stock.

Some investment advisers suggest that an investor shouldn't attempt to build an individual portfolio with less than $10,000.

When a portfolio is to be launched with as few as three to five segments each of those stocks should be in a different industry. The companies and industries should be meticulously selected. Obviously, the value of a small portfolio is especially vulnerable to variations in the price of even one of its holdings.

As more capital becomes available, additional choices can be made, positions can be enlarged, other industry groups can be added, or additional companies can be purchased within an industry that is already represented. If the dollar amount available for investment is large, it can be divided into between seven or more equal parts, depending on the individual. People who manage their investments full time can track more stocks than investors who turn their attention to a portfolio only after a busy workday schedule.

The number of stocks in a portfolio is a highly individual choice, depending on time available and interest in the subject. While a professionally managed portfolio could be larger, a personal portfolio should not include more than 20 different equities. Twenty is enough stocks to afford widespread diversification, but not so many that it is burdensome to keep regular track of the diverse industries, companies and stocks. With a compact group of companies, a monthly or quarterly review generally is often enough to keep a stockholder in close touch with the state of his or her investments.

Some very sophisticated investors with large amounts of capital often choose to have a relatively small portfolio, even though they have enough money to buy as many stocks as they want. If Warren Buffett were Noah, the *Wall Street Journal* once wrote, "he'd fill the ark with a few big animals."

INDUSTRY GROUPS

No matter how many companies are included, at least one of the stocks in every portfolio should be a utility. Then a selection might be made from the food or pharmaceutical groups. These industries are resistant to adverse economic events, and can provide a bedrock on which to build a larger portfolio in the future.

As a portfolio gets larger and more mature, it should gain additional legs on which to stand. Eventually, energy, retail, chemical companies, technology, transportation stocks and the other industry groups should be represented, to be added when those industry groups (or the individual stocks within a group) become undervalued. By picking several different stocks within an industry group, representing different facets of that industry, an investor achieves additional balance in a portfolio.

In the case of utilities, the diversification should also include both geographical locations—to spread the risk created by regional economies, unfriendly regulatory agencies and so forth—and the various primary power sources: nuclear, oil, gas and coal. Each energy source carries its own advantage and disadvantage. The idea of diversification is to spread the risk as far as is reasonably possible so that unexpected events or shocks to a particular industry will not wipe out the value of a portfolio.

General Industrial Categories of Stocks

Basic Energy	Basic Materials	Commercial and Industrial Services
Consumer Cyclical	Consumer Staples	Financial
Health Care	Industrial Manufacturing	Technology
Transportation	Utilities	

Additional guidelines for investing in utility stocks are presented in chapter 12.

DON'T WELD YOUR PORTFOLIO INTO PLACE

A portfolio should not be rigid. It should be flexible and be allowed to change and grow along with the financial circumstances of the investor. The ongoing cyclical changes in stocks and the market should be allowed to influence the portfolio also. When individual stocks become overvalued, they should be sold so that profits can be reinvested in an undervalued stock. Naturally this alters the mix of companies in a portfolio. That means an investor continually has to pay attention to diversification. It's not an evaluation to be performed once and forgotten.

HOLD STEADY

It's important to be flexible and agile in managing a portfolio, but not to the extent that each passing breeze causes doubt or a change of mind. Investors who have stuck to their goals, and who have pursued quality and value, must strive to remain objective when everything they read or hear seems to be going against them.

"Don't panic," advised 84-year-old Joseph S. Nye Sr. when the market came tumbling down in the fall of 1987. "Buy Hercules (Corporation) tomorrow." Nye, who had been a bond trader on Wall Street in 1929, was interviewed in *Financial World* magazine shortly after the recent crash.

The magazine reported that Nye told a visitor on the day of the crash, "Hercules was a good buy at 70, and it's a great buy at 45 7/8—which is what it closed at tonight." His equanimity was based on experience. When the depression was deepening back in 1932, Nye called Dow Jones and had the ticker removed from his office. He instructed his traders to make their stock trades according to what the security was worth, not according to information coming across the newswire.

"I don't know whether the market's going up, down or sideways," Nye told *Financial World* magazine, "so our policy is to keep invested in quality common and let the compound interest on high-yielding bonds take care of the rest. That way there's no reason to panic—even if others do."

HOLDING BACK

All capital need not be invested in the market at once. Some funds always should be kept aside in liquid money accounts to take advantage of investment opportunities in the stock market when they arise.

British economist Lord John Maynard Keynes once said, "To be quiet (in the market) is sometimes the best policy." One of those times during which it is best to watch and wait is when a bull market is at its top, and a turnaround is at hand. Good-value stocks become more scarce at that time.

When the bull market is exhausted and abandoned by others after a big market decline, that's the time for a shopping expedition. Lucky are the investors who first step into the market in a down cycle, for they may pick rosebuds for a bouquet that will later spring into spectacular bloom.

11

Investing in All Kinds of Markets

"It is circumstance and proper timing that give an action its character and make it either good or bad."

—AGESILAUS

"Market Soars as Rates Slide." "Trade Figures Off—Dow Falls Through Floor." "War in Middle East; Stock Market Dives." Radio, television, newspapers and magazines are full of them: headlines blaring out the delicate health of the economy, the state of the oil, paper or insurance industry, reports on the gross national product, prognostications on the direction of interest rates. Economic phases, interest-rate fluctuations and industry cycles battle for attention in the news.

ALL EYES ARE ON THE ECONOMY

If investors are watching interest-rate movements, so are the managers of blue-chip corporations. If consumer sales are in the news, they are also on the minds of the marketing executives of American business. If the economy is turning up or down, the first clues often come in purchase orders, which translate into factory orders, to raw material production and so on, up and down the line. Those trends work their way into the total amount of goods and services produced in this nation—the gross national product.

While this avalanche of information sometimes unnecessarily clouds the vision, it can be helpful if correctly interpreted. Economic activity, some of which was mentioned earlier in this book, does affect the way stocks behave. The trade figures, the oil rig count or the prime rate does not tell when shares are overvalued and should be sold, or when a stock is undervalued and should be bought. That is the information one expects to glean by tracking the dividend yield. But economic, interest-rate and industry movements can help investors understand why stocks perform the way they do. They can help streamline investment timing.

In the intricately woven ways of the economy, information gets translated into activity, activity into profits and profits into dividends. If economic affairs look turgid, management does not foresee rising profits, and so holds off on dividend increases.

Understanding the mood of the market can lead an investor to certain industry groups and away from others. With even a limited amount of information, one can measure the tides and calculate the most advantageous time to dip in and out of the water. Timing, as Benjamin Graham pointed out, is of no value unless it coincides with price. Only if it allows the purchase of quality stocks at a lower price, or the sale of investments at a higher price, is timing worthwhile.

In addition to timing buy and sell orders, through an awareness of economic and other cycles an investor can be psychologically prepared for changes in the return on his or her stocks. Surprises are fun at birthday parties; they are not so entertaining when managing investments.

BETWEEN BOOM AND BUST

First, it's important to consider economic patterns that have dominated this country for dozens of generations. The United States fluctuates between periods of expansion and contraction that generally last from three to five years from the beginning of one cycle to the beginning of the next. Seven of these cycles have recurred without fail in the last 25 years, though they have exhibited various lengths and depths.

These repetitions of recovery and recession in economic activity happen for the same fundamental reasons that stock prices move in wave-like patterns. The cause is a variation on the old supply-and-demand theme. In a simplified scenario, prosperity comes in cycles for a variety of reasons ranging from weather patterns to the timing of flu epidemics. Whatever it is that triggers a cycle, it begins with scarcity.

Scarcity (of food, water, gold, whatever the resource in question) puts pressure on demand, accelerating production, spurring profits and creating a boom.

But as is typical of human nature, the new production usually goes overboard, and an era of plenty turns into an era of too much. Oversupply drives prices down, profits fall, producers stop producing and the economy goes flat. This condition lasts until prices are low enough, at which time the cycle begins again.

This happens over and over, in many different segments of the economy. When all trends, like tributaries, flow to meet one another, they become the great rambling river that is the economy.

While economy-wide accelerations and decelerations have typical durations of three to five years, some economic booms have been known to last for a decade. Remember the fabulous 1950s?

Though busts usually have a shorter life span than booms, the Great Depression of the 1930s gives some idea of how deep and dreadfully long a recessionary spell can become. Happily, eras like the 1930s are rare occasions.

RECESSIONS

Recessions aren't so rare. After all, a standard definition of a recession is simply two consecutive quarters of negative growth in the gross national product. Usually recessions sound trumpets announcing their impending arrival. One of those warnings is the topping out of a bull market. A primary reversal in the stock market does not unerringly mean that a recession will follow, but a substantial market decline does present that ominous specter.

Over the past 40 years, eight recessions have occurred. All but one, in 1980, happened within one year of the onset of a bear market. Again, this is because the stock market continually discounts the future as investors expect it to be. And more often than not, investors have turned out to be correct. Current events are history to the financial markets.

INDUSTRY CYCLES

The fact in itself that the economy is experiencing a boom or bust doesn't mean that all sectors of the economy are experiencing the same state of affairs. The different industry groups have their disparate though interconnected business fluctuations. Industry cycles vary in length and latitude, depending on the role of the industry in the economy.

For example, the aerospace industry moves in an approximate ten-year pattern, tracked with government, military and research spending. When military budgets are big, so are profits for the aviation and aerospace industries. Conversely, when with predictable regularity, an economy-minded administration or leadership dedicated to social programs seizes office in Washington, military budgets shrivel and aerospace profits decline.

Durable goods, such as heavy equipment, planes, boats and trains, move in longer cycles than do disposable and consumer goods such as clothes, food and cosmetics.

Regardless of their duration, the industry cycles affect earnings growth, which in turn establishes the cycles of dividend yields. When industries are in their infancy, such as the semiconductor and computer industries have been, the cycles have not yet emerged. Clumsy timing creates extreme ups and downs, in both profits and share prices, in the formative years of an industry, because there has not been sufficient time to identify patterns by which fluctuations can be predicted. The absence of history is one of the reasons that the dividend-yield theory presented here shies away from very young industries and companies.

A TIME FOR EVERYTHING

"Each investment vehicle—stocks, bonds, gold and money market funds," explains Dr. Lacy H. Hunt in his book *A Time To Be Rich*, "has its own cycle within the broader context of the economy's five [he breaks them into three of expansion, two of contraction] phases."

For the most part, the stock market behaves in just the opposite manner as that of the economy itself. The market may lead the way into a recovery, but when the economy is at its healthiest, the Dow Jones Industrial Average will peak and decline. The economy soon follows. Rallies most often occur at the bottom of recessions. When citizens are most pessimistic, the most convinced that things will never get better, stock prices undergo a swift and substantial upsweep.

VERY JUMPY STOCKS

While all stock prices repeatedly travel between their undervalue and overvalue levels, some industries are labeled "cyclical" because the price of their stocks is hypersensitive to economic change.

Cyclical stocks tend to rise rapidly when the economy turns up and tend to go into a tailspin when it rotates in the opposite direction. Airlines are, by their basic nature, cyclical. In good times people travel more on vacations. When business activities slow down and disposable income shrinks, air travel is one of the first conveniences to hit the road. Housing, automobiles and lumber are cyclical stocks because they rely heavily on consumers' willingness and ability to spend.

For example, Lomas & Nettleton, a real estate company, remained overvalued through the recession of the early 1980s until the beginning of 1983 (see figure 11.1). Preceding the end of the recession, it began to rise, its stair-stepping overvalue line moving higher and higher. In 1987, when the specter of recession and higher interest rates appeared, the share price quickly retreated.

When the economic future is uncertain, the stocks of real estate, automobile and other companies of a highly reactive nature should be sidestepped. Save them for when the economy already has seen the worst and recovery is at hand.

THE PRESIDENTIAL INFLUENCE

Politics also exert a ritual influence on both financial markets and stock prices. The simple fact that a given year is an election year makes a difference. Of the past nine election years, stock prices rose during all but one, and gains were sometimes substantial. In 1980, the year of Ronald Reagan's first presidential victory, the Standard & Poor's 500 index achieved a 25.5 percent gain. By and large, Dr. Hunt pointed out, stocks rise under a pro business president who promises to avoid tinkering with the private enterprise system.

A common pattern can be discerned. A president's political leanings aside, the nation's chief executive tends to exercise a tighter monetary policy and force interest rates higher during the first two years of his administration. As the next election draws near, presidents relax their grip. They ease up, letting interest rates slip and generally making voters more comfortable. It is hoped, apparently, that because voters are more

FIGURE 11.1 Dividend-Yield Chart

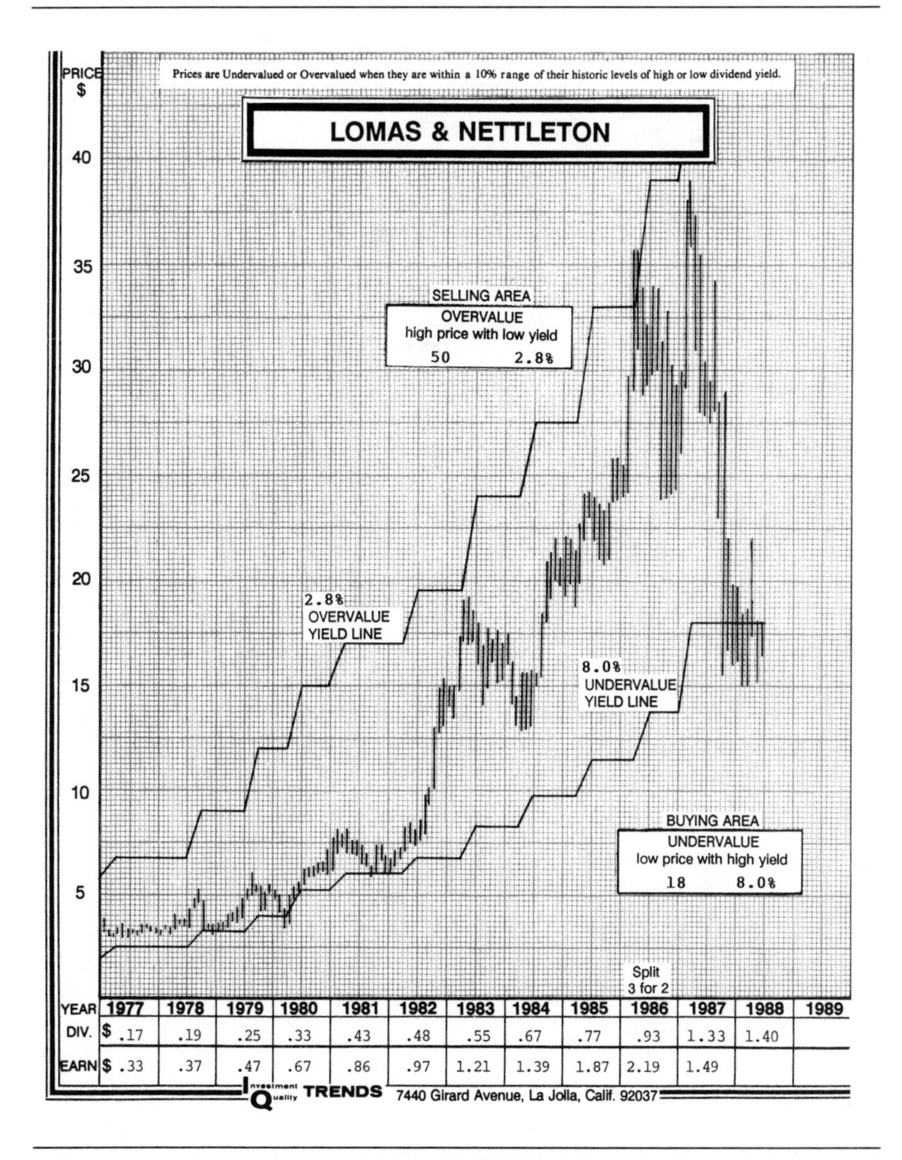

YEAR	1977	1978	1979	1980	1981	1982	1983	1984	1985	1986	1987	1988	1989
DIV.	$ .17	.19	.25	.33	.43	.48	.55	.67	.77	.93	1.33	1.40	
EARN	$ .33	.37	.47	.67	.86	.97	1.21	1.39	1.87	2.19	1.49		

The dividend-yield pattern of Lomas & Nettleton, a real estate company, can sometimes forewarn a coming recession, as it did in the late 1970s and early 1980s. When the recession was nearing an end, the stock shot up.

satisfied with the economy, the incumbent political party will be re-elected.

The technique has obvious merit. Presidents Richard Nixon and Ronald Reagan both had recessions early in their first terms, then were reelected handily. President Jimmy Carter postponed his recession, and was resoundingly voted out of office.

WHEN THE FED SPEAKS, THE MARKETS LISTEN

This manipulation of interest rates, accomplished by a control of the money supply via the Federal Reserve Bank, is felt acutely by the stock market. Interest rates, almost more than any other factor, hold sway over corporate profits and dividends. They make a significant difference in the selection of investment vehicles.

Presidential politics is not the only factor that prompts the Federal Reserve to tighten up on money and spur higher rates. Throughout the 1980s, the identical techniques have been used to curb inflation or to cool an overheated economy.

In times of high interest rates, economic growth is dampened because businesses and consumers are able to spend less money. High rates also put pressure on banks, have traditionally impacted utilities and bring a heightened rate of business failure.

Interest rates that are too low, on the other hand, can create excessive liquidity (too many dollars chasing too few goods and services) and lead to inflation.

INTEREST-RATE SENSITIVITY

When interest rates climb to rarified altitudes, few companies can get the cheap and plentiful credit they like in order to grow and prosper. Because they don't need so much credit, blue-chip companies with low debt, strong earnings, expanding profit margins and improving rates of productivity will be the most stable in terms of share price during these times.

Frantically gasping for air in this thin interest-rate atmosphere will be banks, insurance companies and, until recently, utilities.

In the past two decades, interest rates twice have risen to dizzying heights, throwing interest-sensitive industries into crisis. The first stifling episode was in 1973 when rates hit 12 percent, the highest they had been in this century. The second high-interest-rate shock was in the early 1980s, when this time, bank rates rocketed to 21 percent.

Some interest-rate-sensitive stocks reacted violently, falling through their previously established lows, and landing at new levels of undervalue. Their old undervalue lines become price barrier lines, through which some stocks had much difficulty breaking even as interest rates receded. On the dividend-yield charts in this book, previously established undervalue lines are identified as "intermediate objective" lines. They've acted much like new overvalue lines, however.

While most of the stocks that suffered from high rates were banks and utilities, other stocks also carved new territories of value. Xerox Corporation and Minnesota Mining & Manufacturing (3M) (see figure 11.2 and appendix) are two completely different stocks that reacted in similar ways.

Xerox was vulnerable to interest-rate changes not just because it is in business services and is hit in recessions. Xerox, like banks, also is active in financing, providing credit for the buyers of its products and equipment. It owns an insurance company and an investment banking firm, Van Kampen Merritt, Inc.

It was high interest rates, coupled with the recession and the strong dollar versus foreign currencies, that drove 3M's share price to an exceptionally low level.

Both Xerox and 3M worked diligently to survive the interest-rate crises. They did come through, proving that they were blue chips indeed. If interest rates remain low, both Xerox and 3M could perform spectacularly in the uplegs of the next bull market.

Few stocks of Xerox's quality had its potential when it was charted in March 1987. Though Xerox rose 100 percent from 1984 to 1986 (and that move was corrected along the way), as industry conditions improve, Xerox had the potential to move back to its old overvalue level of a 1.0 percent yield. An advance of that magnitude would represent a gain of some 311 percent.

3M's outlook also was excellent at the time its chart was completed. The downside risk for the company, for example, was extremely low.

FIGURE 11.2 Dividend-Yield Chart

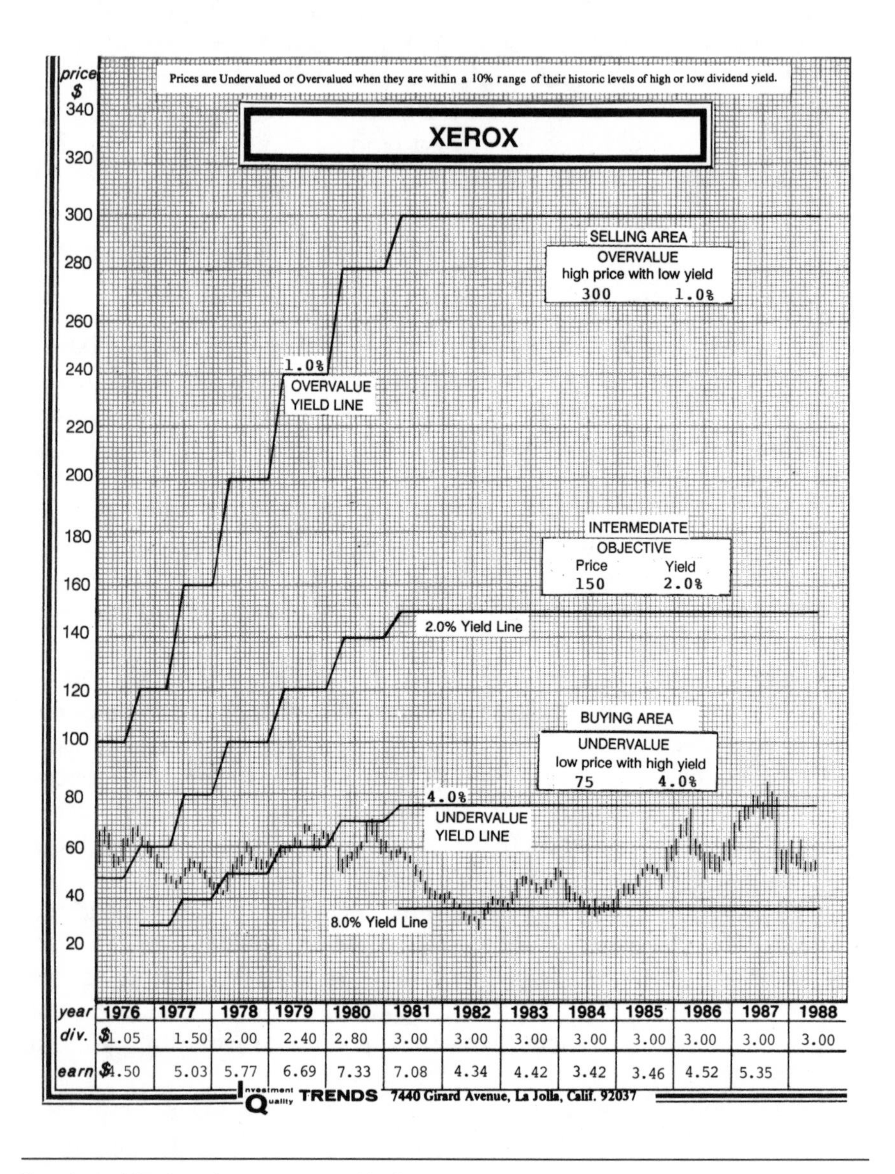

Xerox's stock has been interest-rate sensitive like utilities and banks primarily because it finances much of the equipment it sells.

However, the stock still promised an 89 percent potential rise, once the consolidation of its most recent price gains had taken place.

FINANCIAL INSTITUTIONS

Banks and savings and loan institutions had a painfully difficult time of it when interest rates reached double-digit levels in the early 1980s. They were collecting payments on loans at the old, lower rates, but to attract deposits, they had to pay the new, higher rates. Their profit spread shrank to nearly nothing, and in some instances, it was in the negative realm.

But interest rates were not the only problems banks faced. Increased competition, problems with debts in less-developed countries and the trauma of deregulation put the banking industry in a tentative position. Citicorp is typical of what high interest rates and other industry problems did to the share value of financial institutions. In figure 11.3, Citibank's overvalue trendline, with a dividend yield of 1.5 percent, reflects the top of a rising trend in 1973. Then the stock declined below its historic 4.1 percent undervalue line, establishing a new bottom line of 7.3 percent dividend yield. The former undervalue line became the top beyond which Citicorp has not been able to rise.

In 1987 Citicorp bolstered its loan loss reserves to protect against default on those debts, creating a huge earnings deficit of about $1.1 billion, or $4.26 per share. The reserves hit the bank hard, but they will protect the company from future loan defaults in the less-developed countries. Also on the positive side, the New York–based bank has been aggressive in moving west and seizing market share with new products in new territories.

Citicorp became an attractive buy in 1980 and was still a good value when its chart was completed. When confidence finally returns to the banking industry, Citicorp can be expected to rebound to its overvalue line, where the yield is 1.5 percent. From an undervalue price of $37 per share to an overvalued level of $180 per share, that price appreciation would be more than 486 percent.

Other large, high-quality banks are similarly positioned for growth. If L. William Seidman, chairman of the Federal Deposit Insurance Corporation, is correct, the banks will show earnings improvements in the late 1980s and early 1990s. "Profitability of commercial banks has been

FIGURE 11.3 Dividend-Yield Chart

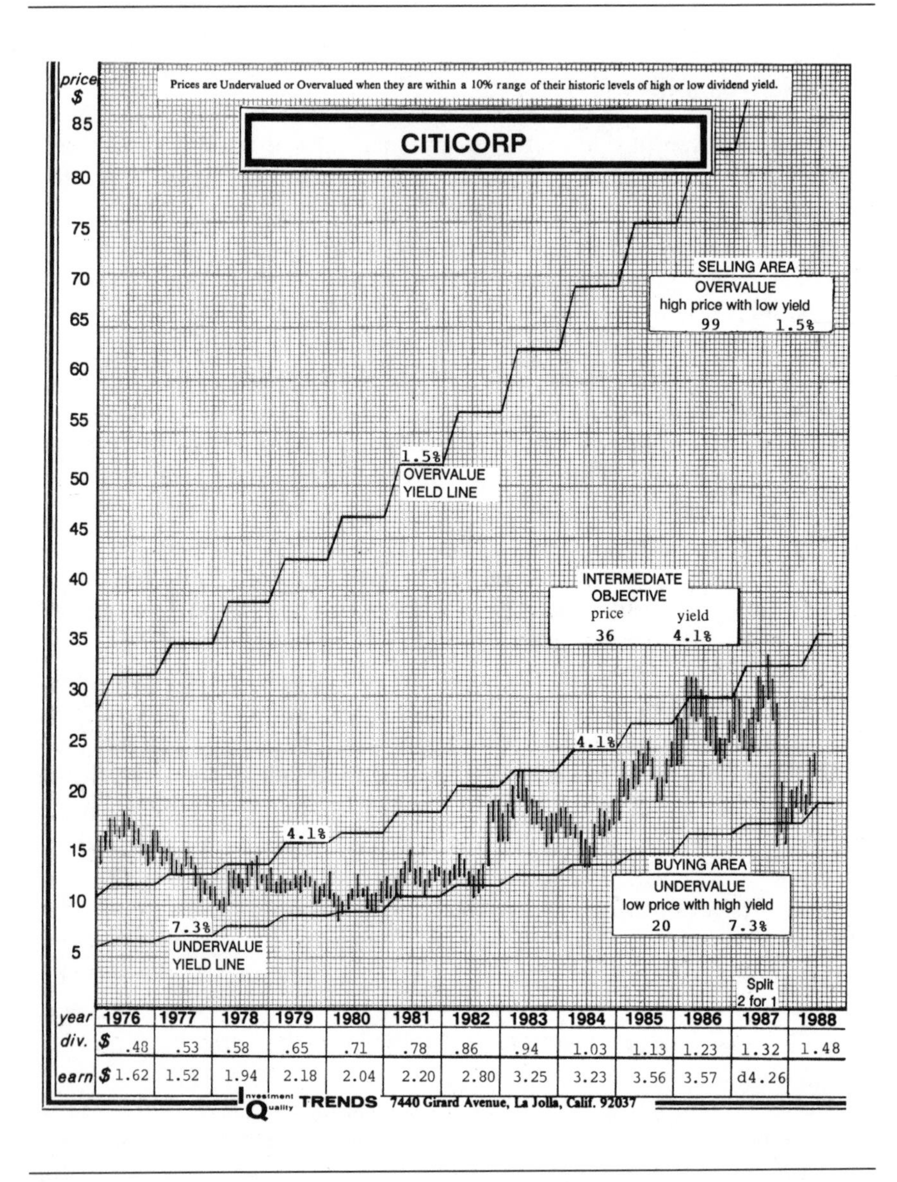

year	1976	1977	1978	1979	1980	1981	1982	1983	1984	1985	1986	1987	1988
div.	$ .48	.53	.58	.65	.71	.78	.86	.94	1.03	1.13	1.23	1.32	1.48
earn	$ 1.62	1.52	1.94	2.18	2.04	2.20	2.80	3.25	3.23	3.56	3.57	d4.26	

Citicorp shared the problems of many other banks in its industry. Dividend yields literally went into the basement, establishing a new, lower range of value.

dropping steadily since 1979," Seidman said in speech to the Conference Board early in 1988, "and the industry's asset growth rate—at eight percent—is far behind other competitors in the financial services industry. If the industry had not set aside reserves of $37 billion on problem loans, including those to less-developed countries, profits from operations would have been about the same as the $13.3 billion reported in 1986. Hopefully, 1988 will be the year this downward trend in bank profits will be reversed."

Some financial institutions have tried to protect themselves from being caught in an interest-rate crunch ever again by increasing their percentage of variable-rate loans, by balancing short-term and long-term accounts and through other risk-management devices.

And though deregulation has presented its own difficulties, legislators and deregulation advocates claim it will allow financial institutions to protect themselves from interest-rate swings by branching out into other lines of work.

THE FLIGHT TO MONEY MARKETS

When interest rates go up, some investors abandon the stock market in favor of money market accounts, Treasury bills and other safe but high-yielding types of investments. The stocks that those income-seeking investors usually evacuate are those that pay high dividends, such as utilities. Thus, as demand for these stocks falls, supply rises, and prices can be driven down. Chapter 12 takes a closer look at utilities.

DOLLAR-SENSITIVE STOCKS

Dollar-sensitive stocks are those that are reactive to currency exchange rates. When the dollar declines in relation to other major foreign currencies, basic industry and capital goods stocks as well as multinational drug and chemical stocks do well. "These industrial companies have products that compete every day against imports," explained Stanley Salvingsen, chairman of Comstock Partners, a New York money-management firm. "Their profit margins should widen enormously as a result of the dollar drop."

This is what happened in the latter part of the 1980s when the dollar declined. The trend picked up steam in 1987 and 1988, when the dollar fell about 44 percent, on an average, against the currencies of America's largest trading partners.

Merck & Company, Inc., a pharmaceutical manufacturer (see appendix), illustrates the point well. Earnings of Merck rose 25 percent in the first half of 1986, partly due to the weakening of the U.S. dollar. Foreign operations account for nearly 50 percent of Merck's total sales.

Paper manufacturers also represent good value when the dollar is weaker, because the United States traditionally has been a low-cost producer of paper.

In adversity is opportunity. This is true in life, and it is also true in investment markets. If a good company has a few problems, look at its history. If it has a record of survival, it may be a wise purchase even in a sour economy.

OUT-OF-FAVOR STOCKS

Never is there a better time to buy a stock than when a basically sound company, for whatever reason, temporarily falls out of favor with the investment community. The best time to have been bullish on oil stocks, for example, was in 1986, when the price of West Texas crude fell from $30 a barrel to under ten dollars. Sad times for Houston, San Antonio and Dallas, and for investors who already owned oil shares; glad times for investors who wanted to own a part of the oil patch. Oil stock prices dropped through the floor.

Then, between mid-year 1986 and mid-year 1987, the price of oil rebounded from ten dollars to $21 per barrel. That spurred an equally sharp recovery in prices of oil stocks. Industry leaders like Exxon, Texaco and Chevron were largely responsible for the early-1987 spurt in the Dow Jones Industrial Average.

Even the declining stock market of late 1987 did not dampen the vigor of those stocks. As the dividend-yield charts for Exxon (see appendix) and Gulf Canada Corporation (figure 11.4) indicate, the general direction continued upward.

STRATEGIES FOR REALLY HARD TIMES

Most people do well in good times; intrepid investors can even do amazingly well. But when jobs are hard to find and bankruptcies dominate

FIGURE 11.4 Dividend-Yield Chart

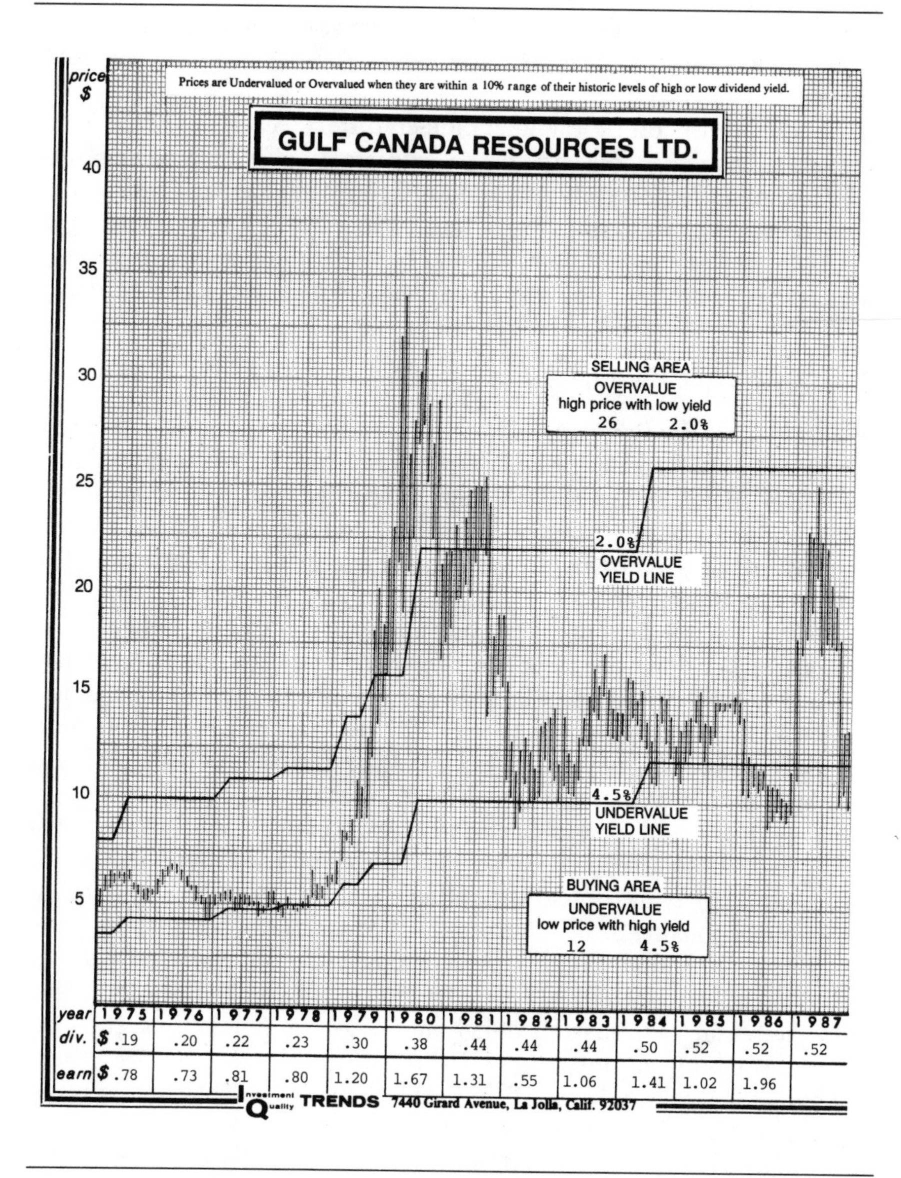

Oil company stocks are frequently driven by factors outside management's control. The volatility that can occur in an international oil crisis is evident in Gulf Canada's chart.

the business pages, fear takes over. Depression, of course, is just as much a state of mind as it is a state of the economy. Fear immobilizes business, industry and investors. But if investors are cognizant of the dangers, hard times offer extraordinary opportunities in the stock market.

These are the times in which blue-chip stocks earn their hue, when corporate managements are put to extreme tests of competency and when some faded blue chips are retired from the game. These are the times when it is especially important to invest only in well-managed, prime-quality, blue-chip companies. The companies of choice must be in good financial condition with low debt and well-protected dividends.

THE DAGGER OF DEBT

In faltering economies, enlightened investors must pay especially careful attention to the percentage of a company's capital structure that is formed by debt, as opposed to equity. Debt includes all money that is owed by the company to its creditors, including bond holders. Equity is the portion of a company's total capitalization that is represented by shares of common stock.

A low ratio of debt to equity, as opposed to high debt, indicates that a company will have an easier time surviving in a high-interest-rate market and will have ballast against a recessive economy. In tough economies, companies that are capitalized with high debt-to-equity ratios can see their earnings drain into the debt market, reducing their ability to employ assets productively and setting the stage for failure.

One quick and easy measure of a corporation's level of debt is a check on its bond rating. Since bond holders get in line along with creditors in case of bankruptcy, the rating agencies keep close tabs on all types of indebtedness.

Blue-chip companies, the focus of this book, generally have a conservative capital structure. They have comparatively little long-term debt. Some, in fact, have absolutely no long-term obligations; these are known as the *royal* blue chips.

While it is certainly an advantage to have little debt in hard times, corporations with 15 percent or less long-term debt still can be considered to be on very sound footing. Some of the companies that traditionally have kept debt at a minimum are John Harland, Dun & Bradstreet, American Home Products, Clorox, DeLuxe Check, NCR Corporation and Snap-On-Tools.

THE PRISTINE COMPANIES

In addition to a low debt-to-equity ratio, investors should look with special favor on undervalued shares that:

- carry the highest Standard & Poor's quality stock ranking, an "A + ."
- have sufficient earnings to cover dividend payout. For example, if the annual dividend payout is $1.25 per share, the earnings per share should be at least that much. Some companies with strong reserves can carry dividends even while reporting annual losses, but this practice cannot continue for any length of time without putting the dividend in danger.

FOUR FAVORED INDUSTRIES

While most corporate managers earn their battle ribbons during recessions and depressions, certain management teams have a natural advantage: They are in the industries that are better able to survive extended periods of hard times than others. In difficult climates, it makes sense to build in additional safety by investing in undervalued blue-chip companies from those industries that are the least affected by swings in the economy.

Although no industry is totally immune to the ravages of recession, four industries that experience the least amount of adversity are pharmaceuticals, food, utilities and oil. This quartet of industry groups is indispensable to the human condition, even during the deepest depression.

One stock that has moved smoothly through its personal cycle of undervalue and overvalue, fairly impervious to incidental influence, is Ralston Purina. Figure 11.5 shows a company that is well diversified but that still concentrates on food-related businesses.

FIGURE 11.5 Dividend-Yield Chart

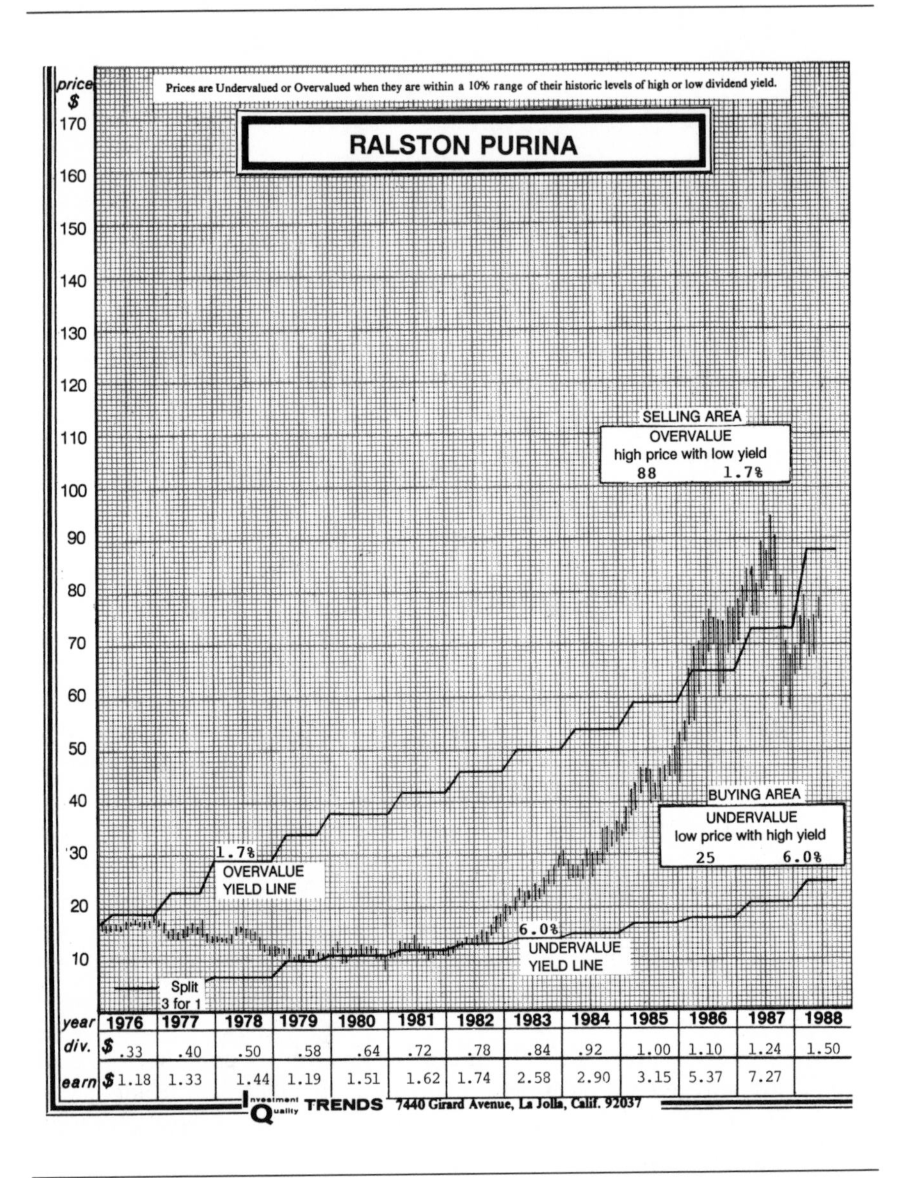

Ralston Purina is diversified enough in its food products to move in a relatively smooth path through its cycle of undervalue to overvalue.

INVESTMENT SAVES THE ECONOMY

Though the mood of the nation is usually against action, it is an opportunity lost to be fearfully immobile when the economy is limping. In fact, the courage to act and to make investments in the market returns the economy to health. Once advantage has been taken of the excellent buying opportunities, and portfolios have been protected against the unexpected, investors should relax and allow themselves the pleasure of optimism. Nothing lasts forever, not even devastating economic phases.

12

The Amazing Opportunity of Utilities

"If one tells the truth, one is sure, sooner or later, to be found out."

—OSCAR WILDE

This prodding and probing of dividend yield and its impact on stocks and the stock market can help in understanding the nature of the market. It allows investors to spot market trends and select individual stocks for the construction of a long-term, stable, high-yielding investment portfolio. It is seen that the dividend-yield theory can also identify both emerging problems and potential opportunities for exceptional total returns.

STELLAR UTILITIES

The utility industry is an example of the opportunity. A series of occurrences in the past two decades drastically changed utilities, an industry that had been stable for 100 years. To start with, utilities went through a ten-year-long bear market that began in 1965 and gave utility stocks a terrible drubbing. In fact, utilities retreated well below their historic undervalued levels of dividend yields, creating a whole new profile of value for themselves.

There is no question that some of the problems of the past decades still exert themselves on some utilities. Public Service of New Hampshire was forced to file for bankruptcy in early 1988, the first utility bankruptcy since the Great Depression. Centerior Energy (figure 12.1), Niagara Mohawk and Rochester Gas & Electric are among a handful of power companies that were forced to reduce their dividends.

But superior values also have been achieved and much money has been made in utilities since the early 1980s. The potential for even greater profits in the next few years is enormous.

A HISTORY LESSON

To comprehend the spectacular potential for future growth in the share price of blue-chip utility stocks, it is helpful to understand what happened to this industry in the 1960s and 1970s. In 1965 utilities across the nation launched massive construction programs, based on the estimated needs of a growing population and the reality of shrinking oil supplies. To move the United States safely away from dependency on foreign oil, many of the new facilities were powered by nuclear energy.

It can take up to ten years to build a power plant, during which time many changes can (and in this case did) occur in the economy.

THE BEST-MADE PLANS

The companies soon found that regulatory agencies were slow to move on rate requests and reluctant to grant needed rate relief, especially during periods of inflation. To make matters worse, the American public never developed full confidence in nuclear energy production. Construction was frequently halted by safety controversies, and costs mounted. Operating licenses were slow in coming. Some plants never even made it into operation.

Then, in 1973, interest rates soared to what until then was their highest level in this decade—12 percent. But the utilities were already committed to their construction programs and to the financing costs attached to them. Management felt it had little choice but to march on and pay the unforeseen high rates for the borrowed money.

Rocketing interest rates created a shock in the utility industry (the first of two interest-rate crises), propelling share prices downward.

FIGURE 12.1 Dividend-Yield Chart

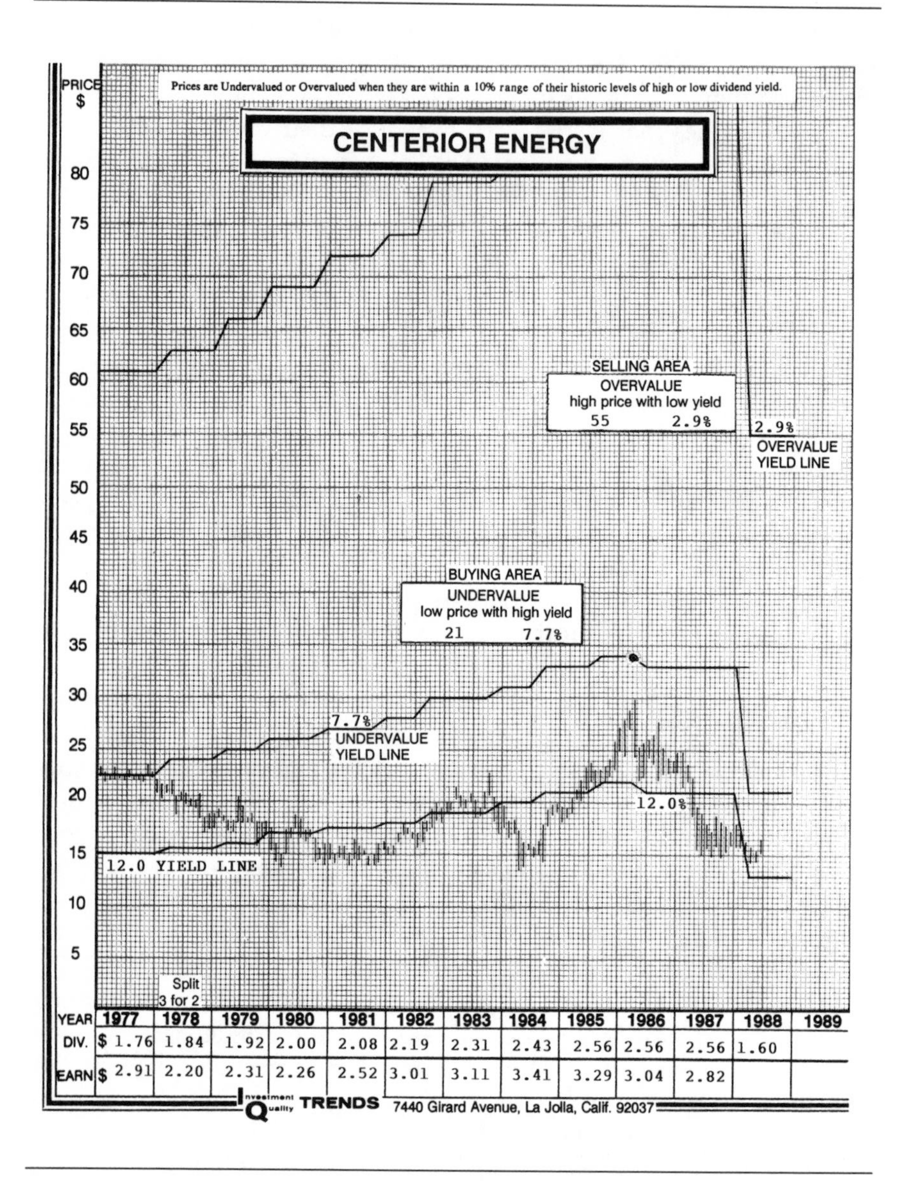

YEAR	1977	1978	1979	1980	1981	1982	1983	1984	1985	1986	1987	1988	1989
DIV.	$ 1.76	1.84	1.92	2.00	2.08	2.19	2.31	2.43	2.56	2.56	2.56	1.60	
EARN	$ 2.91	2.20	2.31	2.26	2.52	3.01	3.11	3.41	3.29	3.04	2.82		

Centerior Energy, plagued by problems with a nuclear generating plant, was forced to cut its dividend. Care should be taken when selecting utilities for purchase, because not all of them have worked through the difficult problems that shake that industry.

Prices dived so low, in fact, that they violated the historic undervalued yields for most utilities.

PLASTIC SURGERY ON UTILITIES PROFILES

During this period, the historical dividend-yield patterns were drastically altered. For most utilities, new bottom lines of undervalue were established. Even those utilities that did not establish new undervalue levels violated to some extent their existing undervalue points, illustrating how painfully sensitive utilities had become to interest rates.

Investors soon realized that when interest rates were high, financial pressure increased on utilities that had sold bonds or were still committed to selling bonds to pay for ongoing building programs.

INTEREST RATES IN THE DRIVER'S SEAT

Utility stocks became harnessed to changes in interest rates, moving up when rates declined and moving down when rates rose. And their dividend yields began to reflect the rates of return in the money markets.

Central and South West, a prominent electric utility holding company with operating units in Texas, Oklahoma, Arkansas and Louisiana, is an example of what happened to utilities at that time. Figure 12.2 illustrates the three major levels of value to which the company's stock has risen or declined in the past. The original 2.4 percent yield at overvalue underscores the high regard once afforded this company by investors.

Most other utilities, and the Dow Jones Utilities Average itself, topped out in 1965 with yields of 3.0 percent.

The 5.5 percent yield line in the center of the Central and South West chart was the undervalue line for the stock in the early 1970s and before. It provided support for this stock for many years before it was obliterated by the onslaught of interest rates. Plummeting prices then established a new undervalued line for Central and South West at 9.0 percent, with prices below that representing a buying area.

EXPECTATIONS CHANGE

Central and South West's old undervalue line at 5.5 percent yield became a temporary overvalue level. This can be called the intermediate goal area. Investors must keep it in mind as an upside objective when considering the purchase of a utility stock.

Paced by a rising dividend trend, the price of Central and South West has more than tripled since 1980, offering excellent value all the while. But only once did it pierce the 5.5 percent yield line. As late as mid-1987 the price to maintain that dividend yield had not been sustainable.

The Dow Jones Utilities Average also established a new undervalue line at the 9.0 percent dividend yield. It now takes that yield, or near to it, to halt and reverse a declining industry trend. Before the interest-rate episode of 1973, the Utilities Average was, like the Industrial Average, undervalued at a six percent yield.

NORMALITY GRADUALLY RETURNED

In the mid-1980s, economic conditions began to look the way they had looked 20 years earlier. Inflation abated and interest rates declined, edging closer to normal levels of the past.

With the new low interest rates, construction costs and debt payments for power projects were handled more comfortably. And at long last, some of those projects were completed, and debts were repaid in full. At that point, most utilities had no major building plans until 1991, and many had none for the balance of the century.

Other changes in the industry began to evolve as well. Due to conservation efforts, the demand for energy was not growing as fast as the utilities had expected. Electric generating capacity, as a result, was high.

With construction costs in remission and the demand for energy on the wane, gone was the need for utilities to issue more stock and dilute current holdings. They no longer needed to go to the bond market in search of financing. By 1987, utilities were able to meet 70 percent of their financial needs from internal cash flow, compared with only 30 percent five years earlier. "Approximately 40 percent of the power companies now have an excess cash flow," wrote H. Bradlee Perry, an analyst for David L. Babson & Co., in the March 1988 issue of *Better Investing* magazine, "and within another year over half of the firms will."

As capital needs of utilities continue to decline, profits will strengthen. As a result, earnings and dividends for utilities are expected to rise, and investment values will improve. Historically, utilities have

FIGURE 12.2 Dividend-Yield Chart

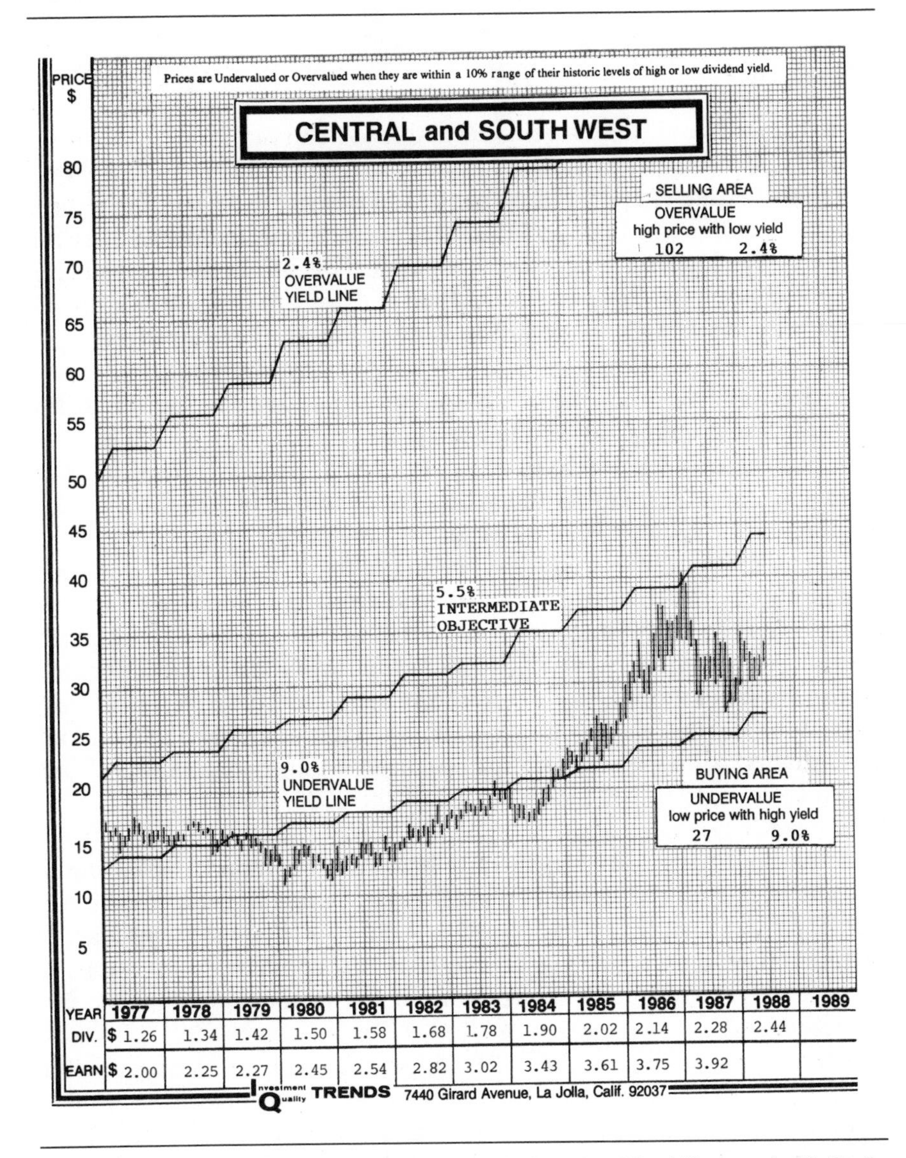

Though investors were given increasingly rising dividends, Central and South West remained in the dividend channels created during the utility crisis.

paid about 70 percent of their profits in dividends, as is shown in figure 12.3.

NEW CASH COWS

Whereas many utilities had not been able to achieve the levels of profitability approved for them by state regulatory commissions, a good deal more are getting nearer to those typical 11 percent to 13 percent returns that have been permitted. Utilities that can show regulators that they are well managed will have access to a great deal of cash in the years ahead.

As a result of this newfound financial freedom, utilities management is experiencing renewed zest. Many companies are inventing creative new sale-and-leaseback plans for solving cost-overrun problems in their nuclear facilities. They also are branching out, buying nonutility subsidiaries to spur earnings and to spread risks.

"There is much more scope for good management in utilities than there used to be," explained analyst Leonard Hyman of Merrill Lynch, in response to a 1988 survey conducted by *Nelson's Directory of Investment Research*. "Managements are discovering what they can do if they take the initiative, instead of waiting for regulators to give orders."

For the first time since the 1920s, utility mergers are taking place, creating companies that are bigger and more cost-effective. In a perspective on electric utilities published in February 1988, Duff & Phelps Inc. acknowledged that many changes had taken place, and analyst William A. Abrams painted a scenario for the future: "The companies best prepared to prosper in the environment of the 1990s will be the low-cost producers."

The Southern Company, a utilities holding company operating in the gulf and southern states, is typical of the advantageously positioned public service company. (See figure 12.4.) It is in a fast-growing part of the nation and is one of the 20 most widely held corporate stocks in America, with 279 million common shares in the hands of 308,000 shareholders.

"We've gone through some difficult years to carry out a construction program that's now moving toward successful completion," Southern Company president Edward Addison told shareholders in 1986. "As a result, we'll be in a solid position to supply the needs of our customers into the 21st century without adding major new capacity. If the future belongs to low-cost producers who can market aggressively and innovate as the situation changes, we expect to do very well indeed."

FIGURE 12.3 Electric Utility Earnings and Dividends

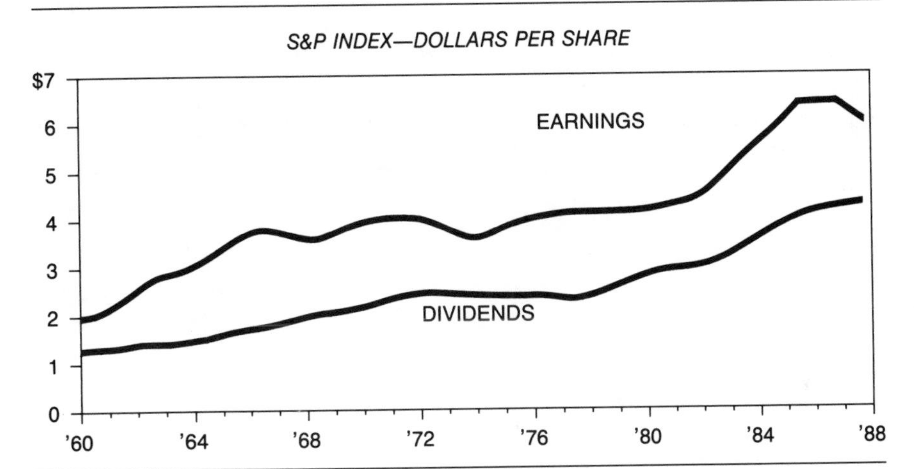

When earnings make a sustainable gain, dividends follow, as is shown here.

SOURCE: Courtesy of David L. Babson & Co., *Better Investing,* March 1988.

OUTDATED IDEAS LINGER

Although the old interest-rate sensitivity is becoming a thing of the past, utilities still are perceived by most investors as being interest-rate-sensitive securities. Actually, interest rates began to lose their grip on utilities stocks in 1977, when construction programs first started winding down. From 1978 to 1981, the prime rate rose from 6.3 percent to a new all-time high of about 21.0 percent. And yet, the undervalue yield line of the Utilities Average never fell below the 12 percent level established a decade earlier.

During that second episode of runaway interest rates, the Dow Jones Industrial Average lost 25 percent of its value. But utilities stocks traded within a ten-point, ten percent range, waiting for value to catch up with price.

THE PATIENT REAP PROFITS

Owners of utilities stocks may have been frustrated and bored with the market during those four years. But those who did not lose patience were rewarded well with a high rate of dividend yield and steady growth

FIGURE 12.4 Dividend-Yield Chart

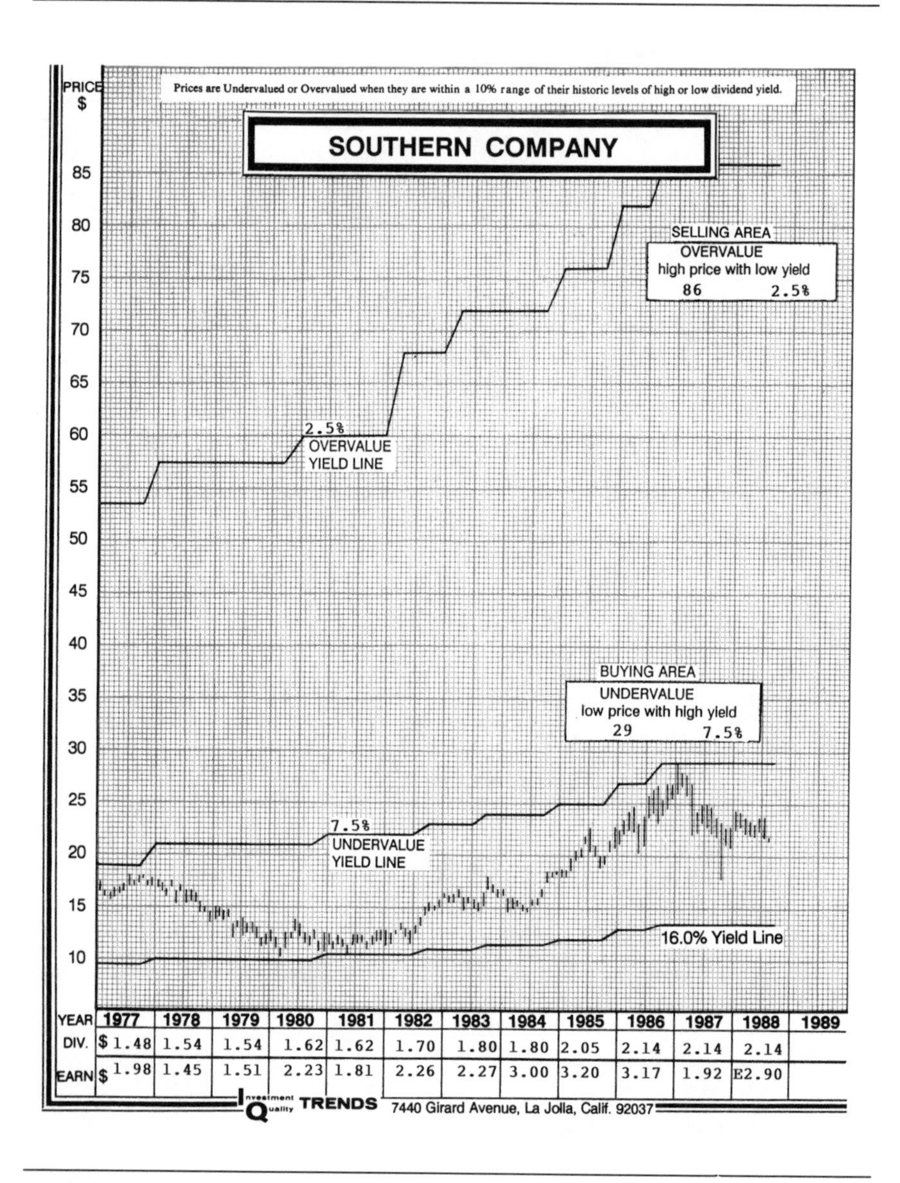

YEAR	1977	1978	1979	1980	1981	1982	1983	1984	1985	1986	1987	1988	1989
DIV.	$1.48	1.54	1.54	1.62	1.62	1.70	1.80	1.80	2.05	2.14	2.14	2.14	
EARN	$1.98	1.45	1.51	2.23	1.81	2.26	2.27	3.00	3.20	3.17	1.92	E2.90	

The Southern Companies has an enormous shareholder base, operates in a high-growth area and frequently offers excellent total return.

of dividend income when the rising trend resumed in 1982. Stock prices soon followed the dividend trend, and utility investors recorded healthy capital gains as well.

THE DEREGULATION WAR

As with many other industries, the trend in utilities has been to unbind company policymakers from state regulatory agencies, giving them more freedom to expand beyond their traditional business boundaries. This deregulation and diversification are coming at a time when utilities have the financial resources to take advantage of new opportunities. "We're being encouraged to compete, and we welcome that," William S. Lee, chief executive officer of Duke Power, commented in 1988. "We're ready to compete with anyone."

Utilities that are participating in these changes are often easy to spot. Any time that a public service company has changed its name, or a utility has deleted the word *gas* or *electric* from its logo, diversification is sure to be under way.

The company charted in figure 12.5, Pinnacle West Capital Corporation, formerly Arizona Public Service then AZP Group, is just such a trendsetter. The name Pinnacle West finally was chosen as the holding company's name to convey the message that the 100-year-old utility was also in the banking business (via its purchase of MeraBank, Arizona's largest thrift institution) and has investments in western real estate, venture capital and the development of natural resources.

Arizona is one of the most rapidly growing states in the nation, and the economy there is strong. With $12 billion in assets and with Arizona Public Service as its largest operating unit, Pinnacle West hopes to match the Southwest's growth and prosperity.

UNKNOWN FACTORS

Whether nonutility operations, in fact, will lead to greater profits for all utilities remains to be seen. It will depend in part on the skill of management in handling the challenges and opportunities that come as the door opens even further. So far, however, none of the diversified utilities have gotten into trouble because of their nonutility expansions.

The California Public Utilities Commission, which for much of the past 15 years has had a reputation for being hostile toward utilities and

FIGURE 12.5 Dividend-Yield Chart

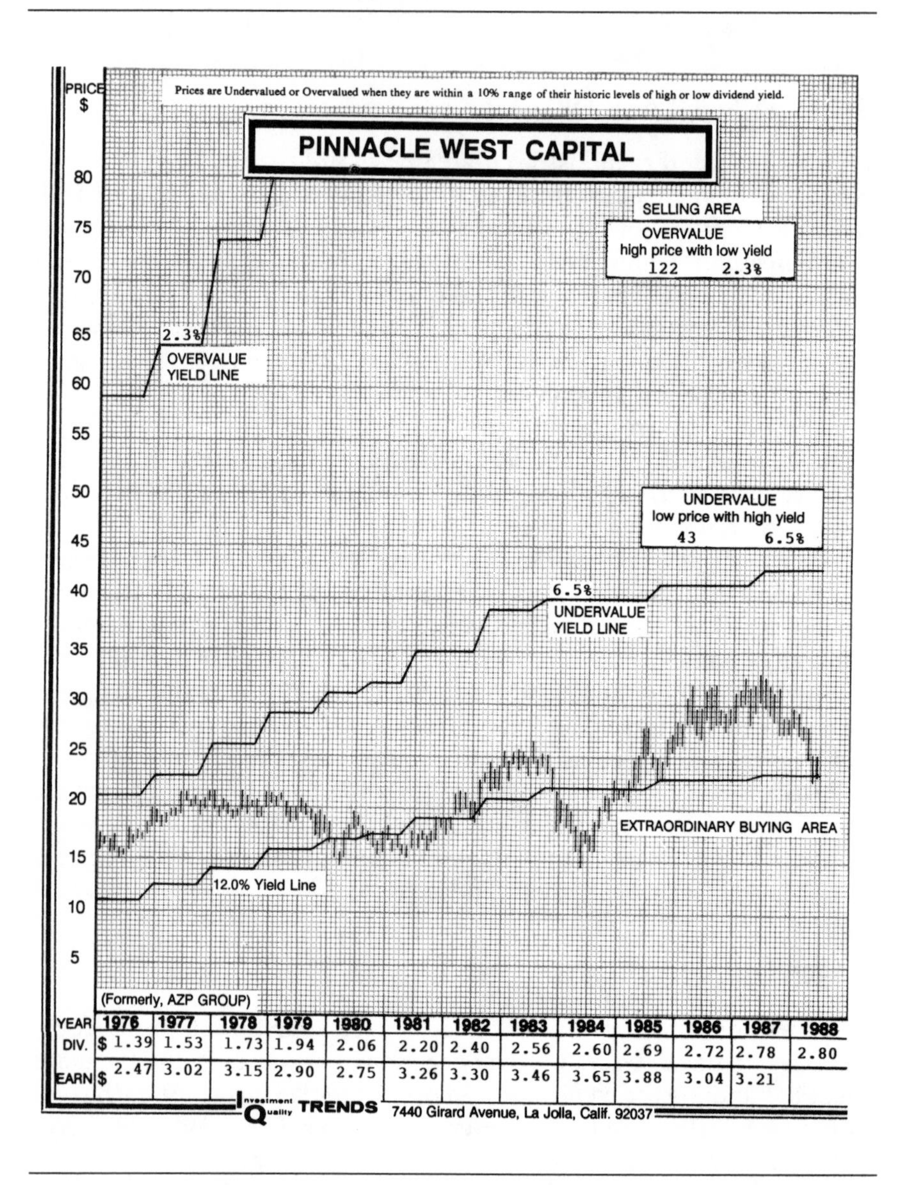

Pinnacle West Capital has become one of the most diversified utilities holding companies in the nation.

restrictive of change, recently approved a utility holding company for Southern California Edison, paving the way for diversification for other California utilities. Some California utilities, such as Pacific Lighting, had moved ahead with diversification without creating a holding company, but such methods were cumbersome.

This spreading of risk to nonutility industries, it is thought, will move power companies even further away from their previous crippling relationship with interest rates. Decoupled from interest rates, utilities have a fascinating investment future. The industry is undergoing a dramatic reformation, from restricted growth due to regulated rates of return, to unlimited growth potentials due to diversification into nonutility, nonregulated subsidiaries. This important change has not been recognized yet by most stock market investors.

A BRILLIANT FUTURE

If interest rates continue to be stable, or even decline as they usually do with a drop in the value of the U.S. dollar, the 7.0 percent to 11.0 percent rates of return from utilities stocks will spark investment attention. Share prices are sure to rise again.

In due time the old perimeters of undervalue and overvalue will be reestablished. Eventually, utilities stocks will again be priced to yield 3.0 percent, as they were in the early 1960s.

At the end of 1987, the Utilities Average yielded 9.0 percent. The full upside potential was roughly 200 percent, to an overvalued price of 530. If utility dividends increase—a very real possibility—the overvalue level for the DJIA could be even higher.

The Dow Jones Utilities Average chart in figure 12.6, completed late in 1987, shows that the DJUA has a long way to go before it reaches overvalued levels, where the yield is 3.0 percent.

WHEN OTHERS CATCH ON

This will be an exciting industry, once investors get used to the revolutionary idea that utility stocks are no longer captives of interest rates. Utilities have been so undervalued for so long that the upward rush to historic yields could push staid utilities into a league with growth stocks. It can be an extremely profitable episode for utility investors.

FIGURE 12.6 DJUA Chart

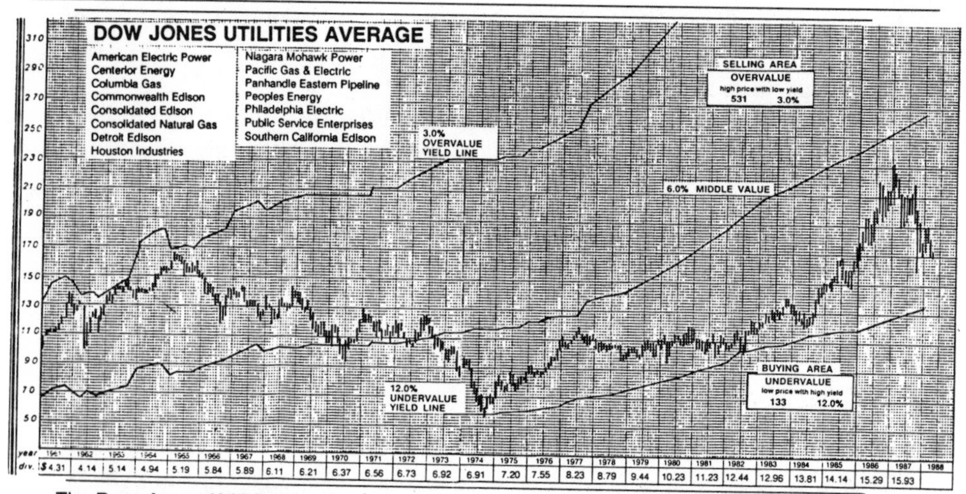

The **Dow Jones Utilities Average** was priced to yield 3.0% in 1961, 1963 and 1965. An ensuing bear market eventually produced a 12.0% yield in 1974. (The 12.0% yield reappeared in 1982 and 1984.) When the DJUA again yields 3.0%, the stocks will be priced more than 150% above current levels, and the group then will be overvalued. As dividends grow, values improve and upside potentials expand.

MEASURES OF THE MARKET

Dividends for the Dow Jones Averages reflect the 12 months through March 1988

Dow Jones Industrial Average	*Current*			*Potential to Overvalue*				*Potential to Undervalue*			
	Price	*Ann. Div*	*Yield*	*Pts. Up*	*% Up*	*High Price*	*Low Yield*	*Pts. Down*	*% Down*	*Low Price*	*High Yield*
	2110	$71.85	3.4%	285	14%	2395	3%	912	43%	1198	6%

Dow Jones Utilities Average	*Current*			*Potential to Overvalue*				*Potential to Undervalue*			
	Price	*Ann. Div*	*Yield*	*Pts. Up*	*% Up*	*High Price*	*Low Yield*	*Pts. Down*	*% Down*	*Low Price*	*High Yield*
	175	$15.90	9.1%	355	203%	530	3%	42	24%	133	12%

DJIA DIVIDEND INCHES UP IN FIRST QUARTER

The composite dividend for the Dow Jones Industrial Average rose 0.9% in the first quarter of 1988. . . from $71.20 for the 12 months through December 1987 to $71.85 for the 12 months through March 1988. Compared to the first quarter in 1987, the increase amounted to a disappointing 3.7%, vs. 7.1% in the previous year. The new dividend changes the price at undervalue to 1198, and lifts the price at overvalue to 2395.

FIGURE 12.7 The Dow Jones Utilities Average Stocks

American Electric Power	Niagara Mohawk Power
Centerior Energy	Pacific Gas & Electric
Columbia Gas System	Panhandle Eastern
Commonwealth Edison	Peoples Energy
Consolidated Edison	Philadelphia Electric
Consolidated Natural Gas	Public Service Enterprises
Detroit Edison	Southern California Edison
Houston Industries	

These stocks are used to compute the Dow Jones Utilities Average.

A BEAR MARKET REFUGE

Furthermore, utilities are a safer harbor than most other blue chips in bear markets. Heat and light are two of life's necessities, no matter how tightly family and business budgets are pressured.

The Dow Jones Utilities Average demonstrated a remarkable relative strength during the October 1987 meltdown in the market, falling only 8.5 percent during the month, versus a 24.4 percent drop in the Dow Jones Industrial Average. On Black Monday, while the Industrial Average lost about 22 percent of its value, the Utilities Average declined a scant three percent.

The Utilities Average had, however, been declining since January 23, when, preceding the Industrial Average to the top, it reached a high price of 230. The Industrial Average did not reach its ultimate level until August 1987. The total decline in the Utilities Average from the January high to the October low amounted to 31 percent, compared with a 39 percent decline in the Industrial Average, from the August high to the October low.

By January 1988, however, utilities had rebounded nine percent at a time when most other stock groups were still falling.

Experienced investors realize that no stock industry group is completely safe in a bear market; but some groups are safer than others. The high-quality utilities offer less risk than most common shares. Their dividends provide steady streams of income at rates that quite often are even higher than returns in the money market. Even when earnings temporarily falter, dividends continue to be paid.

BLUE-CHIP RELIABILITY

Recession or not, dividends from most blue-chip utilities are safe. The companies have long histories of experience on which to draw, as well as seasoned managements who have led them through many past economic climates. Through good times and bad, they have been persistent survivors in an uncertain financial world.

INVESTMENT STRATEGY

Utilities make an excellent foundation or core industry group for investor portfolios. Despite the inherent safety of utilities, though, planning this sector of a portfolio demands the same emphasis on quality and value that other industry groups require. The painful remolding of this industry in the past 20 years has made attention to fundamentals even more crucial.

SPREAD THE RISK

Diversification of stock purchases, as explained in chapter 10, is one way to maximize utility dividend and growth potential and to minimize risks. First of all, a utilities portfolio should be diversified according to sources of power. Some coal, some hydroelectric, oil, purchased power and nuclear generating companies should be among those purchased. Most investors are aware of the risks associated with companies heavily involved in nuclear generation, but all sources of power involve some risk. A war in the Middle East can send oil prices skyward; a drought can curtail the availability of hydroelectric power.

NUCLEAR EXPOSURE

Each fuel source also has its advantages. All of the blue-chip utilities, even those that are involved in nuclear construction, represent values for some time to come. While those with nuclear exposure are a somewhat riskier investment than nonnuclear utilities, they can supply high dividend yields and a higher potential total return to justify the higher risks.

An example is a company mentioned earlier in this chapter, Pinnacle West, which carries a higher degree of risk because of its ownership of the Palo Verde nuclear generating station. The company also offers a higher dividend yield (8.7 percent in mid-1987) and a lower price/earnings ratio than most utility stocks (ten to one). According to the *Rule of 72* (which tells us how long it will take for an investment to double by dividing the yield into 72), it will take little more than 8 years for this investment to double, when the yield is 8.7%. If dividends are increased down the road, that time will be shorter.

In a 1988 poll of utility industry analysts, three utilities with nuclear exposure were rated the best managed of all utilities. Duke Power, Dominion Resources and Wisconsin Energy ranked first, second and third. "Duke is regarded worldwide as a premier utility in the engineering, construction and operation of power plants of all types," noted Prudential-Bache analyst Barry Abramson, in response to the survey.

NUCLEAR AVERSION

Investors who like utilities but abhor risk may want to concentrate on those public services companies in high-growth areas; those diversified enough not to be dependent on any one industry, or those with little or no nuclear exposure.

Plenty of excellent choices meet these criteria. TECO Energy, Idaho Power, Southwestern Public Service and Hawaiian Electric are four such securities that might appeal to extremely conservative investors. Figure 12.8 lists utilities that do not draw from nuclear power sources.

HIGHER GAINS POSSIBLE

Investors with a higher risk tolerance and a greater need for capital gains also can find a variety of utilities that meet their needs. Detroit Edison, for example, a primarily coal-based utility, generally rides the economic cycles of the auto industry that dominates its territory. Because of this dependence on car sales and the automakers, and because of some degree of reliance on nuclear, along with several other problems facing the company, investors have shied away from the stock of Detroit Edison.

The company's dividend was safe at the time its chart, figure 12.9, was completed in September 1987. And the utility was priced at six times earnings, below book value, and it yielded nearly 11.0 percent—a

FIGURE 12.8 Blue-Chip Utilities with No Nuclear Exposure

STOCK	*FUEL SOURCE*
ALLEGHENY POWER	Coal (89%); Hydro & Purchased (11%)
HAWAIIAN ELECTRIC	Oil (93%); Purchased (7%)
IDAHO POWER	Coal (36%); Hydro & Purchased (64%)
IPALCO ENTERPRISES	Coal (100%)
INTERSTATE POWER	Coal (98%); Purchased (2%)
LOUISVILLE GAS & ELECTRIC	Coal (93%); Hydro & Purchased (7%)
OKLAHOMA GAS & ELECTRIC	Gas (51%); Coal (49%)
PACIFIC LIGHTING	Gas (100%)
POTOMAC ELECTRIC	Coal (88%); Oil (12%)
SOUTHWEST PUBLIC SERVICE	Coal & Purchased (81%); Gas (19%)
TECO ENERGY	Coal (98%); Oil (2%)
UTAH POWER & LIGHT	Coal (92%); Hydro (7%); Gas (1%)

rare find in the stock market at that time. Because of its track record, even with certain unresolved questions, Detroit Edison represented a good buy.

A STUDY IN DEMOGRAPHICS

Regional diversification can help ensure that utilities are positioned to make the best of demographics and changing economies. But even for companies in a geographic location that is experiencing serious hard times, dividend yield can signal a turn in the fortunes of a specific stock.

One high-quality operation that has faced the challenge of a weak regional economy is Houston Industries, charted in figure 12.10. Among the most impressively managed and profitable utility holding companies in the United States, by early 1988 Houston Industries had weathered the economic storms in its oil-depressed service area. The rest of Texas was still biting the bullet.

Houston, the fourth-largest city in the nation, enjoys a broader economic base than does the remainder of Texas. It is home to the nation's third-ranking seaport; is an important rail center; and has NASA's Manned Spacecraft Center. A growing tourism industry promotes such attractions as Astroworld, Astrohall, the Astrodome and Sea-Arama.

Houston Industries president and chief executive officer Don D. Jordan explained his company's situation in a 1988 analyst's report. He

FIGURE 12.9 Dividend-Yield Chart

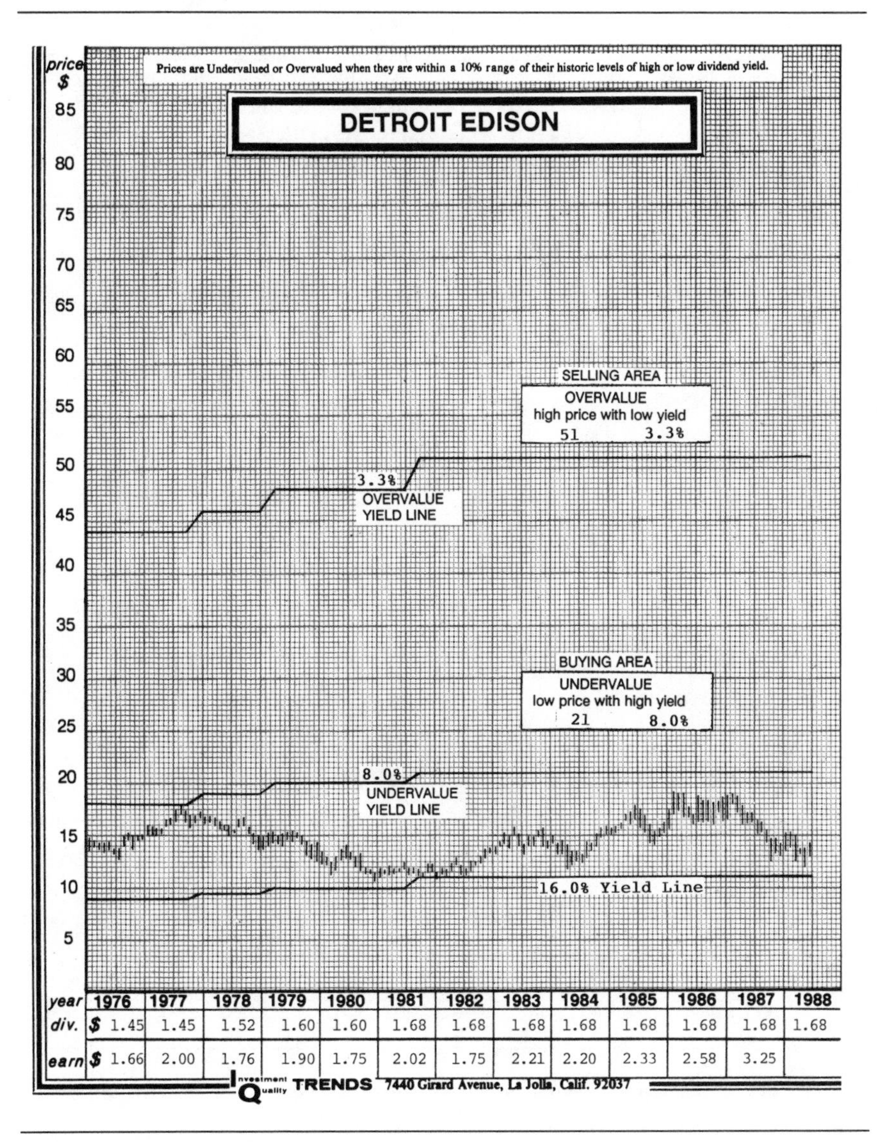

year	1976	1977	1978	1979	1980	1981	1982	1983	1984	1985	1986	1987	1988
div.	$ 1.45	1.45	1.52	1.60	1.60	1.68	1.68	1.68	1.68	1.68	1.68	1.68	1.68
earn	$ 1.66	2.00	1.76	1.90	1.75	2.02	1.75	2.21	2.20	2.33	2.58	3.25	

Regional diversification is essential when building a utilities portfolio because many light and power companies are dependent on local economies. Detroit Edison, for example, operates in a region economically dominated by the automobile industry, and rises and falls with the fortunes of that manufacturing group.

FIGURE 12.10 Dividend-Yield Chart

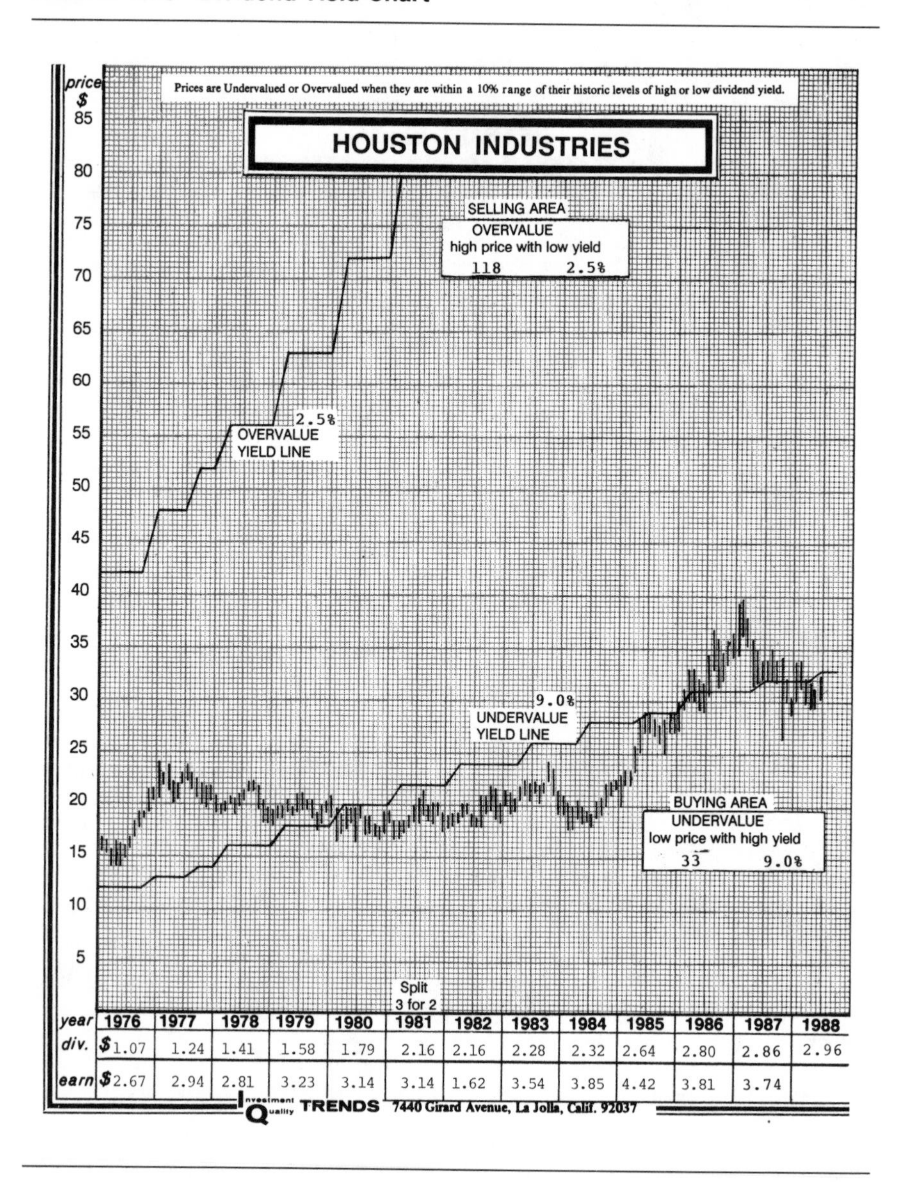

In addition to having to cope with utility industry problems, Houston Industries operated in a depressed Texas economy in the early 1980s. The utility would have been an excellent purchase at the bottom of the cycle shown on this chart.

said that the Houston economy is expected to grow by two percent during 1988 after having bottomed out during 1987. Quoting the University of Houston's Center for Public Policy, Jordan predicted that Houston's economy would also show greater diversity in the future. At the beginning of the decade, 80 percent of its growth was oil-related; by the end of 1987 the oil-dependent sector had dropped to 64 percent. More important, 80 percent of the growth anticipated after 1987 was expected to be non-energy-related.

In 1986, the total return for Houston Industries produced a 34 percent gain, outperforming both the Standard & Poor's 500 and the Dow Jones Utilities Index. Houston Industries' stock lost 4.3 percent of its value in the market meltdown of October 1987, but by mid-February 1988 it had regained the full loss.

The 2.5 percent yield at overvalue on Houston's chart may seem modest for a utility stock, but that is merely the intermediate level, established when interest rates fell in the early 1970s. At the top of the bull market in 1965 Houston Industries was priced to yield 1.3 percent. If interest rates remain stable or decline, and investment popularity returns to utilities as is bound to happen, those low dividend yields will be seen again. Houston Industries' price could then go off the top of this chart.

TIMING

As emphasized in earlier chapters, it is difficult to predict exactly when a stock or an industry group will begin a trend movement in a new direction. When any segment of the market, or the market itself, has been undervalued for an extended period, new trends can begin suddenly, and move forward with dramatic speed. The ascent of utilities stocks could be the next big Wall Street success story.

Anticipating the Future

13

The Market and the Economy

"I know no way of judging the future but by the past."

—PATRICK HENRY

No one knows what lies ahead in the next year, or in the next two years and beyond. Still, investment advisers, journalists and futurists delight in polishing their perceptions, venting viewpoints and attempting to forecast the future. Sometimes they register a hit, sometimes a miss, but no matter. What is really offered is food for thought—an educated guess, based on reasonable assumptions, personal opinions and a lifetime of study and experience.

When delving forward into time, one thing is certain: change. The economy will be wonderful for a time, then for several months or several years it will muddle along in misery. Then that, too, passes. The cycles will have their way. One defense investors have is to anticipate change and to be prepared for it.

The study of individual stocks and the market in general presented here can reveal some trends and provide some useful jewels of wisdom. Certain of the predictions are short-term in nature, while others reach somewhat further down the years.

A CRYSTAL BALL ON THE STOCK MARKET

A primary question is: What can be expected of the stock market?

The stock market will be in a downtrend through the end of the 1980s and possibly lasting until 1993.

The meltdown of the stock exchange in October 1987 left little doubt that the bull market that started in 1974 had ended and a bear market had taken its place. However, relatively strong rallies are possible in bear markets, and 1988 will be a year of the dancing bear.

That does not mean, however, that the Dow Jones Industrial Average is likely to return to its August 25, 1987, record high of 2722.42. Nor is 1988 expected to repeat 1987's lowest level. On October 19, 1987, the Dow landed at 1728.78, wiping out the year's gain and then some.

The important benchmarks to look for are the extremes of dividend yield: three percent at overvalue, six percent at undervalue. Based on the current DJIA composite dividend of $73.92, the price at overvalue is 2464 and the price at undervalue is 1232. Those prices, however, will change when the dividend changes.

Typically, the stock market declines in the year following a presidential election. At best, 1989 will be flat, and boring for traders, with little volatility.

An interesting, and very likely accurate, bit of crystal-gazing was put forth in 1987 by the Foundation for the Study of Cycles, an organization that studies and charts virtually every type of cycle imaginable, from when salmon are going to be abundant in Washington state to when the locusts will swarm.

The Foundation suggests that the absolutely best time to buy stocks in the next several years will be April 1989 or thereabouts. By then, according to the dividend-yield theory, the Dow Industrials will have reached an undervalue of at least six percent, after producing a second bear market rally at the five percent dividend-yield level.

The best time to take profits? Try December 1990 or January 1991, said the Foundation's executive director, Jeffrey Horovitz.

FAVORED INDUSTRIES

In several highly undervalued industry groups, great profits will be possible, and stocks are likely to give respectable returns even in a bull market.

Investors should focus, at least through 1989, on blue-chip companies with multinational operations. The undervalued industry groups most favored are utilities, drugs, hospital management, oil service and computers. For patient investors willing to scrutinize companies for quality, banks also present good investment opportunities.

Banks, because they were hit in the 1970s and early in the 1980s by deregulation, high interest rates and the collapse of many loans to less-developed countries, have been out of favor for a long time. Yet for many financial institutions, the worst times are behind them. While banks' profits aren't dazzling in 1988, it could easily be the year that the downward trend in bank profits is reversed.

The best of the blue-chip banks now represent excellent values for long-term growth. Security Pacific (figure 13.1) and Bank of Boston (figure 13.2) offer particularly good value at their undervalue range. Citicorp, discussed in an earlier chapter, also has a potent future, if purchased at undervalue.

Utilities also offer exceptional values. In the past two decades, big construction projects and record interest rates caused many lean years. But those troubles, for the most part, have been conquered. A long stretch of price appreciation lies ahead.

The March 1988 issue of *Stratagem*, published by the InterCapital Division of Dean Witter Reynolds Inc., put forth the following analysis of the utilities industry:

"There is one sector of the equity market that has historically provided an unmatched compromise between asset growth and volatility: utilities! These stocks have traditionally been the asset of choice for defensive portfolios. But they have also provided above-average long-term returns. While investors gravitate to utilities during times of uncertainty, we doubt that many are aware of the extraordinary long-term attraction of what is normally considered a dull and unexciting group. Incredibly, utilities have substantially outperformed the industrial averages over the last five, ten and fifteen years when including dividends. Moreover, they have done so with only half of the overall market volatility and have paid twice the annual dividend yields!

"The statistical breakdown of the industry's long-term performance is extraordinary. The S&P 40 utilities yield has averaged twice that of the S&P 400 industrials over the last 15 years, ranging between 1.5 and 2.6 times."

Investors can consider a variety of eye-catching utilities. Among the best values are Florida Progress—well managed, high yield, rate base is settled—(figure 13.3); Texas Utilities—safe dividend, recently yielding 11 percent—(figure 13.4); Houston Industries—raised its dividend in

FIGURE 13.1 Dividend-Yield Chart

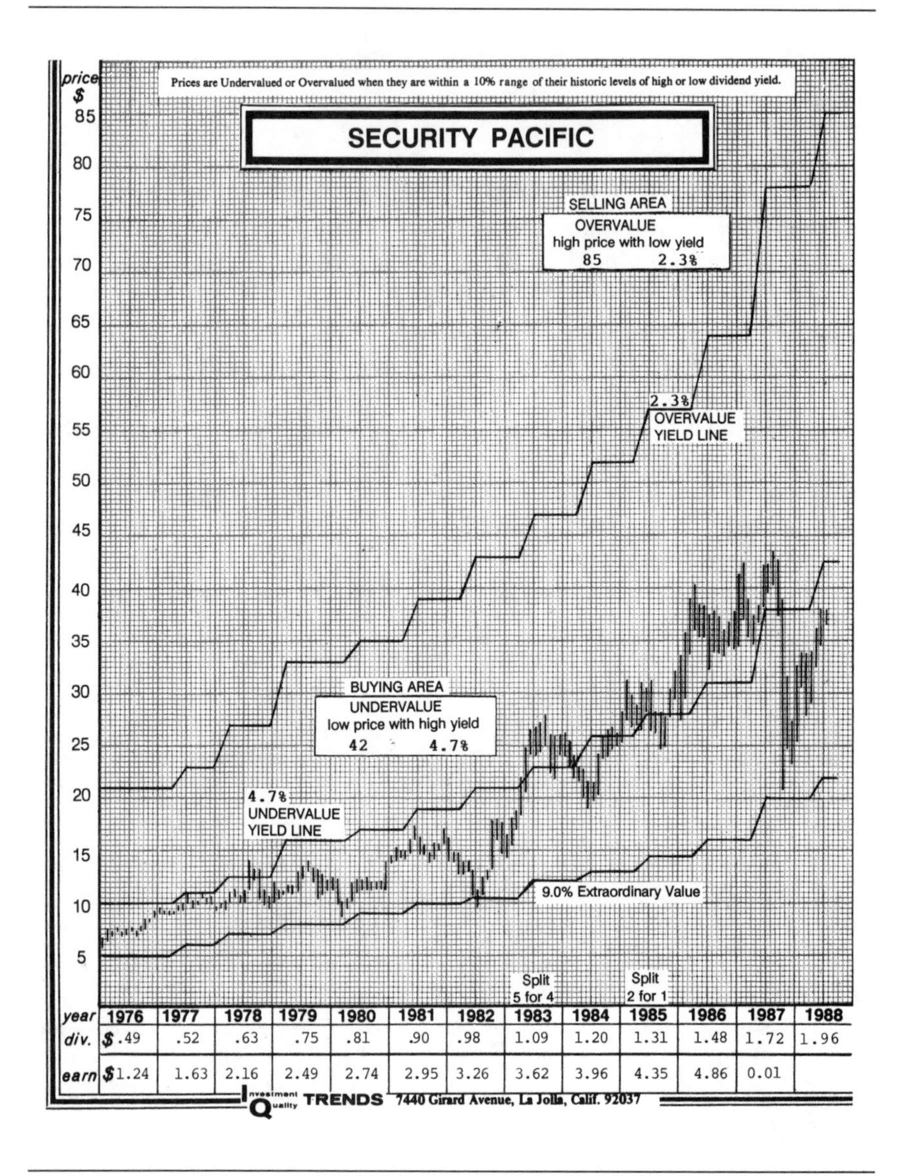

year	1976	1977	1978	1979	1980	1981	1982	1983	1984	1985	1986	1987	1988
div.	$.49	.52	.63	.75	.81	.90	.98	1.09	1.20	1.31	1.48	1.72	1.96
earn	$1.24	1.63	2.16	2.49	2.74	2.95	3.26	3.62	3.96	4.35	4.86	0.01	

Security Pacific has been one of the strongest banks in the high-growth, western United States. At undervalue, it has been an excellent buy.

FIGURE 13.2 Dividend-Yield Chart

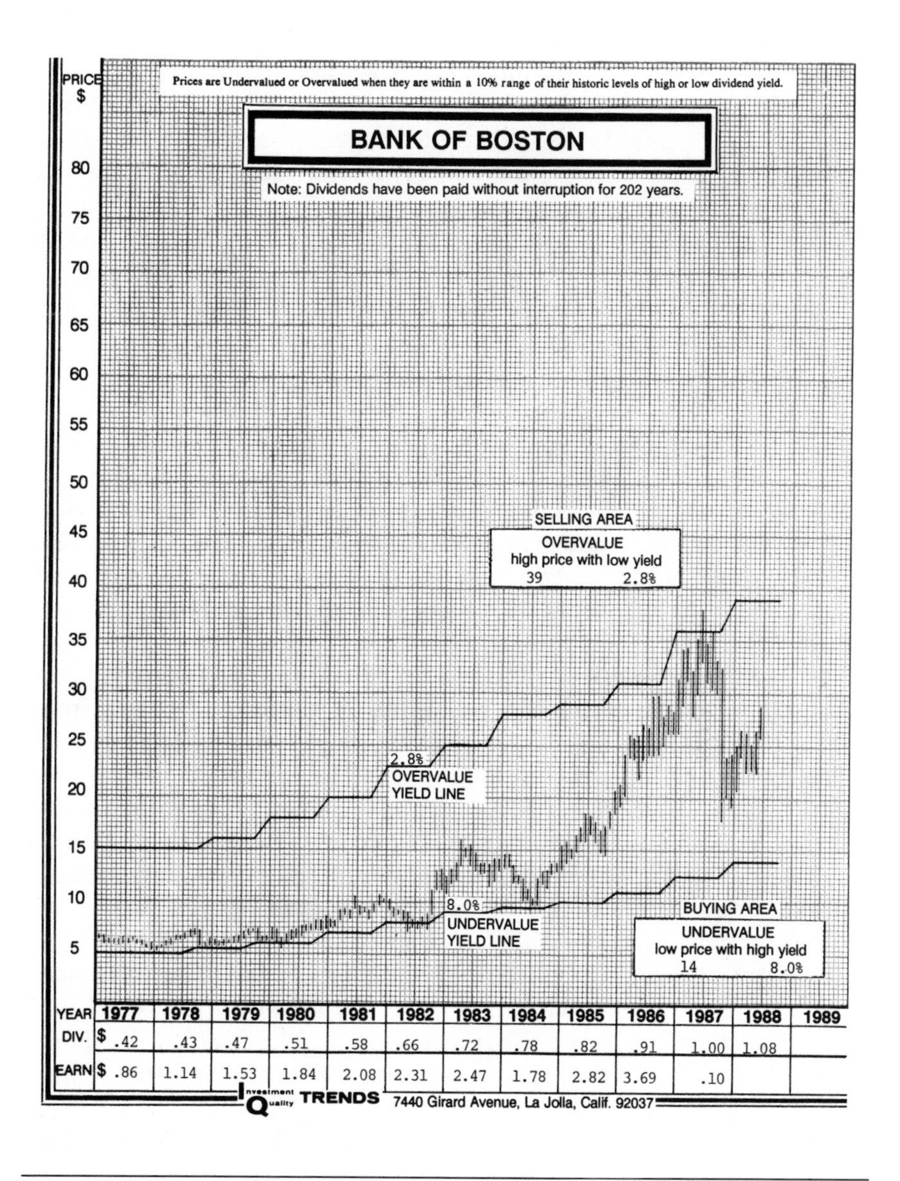

YEAR	1977	1978	1979	1980	1981	1982	1983	1984	1985	1986	1987	1988	1989
DIV.	$ .42	.43	.47	.51	.58	.66	.72	.78	.82	.91	1.00	1.08	
EARN	$ .86	1.14	1.53	1.84	2.08	2.31	2.47	1.78	2.82	3.69	.10		

Bank of Boston has a lengthy history. At the proper dividend yield, it can be an advantageous purchase.

1988, recently yielding 10.0 percent—(figure 12.10); Pinnacle West Capital—diversified, double-digit dividend yield—(figure 12.10); and Pacificorp—no nuclear exposure, acquiring Utah Power & Light, excellent long-term growth potential—(figures 10.2 and 13.5).

Though utilities are no longer as interest-rate-sensitive as they once were, both utilities and banks will be even greater buys if interest rates remain at single-digit levels. Although temporary uptrends will appear from time to time, the major trend of interest rates, at least through 1989, will be down.

In the other favored industry groups, certain stocks show specific promise. Among them are IBM (see appendix), Xerox (figure 11.2), Bristol-Myers (figure 3.2), Eastman Kodak (see appendix), American Medical International (figure 5.3) and Pfizer (figure 13.6).

OUTLOOK FOR THE ECONOMY

What lies ahead for the economy? Again, the best of times don't last forever. The economy had experienced more than six years of expansion in 1988, much of it financed by overseas capital. Typically, such economic cycles last four years. A cooling-off period would be normal and natural.

Investors worried about the impact of computerized and program trading on the stock markets long before their swift and deadly influence was felt during the frantically volatile month of October 1987. When a new and unmeasured factor enters the market, uncertainty always exists until the changes are tested. So it is with the recent internationalization of world economies and stock markets. Electronic linkups make the United States, Europe and the Far East infinitely more interconnected and dependent on one another for stability.

A disturbing imponderable that weighs heavily on the future is the Japanese economy. In Japan, both the real estate market and the stock market are out of touch with reality. Total land value in Japan in 1987 was reported by *Forbes* to be $8 trillion—more than double the value of all land in the United States. This is especially startling when one realizes that the United States is 30 times the size of Japan.

Stocks in Japan were selling at 70 times earnings at the beginning of 1988, with overvalued real estate being used as collateral for loans to buy overvalued stocks. When the bubble bursts—and it will—the effects will be felt in financial markets around the world.

While our economy appears headed for danger, if Japan stays afloat throughout 1988, the U.S. stock market could do very well, despite the down pressure of a bear market.

How is it possible for the stock market to go up while the economy goes down? It is not only possible, it is probable: A recession of considerable magnitude already was discounted in the stock market on October 19, 1987, when investors lost more than $500 billion in equity assets. A perception of improvement in either trade or budget deficits would change the mood of investors worldwide, and could spur a strong stock market rally.

However, there is little chance of the budget deficit's being reduced meaningfully in an election year, and reductions in the trade deficit have been slow in coming.

Economists have been looking for reductions in the trade deficit for more than two years as the dollar has fallen to 40-year lows against foreign currencies. The dollar now has fallen so low that the end of the decline should have been seen. The trade deficit should now improve, as goods and services from the United States are attractively competitive in overseas markets. In fact, manufacturing companies began showing sales and profit improvements during 1988.

This, in a nutshell, is what the authors of this book see in the future. We know that the economy will present challenges in the years ahead. We know that the stock market will present opportunities. Successful investors will meet the challenges and seize the opportunities.

FIGURE 13.3 Dividend-Yield Chart

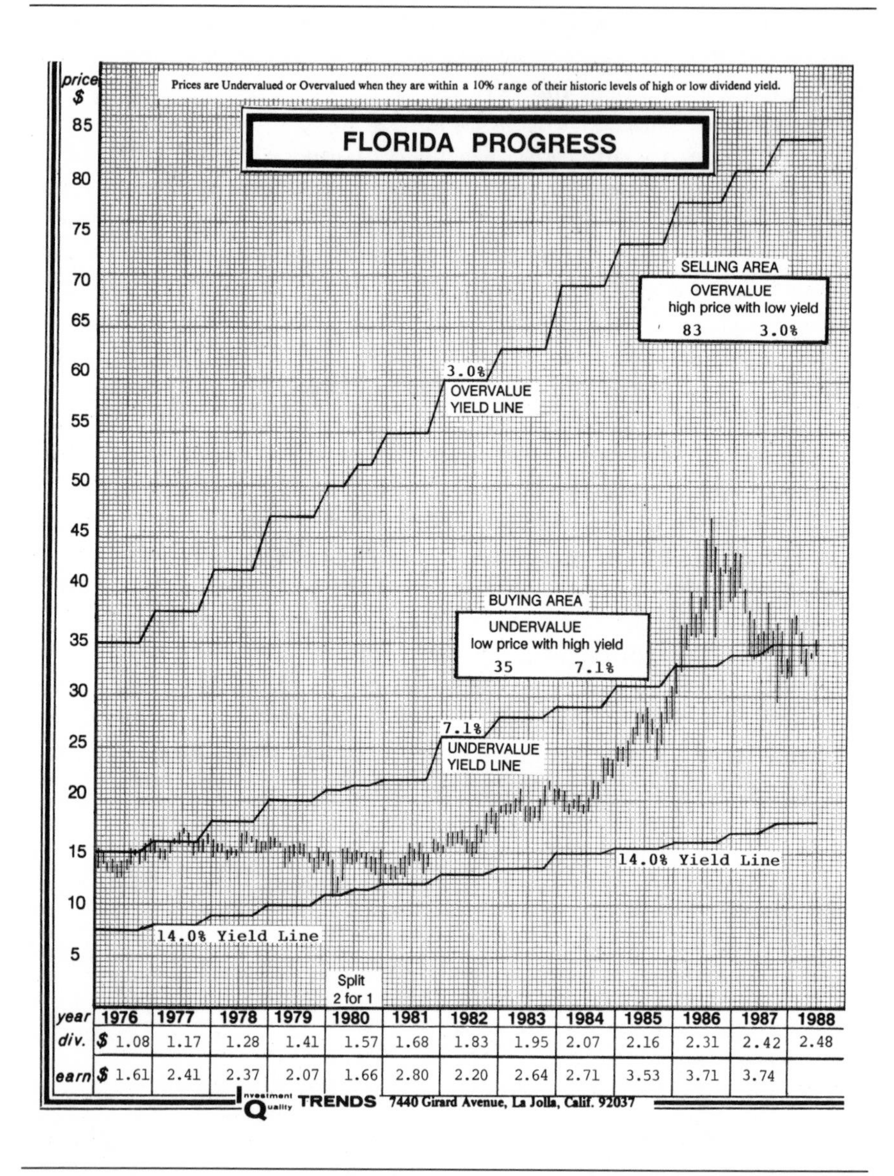

Florida Progress has a reputation for being well managed. It does business in a growing region, and it is expected to have few, if any, regulatory problems.

FIGURE 13.4 Dividend-Yield Chart

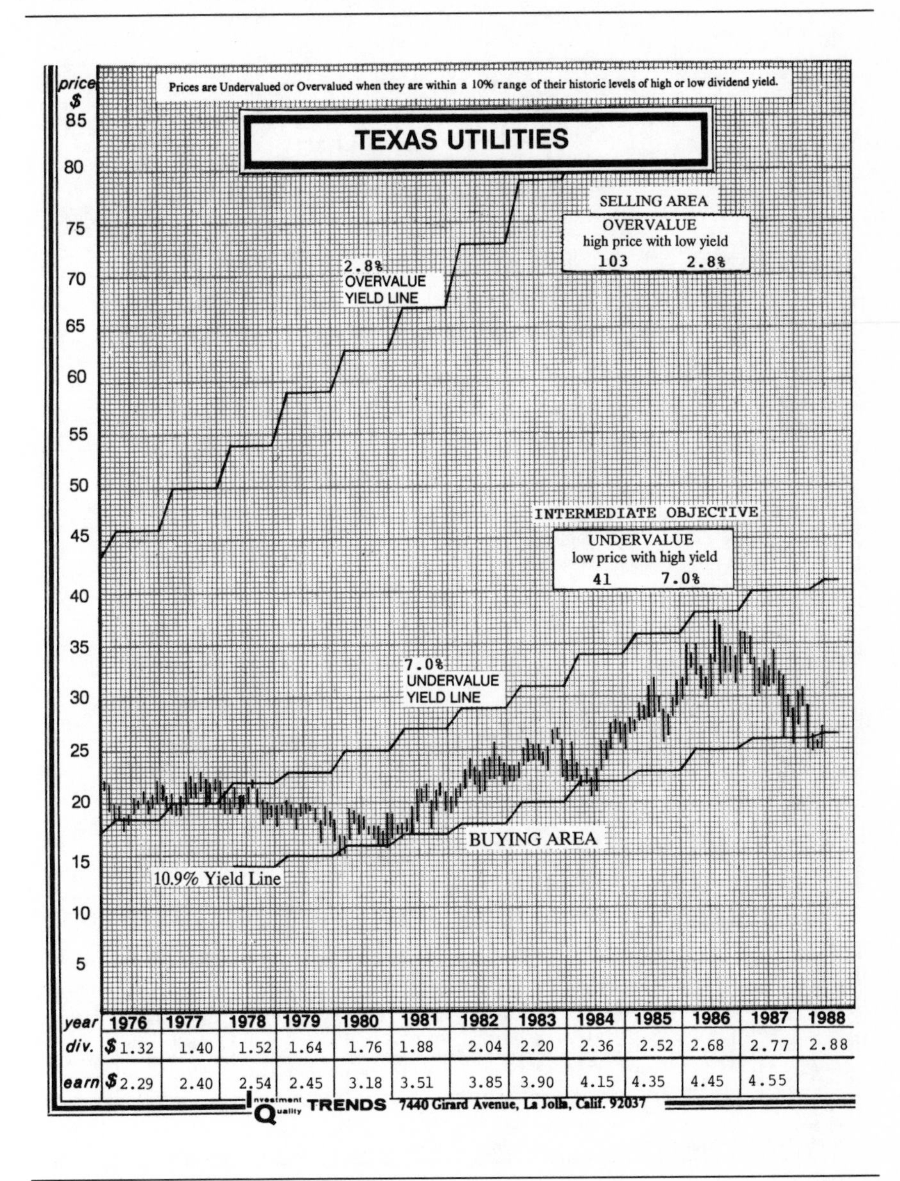

Texas Utilities' price remained undervalued even after the Texas economy began its recovery. Texas Utilities has often been a bargain stock.

FIGURE 13.5 Dividend-Yield Chart

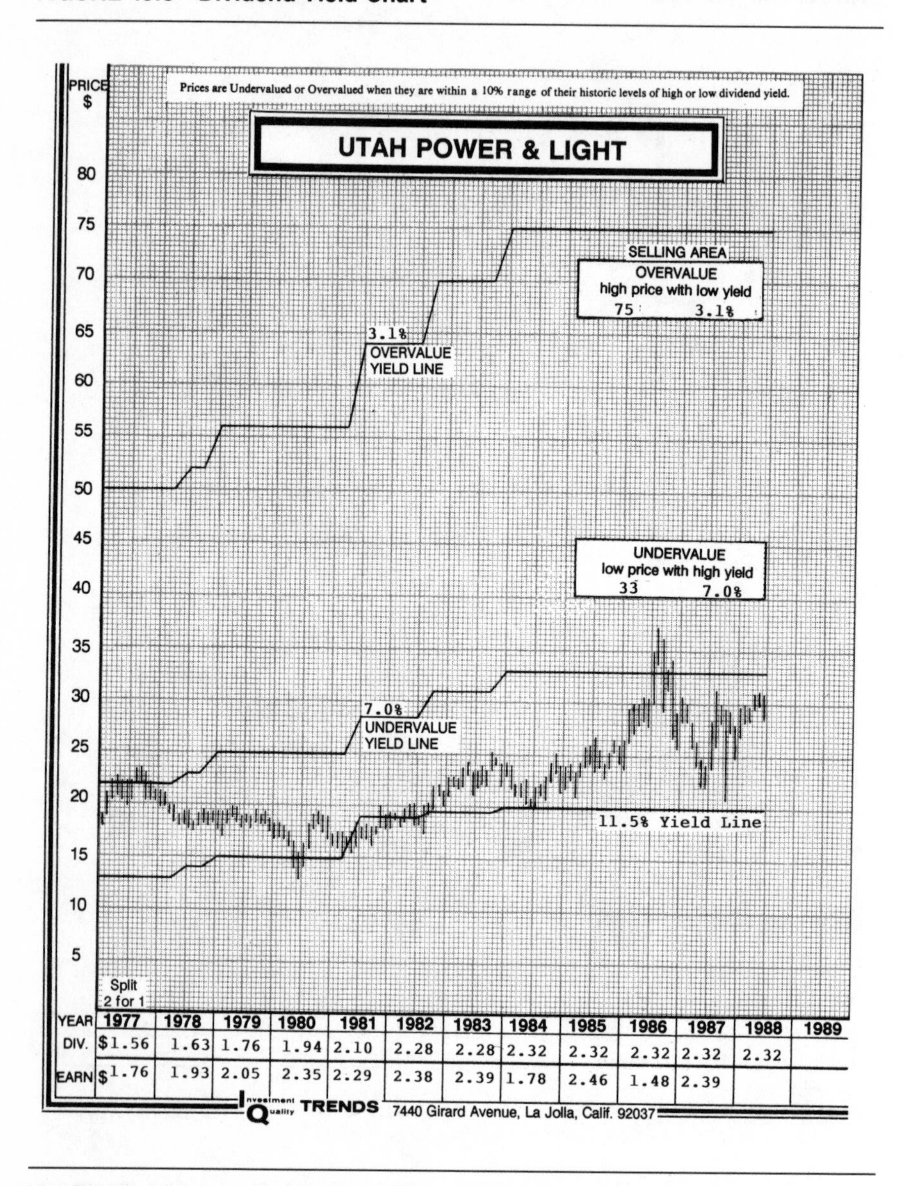

Utah Power and Light developed a reputation for reliable share price growth and enviable dividend payouts. Its stability is based on a remarkable mix of raw materials from which electricity is generated, including hydroelectric and coal.

FIGURE 13.6 Dividend-Yield Chart

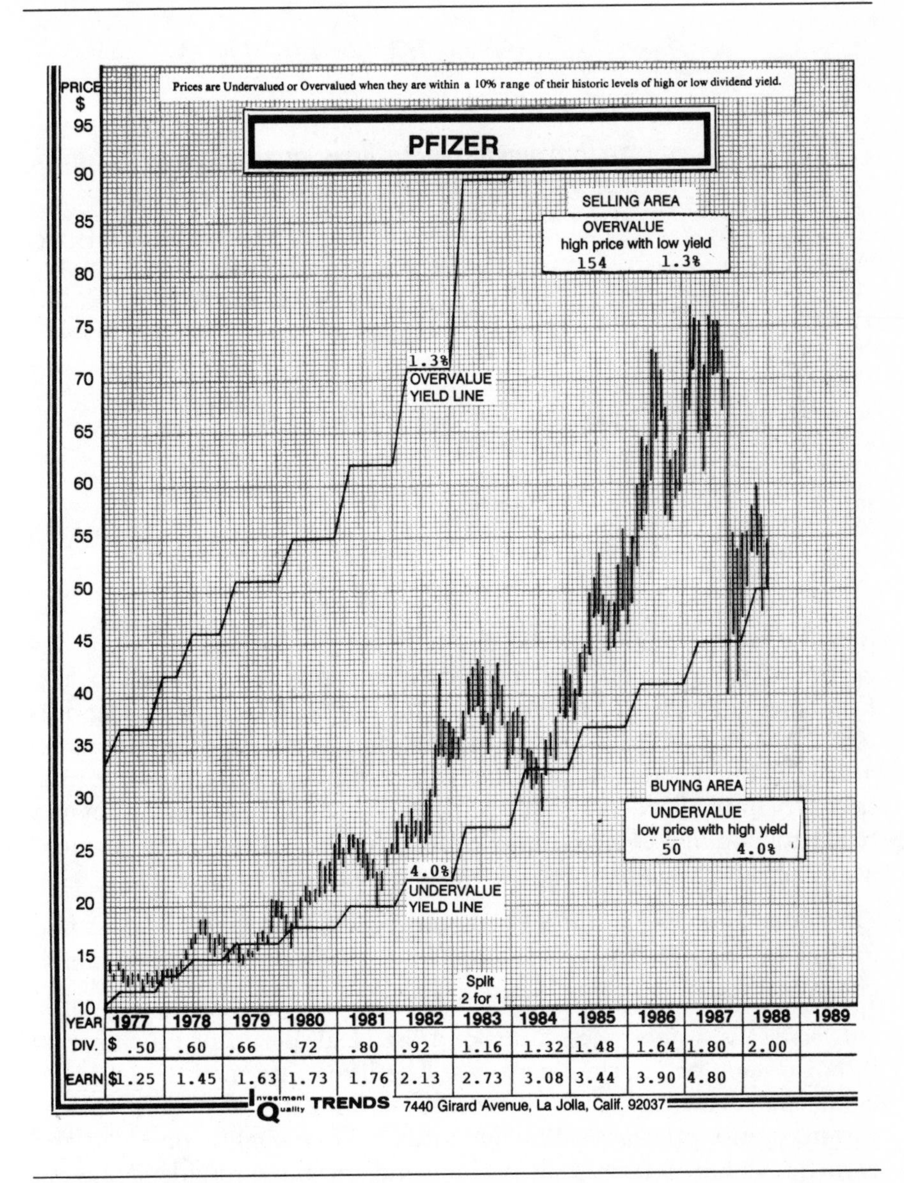

Productive and well managed, Pfizer's earnings have increased at an average annual rate of 20 percent since 1979. Pharmaceuticals, in general, have a good long-term outlook.

14

Questions and Answers

"Man is not a circle with a single center; he is an ellipse with two foci. Facts are one, ideas are the other."

—VICTOR HUGO

It is the crazy paradox of the learning experience that the more one knows about a subject, the more questions one is compelled to ask. Even after the extended discussion of the dividend-yield theory and its role in the analysis of the stock market, an assortment of questions remains. To build and manage a blue-chip portfolio, a little more information is helpful. Readers of "Investment Quality Trends" have shown a talent for looking at investment problems with a fresh point of view. Many of the following questions were posed by those readers.

Question: *How can an investor choose among three or four stocks that look alike? Sometimes different undervalued stocks have very similar characteristics.*

Answer: It is a good idea to make a list of all pertinent fundamental facts for each of the similar stocks. The listed information would include the dividend, yield, percentage of institutional interest, price/earnings ratio, price-to-book-value ratio, relative quality, dividend and earnings stability, frequency of dividend increases, dividend payout ratio and other relevant statistical information. When these are listed side by side and compared, differences among several stocks that superficially look alike will become apparent. The differences then must be weighed on a scale that balances this raw material with the personal investment objectives and the temperament of the investor.

For example, suppose an investor is interested in purchasing the stock of a company in the hospital management industry and has narrowed the choices to Hospital Corporation of America, Humana and National Medical Enterprise. The investor should list price, dividend yield, potential price increase, quality ranking and blue-chip status. When this information is compared, one of the three companies may appear to be stronger or have a greater potential for share-price growth. In addition, an investor may want to examine the comparative size of each company, the amount of debt carried and the length of time the company has been paying uninterrupted dividends. After this analysis, differences frequently begin to emerge and the investor develops a better sense of the relative strengths of each company. The choice then becomes easier.

Assuming that relative quality and value are comparable between stocks that are being considered, a selection can (and should) be made on the basis of personal preference. Perhaps the investor prefers the services of Hospital Corporation of American over Humana or National Medical Enterprise. Perhaps he or she has heard or read good reports of that particular management team. It even may be a frivolous reason that tips the scale in favor of one company or another.

In any event, when the selections are close in the important categories of quality and value, the company preferred by the investor should be the stock of choice. Investors must be comfortable with their holdings. Above all, they must have confidence in the futures of the companies in which they assume stock ownership. An investor who, even after weighing all of these considerations, cannot decide between two or three comparable stocks probably should try to buy each.

Obviously, no one answer, no one route, can be applied alike by all investors when making close choices in the stock market. Investors have diverse investment objectives. They have different likes and dislikes. However, the most important step toward making successful investment choices is self-examination. Only after understanding his or her own motivations and objectives can an investor devise the correct plan for himself or herself, and then develop a portfolio of undervalued, blue-chip stocks with which the investor can be comfortable and feel secure.

Question: *Many companies don't pay dividends, their justification being that they are growth stocks. Does a stockholder have a right to dividends?*

Answer: Stockholders are owners of the company. They receive no salary, no group insurance rates, no health or pension benefits. They hope to see growth in their company so that the value of the stock will increase. However, they also have every right to expect a tangible cash return on their investment in the form of dividend income. Earnings per share and price/earnings ratios are not accepted as currency at the grocery store. Dividends are.

By the way, the adjective *growth* in relation to stocks has been in vogue at various times. Brokers have used the word like a carrot to attract customers to the stock market. In the late 1950s throughout most of the 1960s, investors could be persuaded to buy virtually any stock that bore the growth label. It was a marketing gimmick. True growth stocks have very specific characteristics, the most important of which is a ten percent compounded annual dividend growth rate.

Question: *How do you know when a company is being too stingy with its dividends—or when it is returning so much cash to investors that future growth is jeopardized?*

Answer: By the time a company is producing profits regularly and retaining enough capital to cover its operating expenses, a dividend payout policy is set by management, based on a percentage of net earnings. The average payout of mature companies, such as the ones that fit the criteria listed in this book for blue-chip stocks, is 50 percent.

If the payout is below 50 percent, stockholders should wonder why. It could be that the company is just plain stingy. But it also could be that an expensive new project will require additional cash, or that capital is needed to reduce debt, repurchase stock or make an acquisition.

If the payout of a nonutility is more than 50 percent of earnings, the company may be undergoing a restructuring or may be experiencing an earnings decline. Most blue-chip companies aim for 50 percent payout. Sometimes it will be a bit less, sometimes a bit more.

Of course, exceptions exist. Utilities, with guaranteed rates of return and general cash flows, typically pay out more than 50 percent of earnings. The industry average for utilities is 70 percent of profits. Drug and high-technology stocks generally pay out less, due to higher cash requirements for research and development.

Question: *What is an appropriate annual dividend increase?*

Answer: Dividend increases vary from year to year, from industry to industry, and from company to company. As pointed out in earlier chapters, boards of directors base dividends on their expectations for the future. When they feel good about the economy or about their own company's future profitability, they tend to be more generous with the payout.

As a gauge of how other companies handle dividend increases, investors can watch the annual composite dividend increases for the Dow Jones Industrial Average. Figure 14.1 shows the average increases from 1974 through 1987.

Question: *Of what value are stock dividends? Don't they just dilute the shares a person already owns?*

Answer: You are right. While they increase the number of shares outstanding, stock dividends do not increase the value of the holdings. They often are paid by companies in lieu of cash dividends to make the stockholders feel that they are getting a "bonus," and to increase the base of common shares. This also lowers the price of a stock to make it more accessible to a greater number of new purchasers.

Question: *In regard to quality, what emphasis do you place on stock splits?*

Answer: A stock split increases the number of shares outstanding and makes the price more attractive to potential investors, but it changes neither the quality nor the value of an investment. Earnings, dividends and book value figures all are split along with the price, and the fundamental value of the holding is unchanged. If a company was undervalued before the split, it will be undervalued after the split.

However, if a split occurs when the price is overvalued (as often happens), it can trigger a decline. Investors are more apt to sell split shares to establish capital gains when the price is overvalued and there is a profit to protect.

Question: *When a company buys back its own shares, is this a positive sign, or is it a desperate attempt to boost up the price of a sagging stock?*

Answer: It could be either, or both. A buyback increases stock values. With fewer shares outstanding, earnings per share rise, and price/

FIGURE 14.1 DJIA Dividend Record

The table below reviews the annual composite dividends for the Dow Jones Industrial Average, stretching back to 1974, at the start of the bull market. It also shows the percent of dividend increase or decrease for each year, and the annual perimeters of undervalue and overvalue. The largest dividend increase was in 1977, when the payout jumped 10.7%, following a 10.5% boost in 1976. The worst year for dividends was 1982 (a recession year), when the payout for the Dow Jones Industrial Average declined 3.7%. We expect the dividends of U.S. blue chips with multinational operations to increase in 1988 along with stronger-than-expected earnings gains from overseas orders and currency translations.

ANNUAL DIVIDENDS AND PERIMETERS OF VALUE FOR THE DOW JONES INDUSTRIAL AVERAGE

Year	*Ann. Div.*	*% Increase*	*6.0% Undervalued Price*	*3.0% Overvalued Price*
1987	71.20	+ 6.2%	1187	2373
1986	67.04	+ 8.1	1117	2235
1985	62.03	+ 2.3	1034	2068
1984	60.63	+ 7.6	1011	2021
1983	56.33	+ 4.0	939	1878
1982	54.14	− 3.7	902	1805
1981	56.22	+ 3.4	937	1874
1980	54.36	+ 6.6	906	1812
1979	50.98	+ 5.1	850	1699
1978	48.52	+ 5.8	809	1617
1977	45.84	+10.7	764	1528
1976	41.40	+10.5	690	1380
1975	37.46	− 0.7	624	1249
1974	37.72	+ 6.8	629	1257

Average annual dividend increase, 1974 to 1987 = 5.2%

SOURCE: "Investment Quality Trends," January 1988.

earnings ratios shrink. If the stock is undervalued, a buyback is a good investment and a prudent use of capital. If the stock is overvalued, the company is wasting its money.

Question: *I recently noticed that accompanying my Citicorp credit card bill was an offer to allow me to buy Citicorp stock directly from the company without brokerage fees. I have to enroll in the company's dividend reinvestment plan to take advantage of the offer. Is there a catch here?*

Answer: Not necessarily. Any time you can save costs in purchasing a stock that is undervalued, you have found a good deal. Dividend reinvestment plans can be useful, but caution is necessary here. They are great while a stock is undervalued or in its rising trend. However, once the stock becomes overvalued, or trips over into a declining mode, it is prudent to withdraw from the dividend reinvestment program. Citicorp is one of many companies now offering stock purchase and dividend reinvestment programs. At last count, stock could be purchased directly from W. R. Grace, Great Northern Nekoosa, Pinnacle West Capital and Johnson Controls, to name just a few. To find out if a company in which you want to invest has a similar program, contact the company's investor relations office. The corporate address and telephone numbers can be found in Standard & Poor's *Register of Corporations,* and from several other library sources.

Question: *Dividends always were an important factor in the stock market. What impact did the new tax law passed in 1986 have on dividends and dividend-paying stocks?*

Answer: Under the Tax Reform Act of 1986, which taxes capital gains and dividend income at the same rate as regular income, dividends became even more important. Previously, capital gains were given a preferential 20 percent maximum tax, making growth in stock price a more attractive source of gains from a taxation point of view. Under the old tax law, the highest tax bracket was 50 percent, and for investors in that maximum bracket, dividends were taxed at 50 percent. Under the revised 1986 tax law, both capital gains and dividends were taxed at a maximum rate of 28 percent. In other words, the 1986 tax bill made conservative investments, which stress safety of capital and income, far more desirable than risky, non dividend-paying securities.

The corporations themselves also will benefit, because corporate tax rates were cut from 46 percent to 34 percent.

While the tax law can be good for investors seeking dividends, it may make it more difficult for innovative, younger companies that are oriented toward research and development to raise capital. In the long term, this may not have been a good move for the nation, which needs innovation to remain competitive.

Question: *What emphasis would you place on the amount of money a company spends on research and development?*

Answer: While expenditures on research and development do not guarantee growth, they do enhance that likelihood. Like dividends, the amount of money spent by a company on R&D generally is based on a percentage of earnings. Some companies, like those in consumer products, pharmaceuticals and high-technology industries, spend a greater percentage of earnings on R&D than do companies in industries for which new products are not so important to sales and earnings growth. Generally, the more a company spends on R&D the more likely it is to stay competitive within its industry and to grow and prosper.

Minnesota Mining & Manufacturing (3M) is an outstanding example of a company that has kept apace of research and development, and still managed to increase dividends for the past 29 years. Key to 3M's success has been its dedication to the development of new products, markets and businesses. In 1986, 3M increased its R&D spending by 11.3 percent, or 6.6 percent of sales. That percentage far surpassed the average for U.S. companies and was the highest for 3M in many years.

At all times, 3M has about 1,000 products in various stages of testing and development. They ultimately give birth to perhaps 100 new products each year, 50 to 70 of which are commercial winners. A strong emphasis is placed on the development of proprietary, high-technology products. It has been 3M's long-standing goal to generate at least 25 percent of sales from products introduced within the past five years. The chart for 3M is figure 11.5.

At Procter & Gamble, another good example, about 5,700 employees worldwide—or just under 8 percent of the company's total work force—are engaged in R&D. "We pay a great deal of attention to trying to understand technological possibilities, and understand market forces—all well enough to intelligently focus our technical resources," said John Smale, chairman and chief executive of Procter & Gamble.

Question: *Is it necessary that a company be a leader in its field to be a blue-chip stock?*

Answer: A blue chip may or may not be a leader in its industry. This is especially true in sectors that comprise many companies.

Question: *When a takeover occurs, do the undervalued and overvalued yield lines change for the dominant company?*

Answer: The acquirer in a corporation typically is larger than the acquired in terms of capitalization and number of shares outstanding.

Therefore, the dominant company has the most influence on the patterns of undervalue and overvalue, and perimeters of dividend yield follow the pattern of the surviving entity, or the dominating partner.

Question: *Some market watchers religiously follow insider trading. Do you think it matters at all? Why?*

Answer: Insider trades (the purchase or sale of a company's stock by its officers and directors) have little or no bearing on either the future of a company or the performance of its stock.

Many times those trades are nothing more than the exercise of stock options before they expire. Sales can represent the need to raise cash for something unrelated to either the company or the stock—like the purchase of a home. Other times, a corporate officer may be acting on news that, when made public, is largely ignored by investors, or that produces an entirely unexpected reaction. How many times have stock prices been seen to rise on bad news, or decline on good news?

Corporate insiders may understand their companies and their products, but when it comes to understanding the stock market, they have no greater insights or information than the rest of us. Success in the stock market has far more to do with following value than following insider trades.

Question: *Rumors about companies in which I've invested make me nervous. When a competitor is expected to introduce a superior product, a takeover is in the wind or the government is about to fine the company, these events are often reported as rumors. How should I react?*

Answer: Enlightened investors do not buy or sell on rumors; they base their decisions on information. When something surprising has happened, they make decisions after the smoke has cleared and the stock price has settled.

Question: *In recent years, foreign investment has flowed into the United States at record levels. What does that mean to my investment decisions?*

Answer: This liquidity, created by an influx of foreign money, has sometimes driven U.S. stocks up beyond their overvalued perimeters. Rapid withdrawals of such invested funds could drive the market sharply down. But overall, the United States has one of the most stable governments in the world and one of the most dependable economies.

Foreign investors come here for safety as much as for high return. This tends to keep foreign money in U.S. markets, especially when economic or political unrest exists elsewhere.

Not all foreign investment takes place on Wall Street, though. Many prime quality stocks that represent U.S. companies also trade on foreign stock markets. On the Tokyo Exchange, for example, we find such U.S. investment luminaries as American Express, Chase Manhattan, Dow Chemical, Eastman Kodak, Exxon, General Motors, IBM, Eli Lilly, McDonald's, Minnesota Mining & Manufacturing, Pepsico, Philip Morris, Procter & Gamble, Sears, Roebuck and Waste Management, among others.

And remember, foreign investors who turn to the U.S. stock market also tend to select stocks of well-known blue-chip companies, the makers and suppliers of goods and services with which they are familiar. For this reason, blue chips are at the forefront when the market turns up. Blue chips are held longer, so those stocks decline more slowly than does the rest of the market.

Question: *Do you ever recommend mutual funds?*

Answer: No. The emphasis of this book and of "Investment Quality Trends" is on the performance of stocks and corporations, not on the performance of mutual fund managers. Investors who are willing to devote a small amount of time and attention to building a portfolio of undervalued blue-chip stocks are likely to do better in the long run than any mutual fund, where investors control neither the stock sales nor the selection of stock purchases. Investors who take charge of their own financial futures generally have a better chance for success.

15

Conclusion

"Knowledge comes, but wisdom lingers."

—ALFRED, LORD TENNYSON

"There are two times in a man's life when he should not speculate," wrote Mark Twain in *Pudd'nhead Wilson's New Calendar,* "when he can afford it and when he can't."

Twain lived during a time when investors, promoters, adventurers and gamblers got rich quick and frequently got poor even quicker. Along the Mississippi River and later in the silver boom camp of Virginia City, Twain saw the end results of speculation. His observation was true on the frontier, and it's true in the stock market.

LOVE AND DESPAIR IN THE MARKET

It's not easy to avoid getting caught up in the excitement of speculation. Stories about people who made a lot of money abound. The losers aren't out crowing about it. Even stock market investors who keep a tight rein on their racetrack instincts can, at times, wonder if they did the right thing. Imagine how confused a reader might have felt about being in or out of the market in 1928, when *Forbes* magazine ran this item:

"Most of the old-timers in the Street are looking for a crash, especially the more conservative ones. But the more conservative ones have been looking for a crash for the better part of a year—and instead stocks have soared to new high records for all time. The 'conservative old-timers' have lost millions of dollars not merely in profits that the 'young fools' have stepped in to take while they hesitated, but also by losses on the short side. The more sober-minded speculators have taken not merely a financial but a psychological beating in the past year or two, and the 'awful examples' have discouraged analysts in general from ever becoming out-and-out-bearish."

Maybe the conservative investor could have timed the market somewhat better, getting out closer to the top. On the other hand, not many old-timers who got out early were leaping out of windows in Manhattan when the tide turned.

Yet no one is ever quite satisfied with the stock market. If the stock we buy goes up, we wish we had bought more; if it goes down, we wish we had bought less, or none at all. We are remorseful if we get in a bull market a little late or bail out before every last dollar of profit has been realized. Despite all of the perplexities and frustrations of the stock market, though, no other place offers such rewarding opportunities—to such a wide variety of investors, with such divergent sums of capital, and such varied investment objectives.

For the professional investor as well as the serious part-time investor, the stock market easily can become a lifelong passion. Even for the person who has other pressing demands but may need the stock market as a financial refuge, the market can be a fascinating secondary career.

COMPLEXITY AND CONFUSION

To be successful, an investor needs to set goals and to work out a plan of how to reach those goals. In recent years, however, investment theories and procedures have become so complex, so ponderously upholstered with technical indicators, confusing new products, tedious statistics and superfluous rhetoric, that simple answers, as the product of ordinary common sense, seem to have become obsolete. Many investors now believe that financial success in the stock market requires, at the very least, an application of intricate formulas, privileged information and rare investment wisdom.

Not so. Though many pages have been devoted to describing, explaining and proving that the dividend-yield theory works, at its heart the technique is quite simple.

SIMPLE AND CLEAN

Simply stated, when all other factors that merit analytical consideration have been digested, the underlying value of dividends, which determines yield, will in the long run also determine price. If one accepts the concept, then everything else falls into place.

Tracking dividend yield and using it as a road map for investment decisions is basically what the process is about. The other considerations mentioned are there to confirm uncertain indications, enhance and maximize profits and, when possible, provide a rational explanation for what is happening to a stock and to the market.

KNOW A COMPANY BY THE VALUE OF ITS STOCK

The primary analytical considerations mentioned earlier—the fundamentals—relate to the value of the stock. The three traditional indicators of investment value are:

- price, as it relates to earnings;
- price, as it relates to book value and
- price, as it relates to dividends.

The price/earnings ratio measures the multiple of current earnings at which a stock is priced. Because average annual earnings generally trend upward, investors also factor an earnings growth potential into the price of every stock.

Differences in the premium above current earnings that investors are willing to pay for different companies reflect various rates of earnings growth. A company with average annual earnings growth of ten percent, for example, will command a higher price/earnings ratio than a company in which average annual earnings grow at a rate of five percent.

Enlightened investors look for stocks that have relatively low price/earnings ratios and relatively high rates of earnings growth. Relative comparisons generally are made with other stocks in the same industry, and with stocks in the Dow Jones Industrial Average. However, no single standard applies to all stocks. Each company must be viewed in the light of its own historical past.

Next, book value indicates the net asset value of a company, less depreciation and preferred stock, at liquidation or redemption value. Theoretically, net assets are supposed to produce net long-term profits. With blue-chip stocks, generally they do.

Therefore, the ratio ordinarily reflects a potential growth percentage of price over book value. Sometimes, however, in a severely depressed market, prices fall close to, or below, book value. A low price-to-book-value ratio signifies rare investment value.

Third, dividend yield represents the current, annual cash return to stockholders on their investment capital. The yields can be influenced by prevailing interest rates, but a more important influence is average annual rates of dividend growth. The stocks of companies with higher-than-average growth rates ordinarily have lower-than-average current yields but better-than-average "total return" potentials.

A relatively high dividend yield, in a stock that has a relatively high dividend growth rate, is an excellent investment value, providing a generous base of income on which future dividend increases can produce even higher returns. Stocks with superior dividend growth enable shareholders to increase their investment income at a rate that matches or exceeds the rate of inflation. It is by tracking and evaluating the most important of these three measures of value, the dividend yield, that success in the stock market is enormously enhanced.

MEASURE THE MARKET BY VALUE

By applying these three indicators of investment value to the Dow Jones Industrial Average, investors can determine if the market itself is undervalued or overvalued, thereby improving their timing of stock purchases and sales, and reducing their margin of investment error. Again, it is in the patterns of dividend yield that investors should ultimately place their faith. This approach has proved to be the most reliable of all investment philosophies for determining value in the stock market.

FINDING STRENGTH IN QUALITY

The concept of identifying undervalued and overvalued stock prices according to historic patterns of dividend yield can be applied to any stock with a reasonably long dividend history. However, investors who make the decision to include only high-quality, blue-chip stocks in their considerations will probably never regret it.

Careful attention to quality, as well as to value, can result in outstanding long-term performance. The record proves that superior investment growth can be achieved in blue-chip stocks with far less risk to capital, particularly if the blue chips are purchased at undervalued levels.

Buying shares when they are undervalued, selling when the stock reaches overvalue in terms of dividend yield, and reaping dividends in the interim sounds simple. It does require patience, however, as well as collecting and interpreting a certain amount of financial information on the corporations involved.

Probably no company better exemplifies the benefits of studying dividend yield than Winn-Dixie, the nation's fourth-largest supermarket chain, charted in figure 15.1. In fiscal year 1987 the company scored its 53rd year of consecutive sales increases, and the dividend was boosted for the 44th consecutive year, making Winn-Dixie the champion dividend-payer on the New York Stock Exchange.

Even more important, though, is that the profile of value for Winn-Dixie, established over many years, has been remarkably constant. Every major decline in more than three decades has been halted and reversed in the 6.0 percent yield area. Every major rise has ended when the dividend yield was at 3.0 percent. With this sort of predictability, no investor should fear being overwhelmed by a suddenly reversing market.

SPECULATION AND FAST TRADING DON'T PAY

The use of hyperbole and high-powered techniques is second nature to some salespeople, and it's not unheard of among securities salespeople. The investment adviser who uses these techniques to tout questionable stocks is appealing to the enthusiasm, optimism and, sorry to say, greed in each of us.

FIGURE 15.1 Dividend-Yield Chart

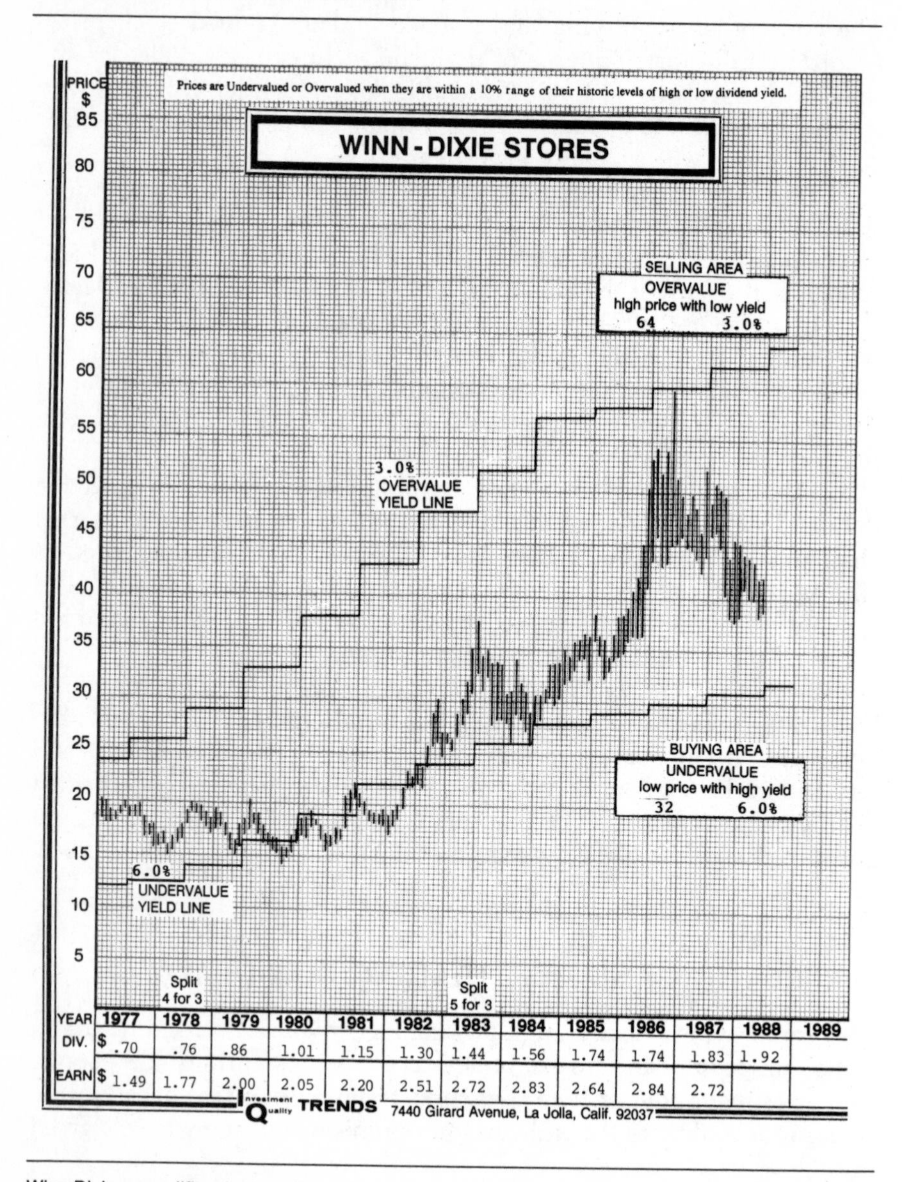

Winn-Dixie exemplifies the benefits of using the dividend-yield theory. In 1987 the dividend was raised by the 44th consecutive year, and the dividend yield has consistently signaled the time to maximize profits by buying and selling this stock.

The best defense against speculation, or the practice of taking inordinate risks in the hope of exceptional returns, is knowing better. Studies have shown that conservative investors, those who seek quality and value and invest for the long term, ultimately achieve higher returns than do those who might be described as traders. Traders attempt to profit from the short-term peaks and valleys of the market.

"It is just appalling," said the eminent investment counselor Philip Fisher in a 1987 *Forbes* magazine interview, "the nerve strain people put themselves under trying to buy something today and sell it tomorrow. It's a small-win proposition. If you are truly a long-range investor, of which I am practically a vanishing breed, the profits are so tremendously greater."

Mr. Fisher's philosophy received confirmation in the October 1987 stock market crash. High-dividend stocks outperformed the market during that wrenching episode. While the Standard & Poor's 500 stock index slumped 22 percent that October, high-yielding stocks slipped only six percent.

In such times, high-yielding stocks offer refuge. In a soaring market, well-timed purchases of blue-chip stocks are also the stellar performers. By tracking dividend yield, an investor finds order in what may seem like a random and chaotic market.

In conclusion, we again assert that when all factors which rate analytical consideration have been digested, the underlying value of dividends which determines yield, will in the long run also determine price. Price increases plus growth of dividends will provide enlightened investors with the greatest possible total return.

We also again remind our readers of Charles Dow's words, "To know values is to know the meaning of the market." Success in the stock market lies in the ability to recognize values—the courage to buy stocks when they are undervalued; the patience to hold stocks while their prices rise; and, the wisdom to sell stocks when they are overvalued. Investors who adhere to this concept will experience a lifetime of worry-free investment growth and long-term financial satisfaction.

APPENDIX

Charts of 30 Dow Jones Industrial Stocks

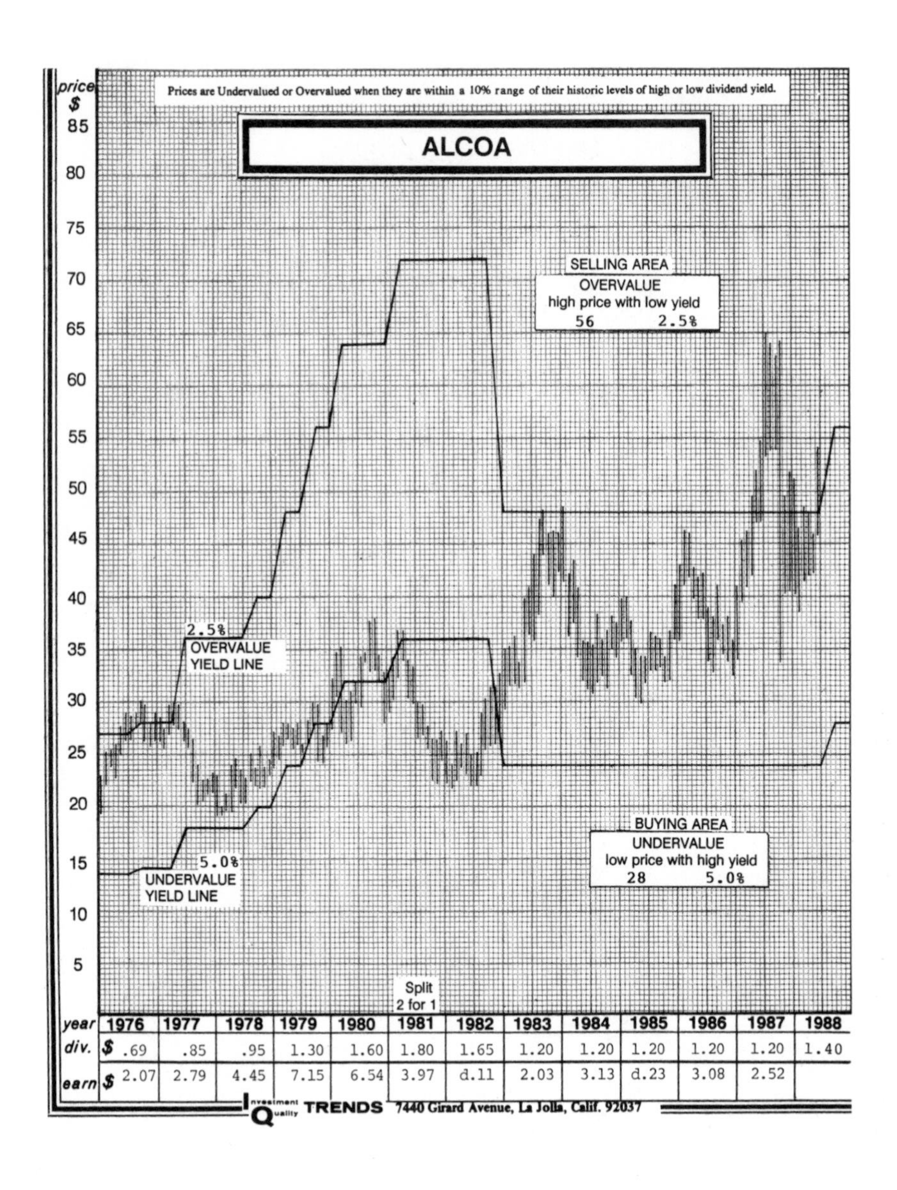

price $
Prices are Undervalued or Overvalued when they are within a 10% range of their historic levels of high or low dividend yield.
ALCOA
85
80
75
70
65
60
55
50
45
40
35
30
25
20
15
10
5
SELLING AREA
OVERVALUE
high price with low yield
56 2.5%
2.5%
OVERVALUE
YIELD LINE
5.0%
UNDERVALUE
YIELD LINE
BUYING AREA
UNDERVALUE
low price with high yield
28 5.0%
Split
2 for 1
year 1976 1977 1978 1979 1980 1981 1982 1983 1984 1985 1986 1987 1988
div. $ .69 .85 .95 1.30 1.60 1.80 1.65 1.20 1.20 1.20 1.20 1.20 1.40
earn $ 2.07 2.79 4.45 7.15 6.54 3.97 d.11 2.03 3.13 d.23 3.08 2.52
Investment Quality TRENDS 7440 Girard Avenue, La Jolla, Calif. 92037

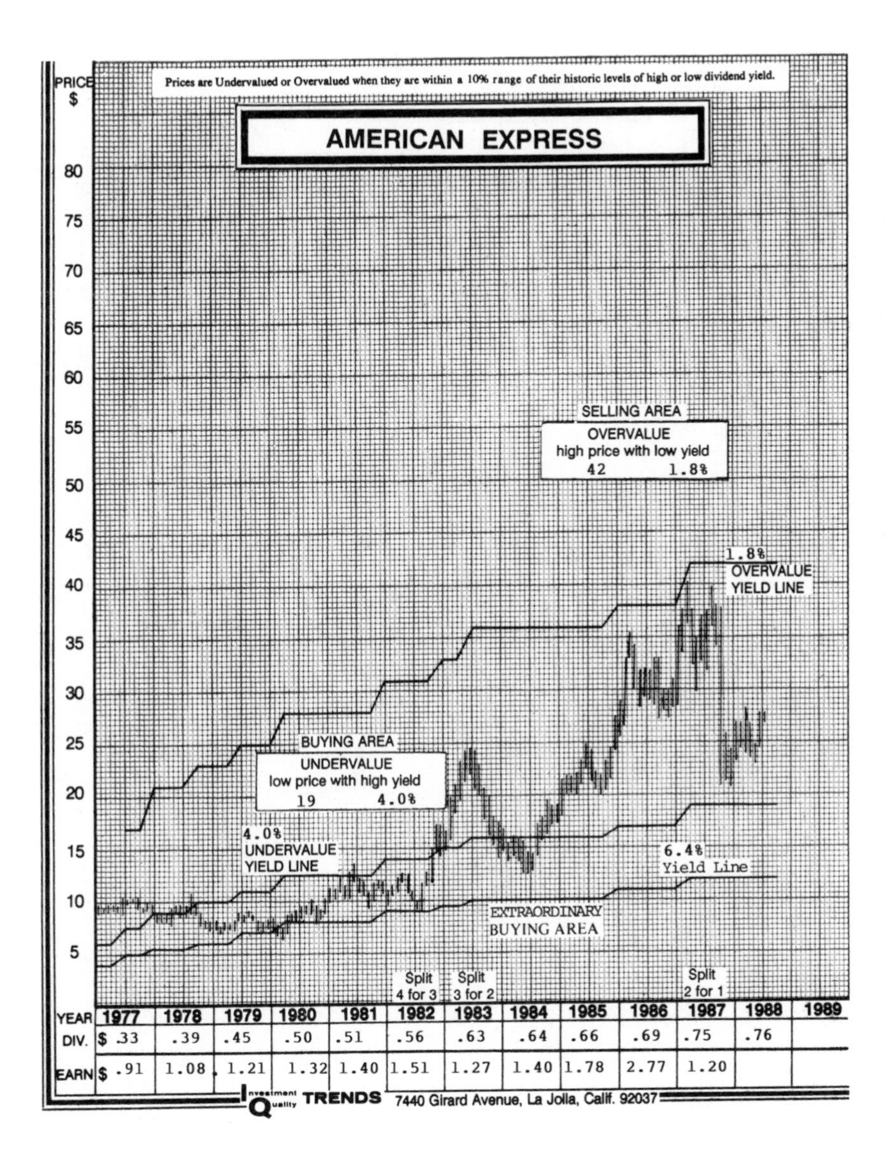

YEAR	1977	1978	1979	1980	1981	1982	1983	1984	1985	1986	1987	1988	1989
DIV.	$ .33	.39	.45	.50	.51	.56	.63	.64	.66	.69	.75	.76	
EARN	$ .91	1.08	1.21	1.32	1.40	1.51	1.27	1.40	1.78	2.77	1.20		

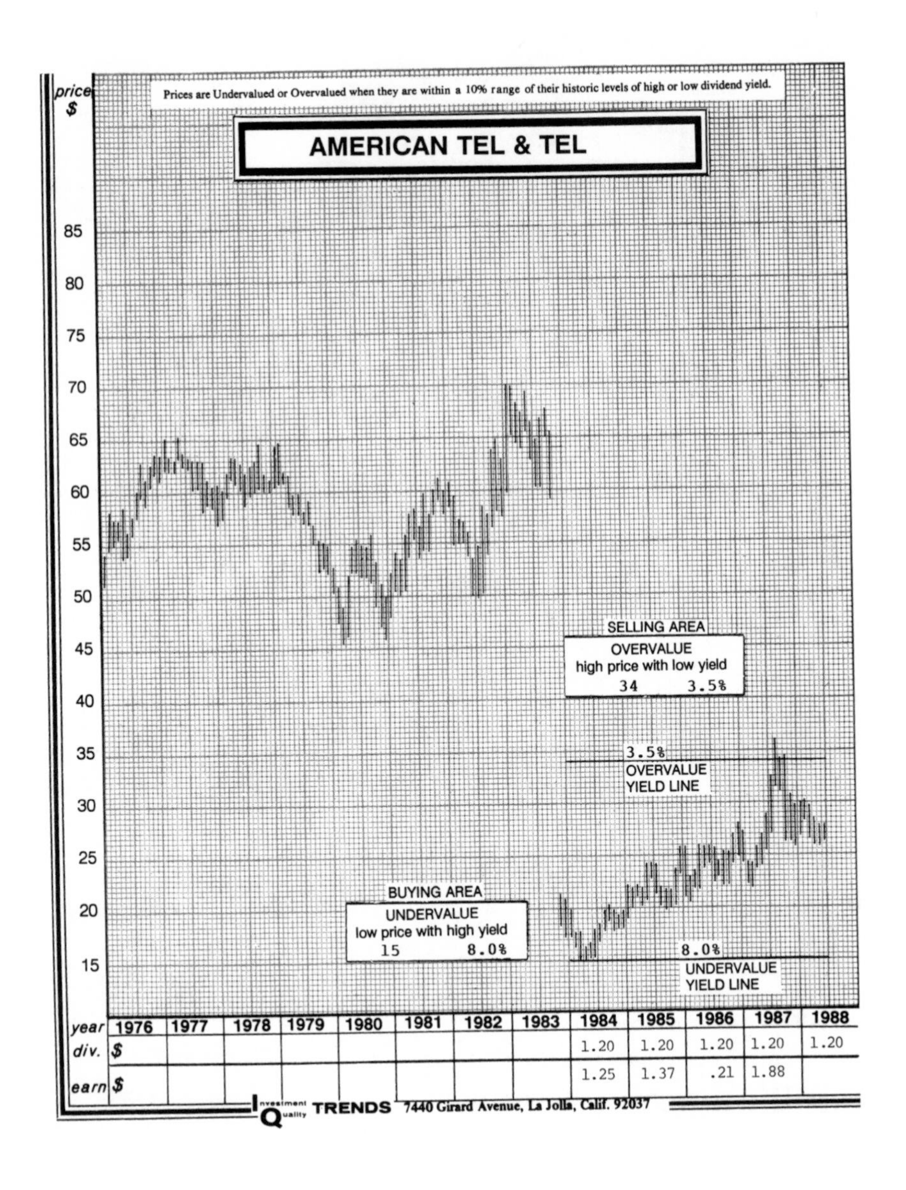

Prices are Undervalued or Overvalued when they are within a 10% range of their historic levels of high or low dividend yield.
AMERICAN TEL & TEL
price $
85
80
75
70
65
60
55
50
45
40
35
30
25
20
15
SELLING AREA
OVERVALUE
high price with low yield
34 3.5%
3.5%
OVERVALUE
YIELD LINE
BUYING AREA
UNDERVALUE
low price with high yield
15 8.0%
8.0%
UNDERVALUE
YIELD LINE
year 1976 1977 1978 1979 1980 1981 1982 1983 1984 1985 1986 1987 1988
div. $ 1.20 1.20 1.20 1.20 1.20
earn $ 1.25 1.37 .21 1.88
Investment Quality TRENDS 7440 Girard Avenue, La Jolla, Calif. 92037

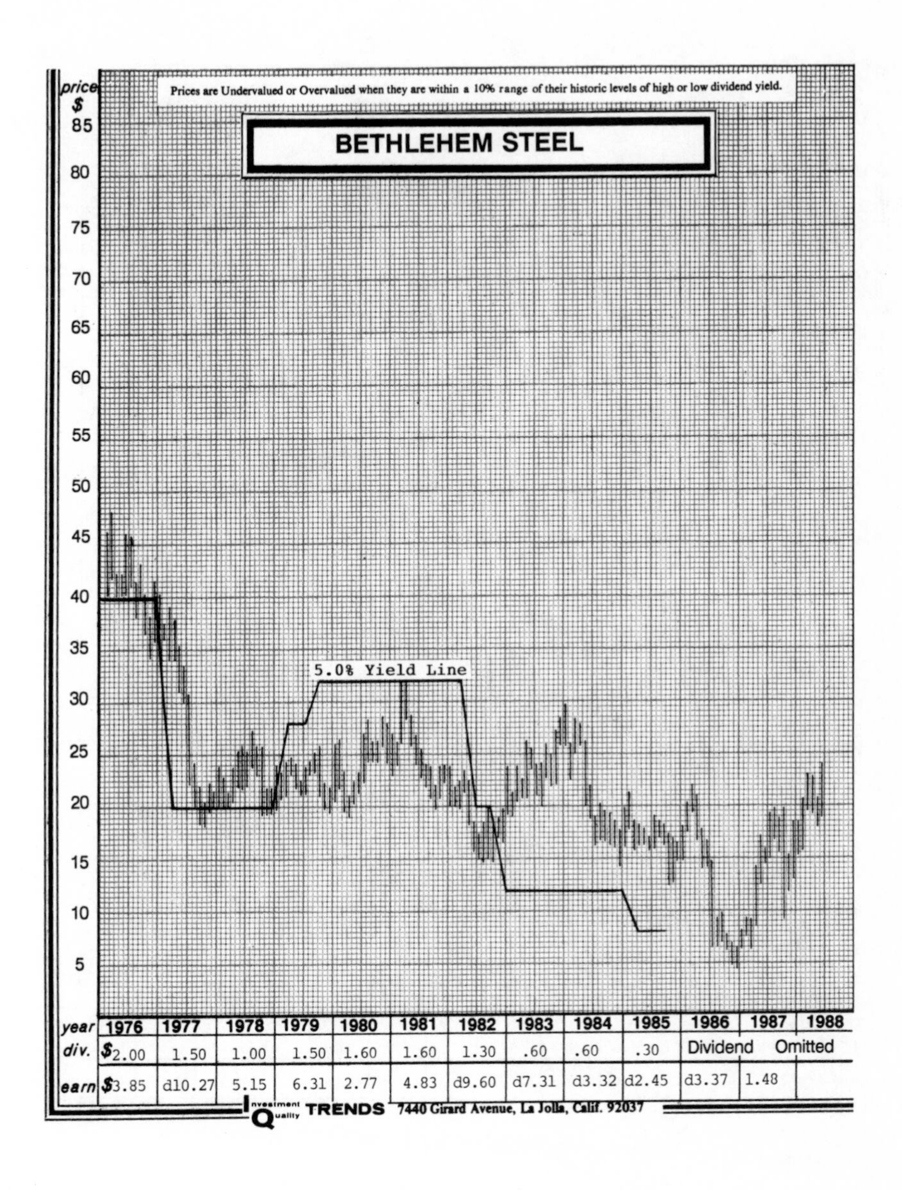

Prices are Undervalued or Overvalued when they are within a 10% range of their historic levels of high or low dividend yield.
BETHLEHEM STEEL
price $
85
80
75
70
65
60
55
50
45
40
35
30
25
20
15
10
5
5.0% Yield Line
year 1976 1977 1978 1979 1980 1981 1982 1983 1984 1985 1986 1987 1988
div. $2.00 1.50 1.00 1.50 1.60 1.60 1.30 .60 .60 .30 Dividend Omitted
earn $3.85 d10.27 5.15 6.31 2.77 4.83 d9.60 d7.31 d3.32 d2.45 d3.37 1.48
Investment Quality TRENDS 7440 Girard Avenue, La Jolla, Calif. 92037

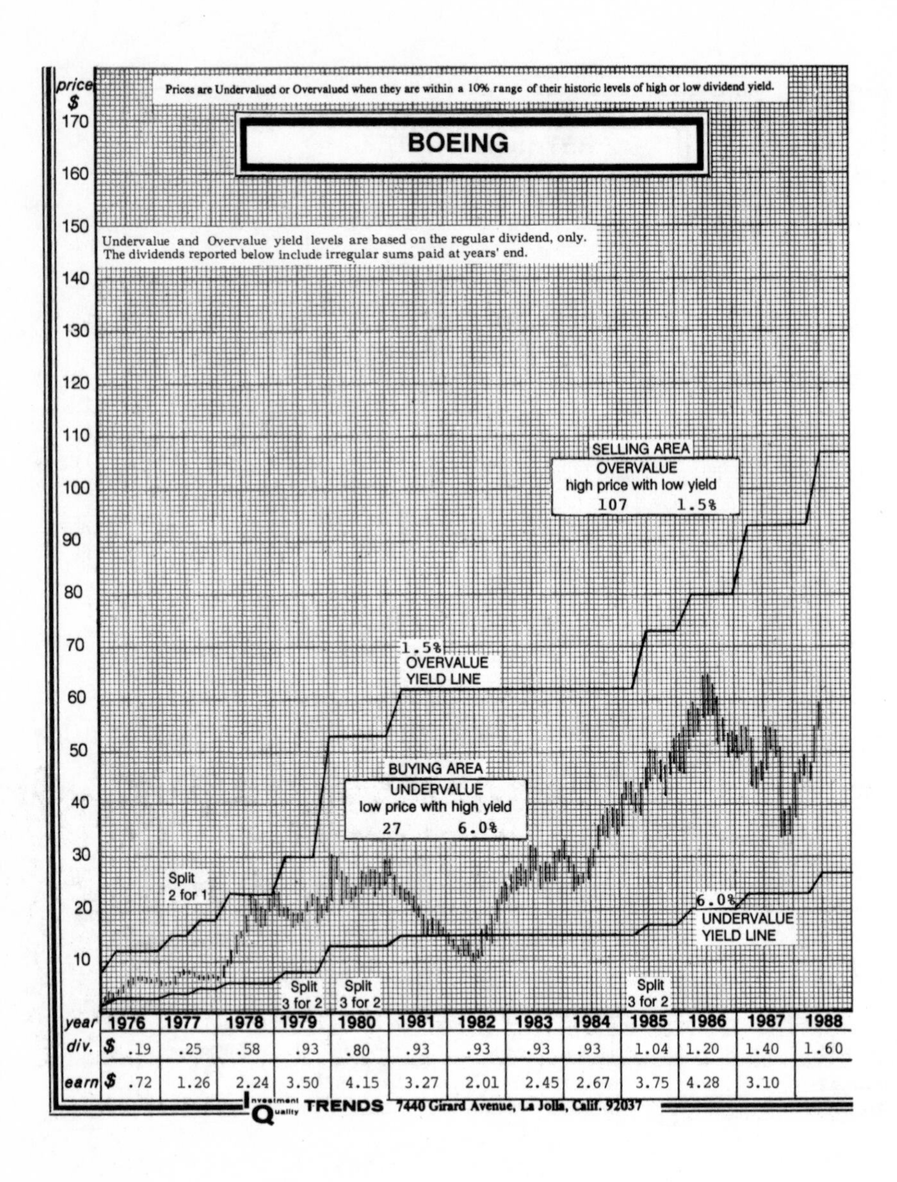

year	1976	1977	1978	1979	1980	1981	1982	1983	1984	1985	1986	1987	1988
div. $	.19	.25	.58	.93	.80	.93	.93	.93	.93	1.04	1.20	1.40	1.60
earn $	.72	1.26	2.24	3.50	4.15	3.27	2.01	2.45	2.67	3.75	4.28	3.10	

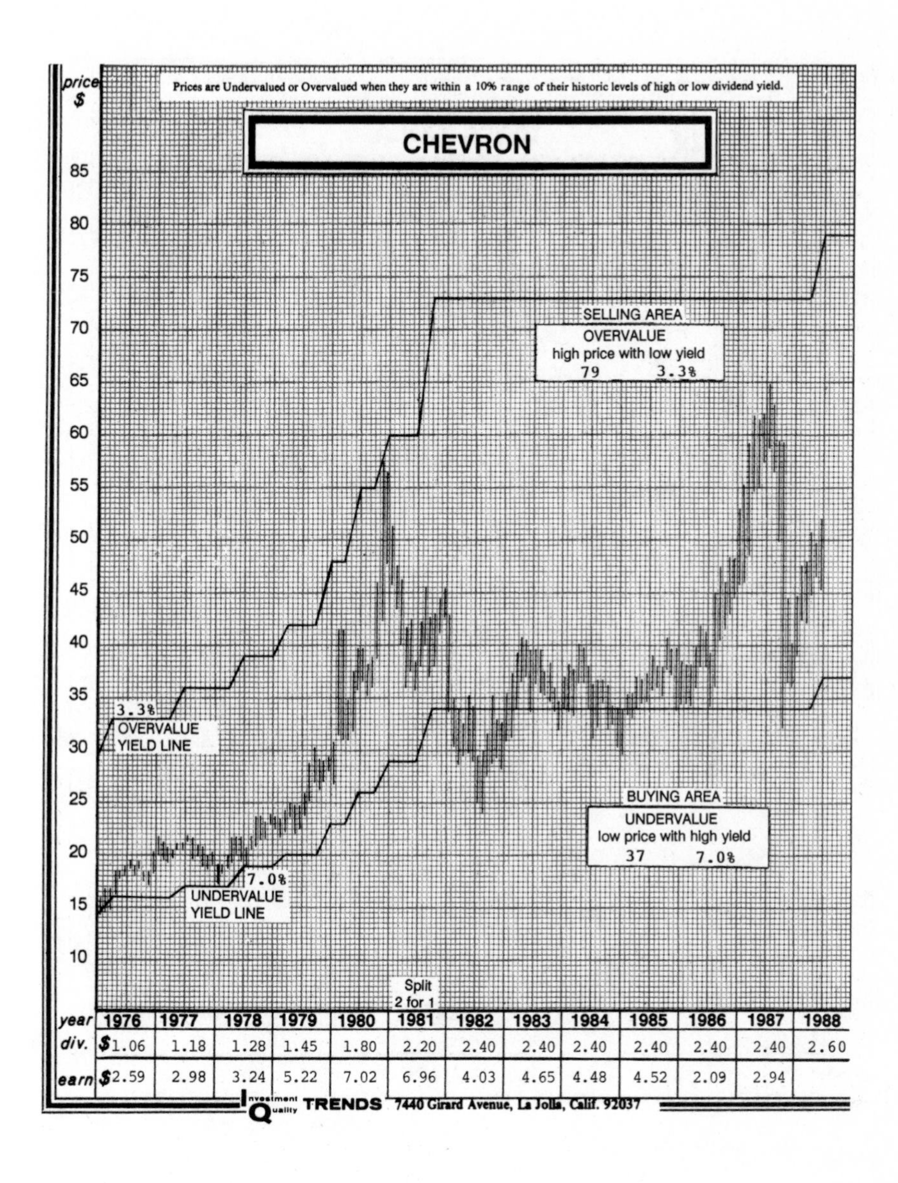

year	1976	1977	1978	1979	1980	1981	1982	1983	1984	1985	1986	1987	1988
div.	$1.06	1.18	1.28	1.45	1.80	2.20	2.40	2.40	2.40	2.40	2.40	2.40	2.60
earn	$2.59	2.98	3.24	5.22	7.02	6.96	4.03	4.65	4.48	4.52	2.09	2.94	

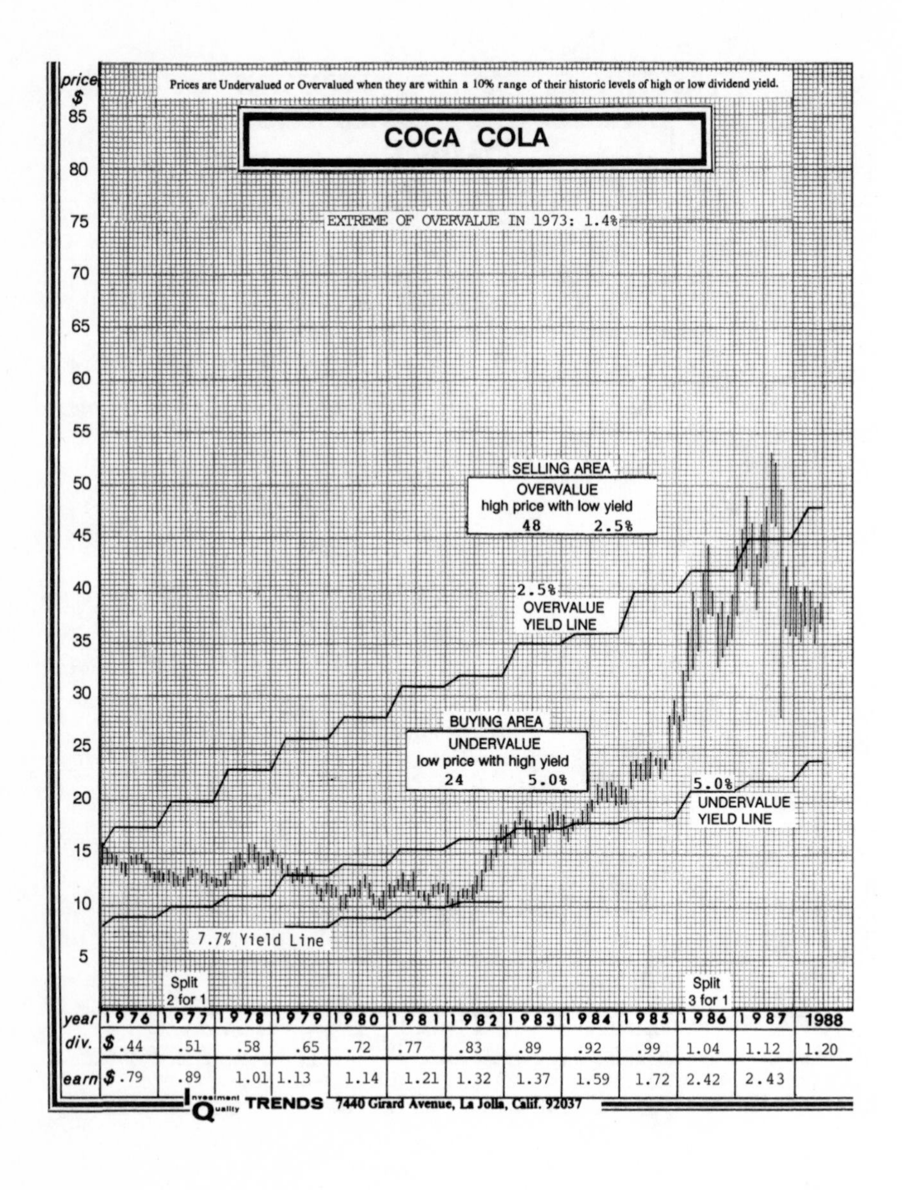

year	1976	1977	1978	1979	1980	1981	1982	1983	1984	1985	1986	1987	1988
div.	$.44	.51	.58	.65	.72	.77	.83	.89	.92	.99	1.04	1.12	1.20
earn	$.79	.89	1.01	1.13	1.14	1.21	1.32	1.37	1.59	1.72	2.42	2.43	

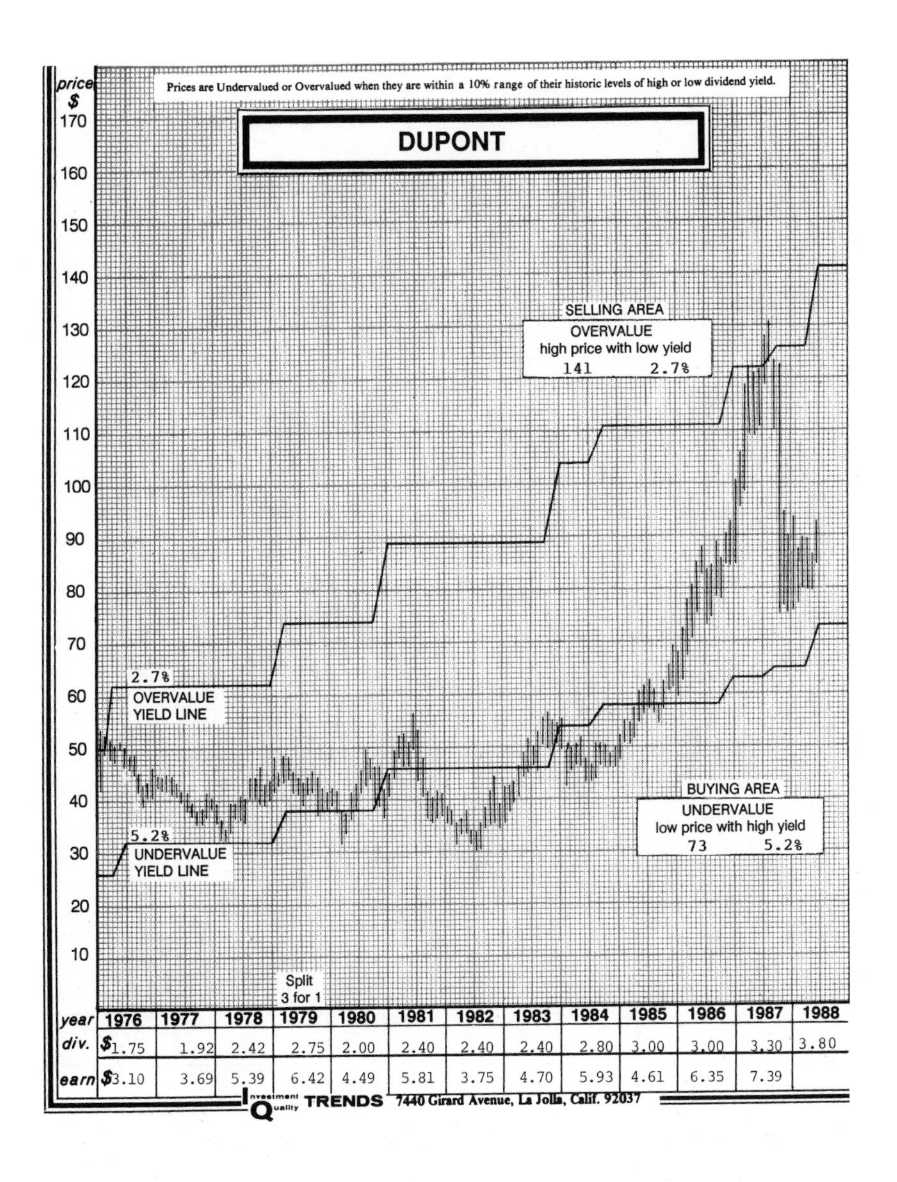

Prices are Undervalued or Overvalued when they are within a 10% range of their historic levels of high or low dividend yield.
DUPONT
price $
170
160
150
140
130
120
110
100
90
80
70
60
50
40
30
20
10
SELLING AREA
OVERVALUE
high price with low yield
141 2.7%
2.7%
OVERVALUE YIELD LINE
5.2%
UNDERVALUE YIELD LINE
BUYING AREA
UNDERVALUE
low price with high yield
73 5.2%
Split 3 for 1
year 1976 1977 1978 1979 1980 1981 1982 1983 1984 1985 1986 1987 1988
div. $1.75 1.92 2.42 2.75 2.00 2.40 2.40 2.40 2.80 3.00 3.00 3.30 3.80
earn $3.10 3.69 5.39 6.42 4.49 5.81 3.75 4.70 5.93 4.61 6.35 7.39
Investment Quality TRENDS 7440 Girard Avenue, La Jolla, Calif. 92037

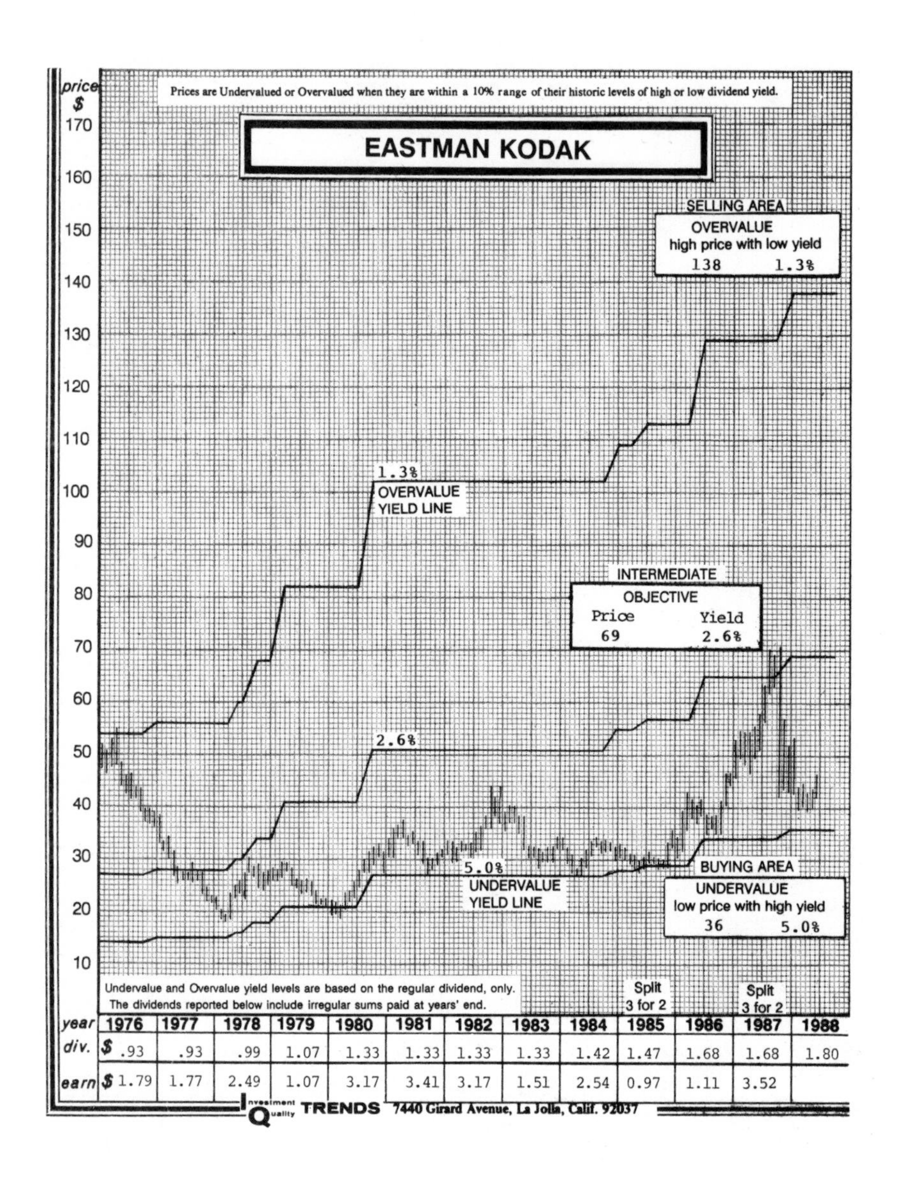

year	1976	1977	1978	1979	1980	1981	1982	1983	1984	1985	1986	1987	1988
div.	$ .93	.93	.99	1.07	1.33	1.33	1.33	1.33	1.42	1.47	1.68	1.68	1.80
earn	$ 1.79	1.77	2.49	1.07	3.17	3.41	3.17	1.51	2.54	0.97	1.11	3.52	

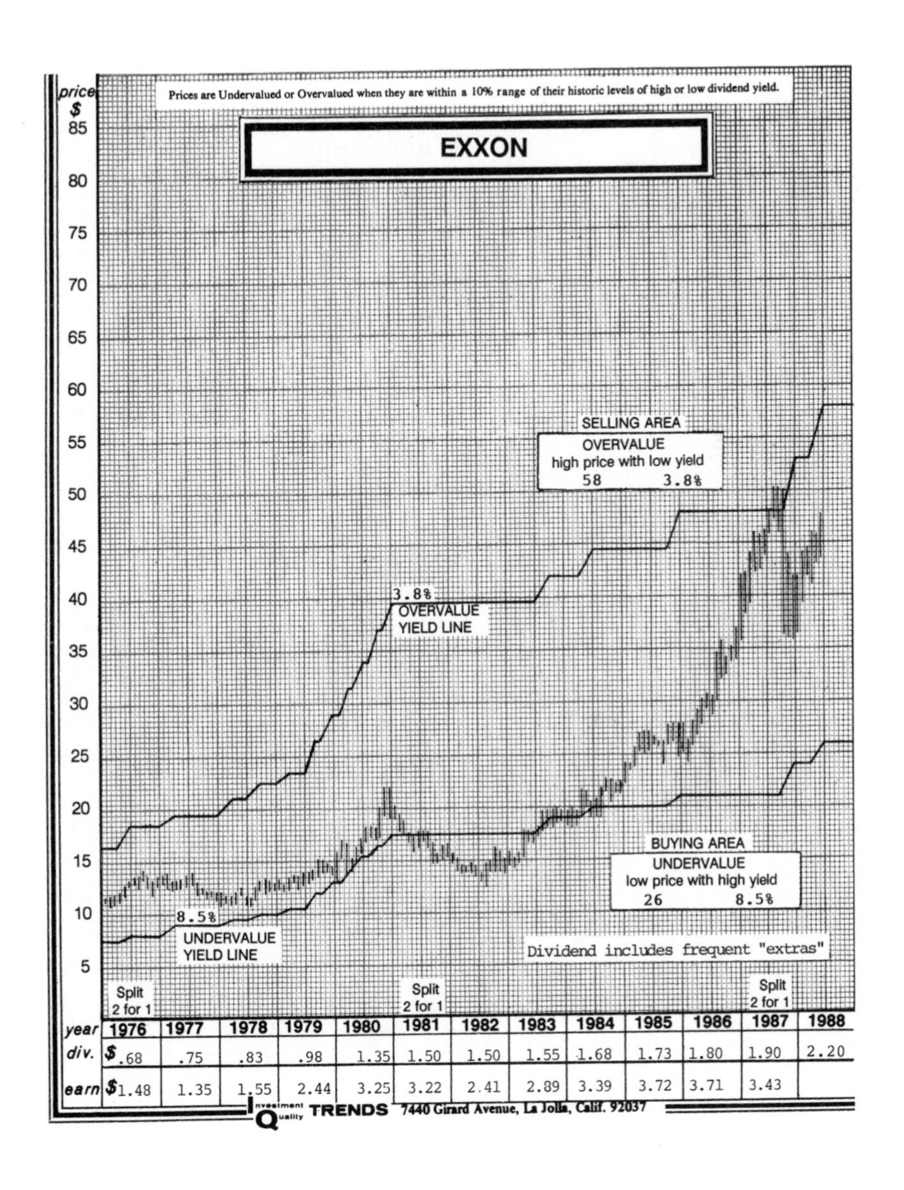

year	1976	1977	1978	1979	1980	1981	1982	1983	1984	1985	1986	1987	1988
div.	$.68	.75	.83	.98	1.35	1.50	1.50	1.55	1.68	1.73	1.80	1.90	2.20
earn	$1.48	1.35	1.55	2.44	3.25	3.22	2.41	2.89	3.39	3.72	3.71	3.43	

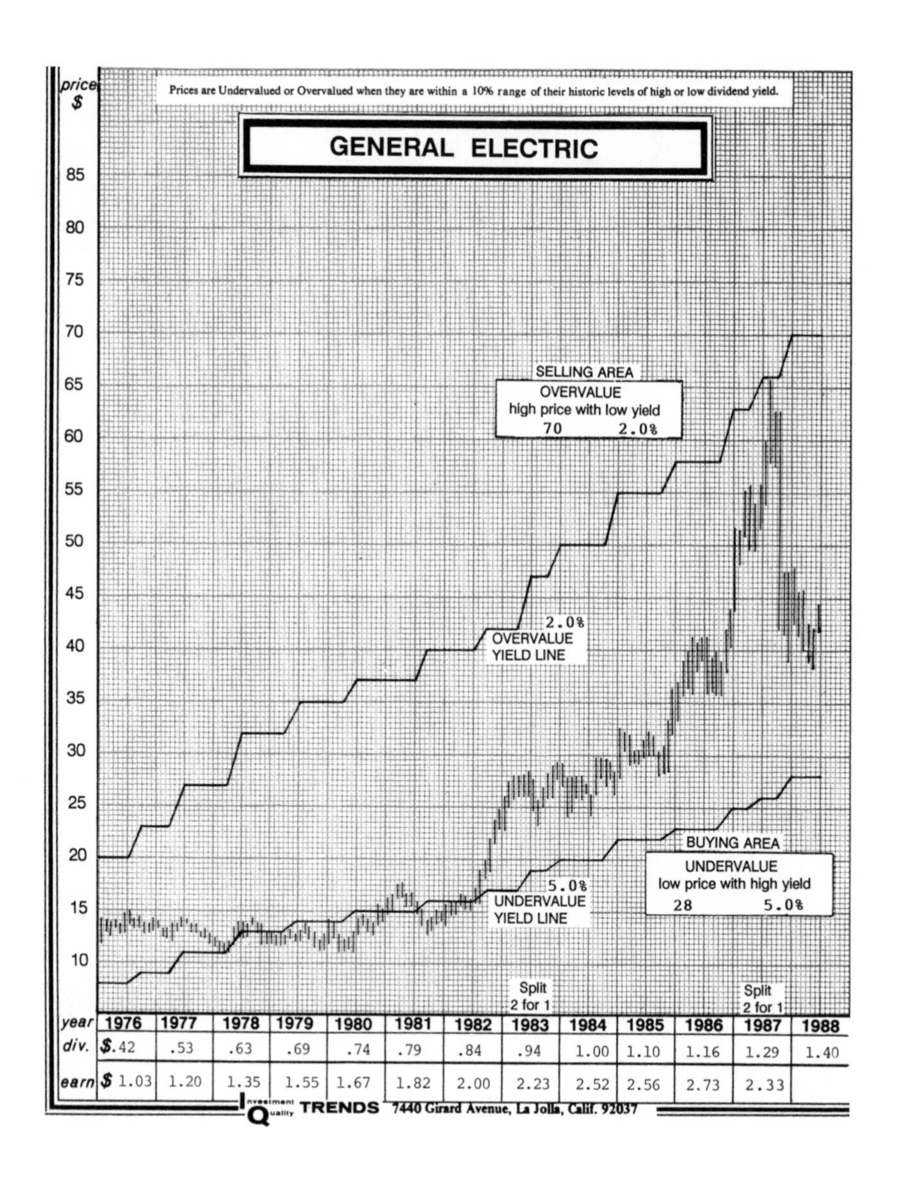
price $
Prices are Undervalued or Overvalued when they are within a 10% range of their historic levels of high or low dividend yield.
GENERAL ELECTRIC
85
80
75
70
65
60
55
50
45
40
35
30
25
20
15
10
SELLING AREA
OVERVALUE
high price with low yield
70 2.0%
2.0%
OVERVALUE
YIELD LINE
BUYING AREA
UNDERVALUE
low price with high yield
28 5.0%
5.0%
UNDERVALUE
YIELD LINE
Split
2 for 1
Split
2 for 1
year 1976 1977 1978 1979 1980 1981 1982 1983 1984 1985 1986 1987 1988
div. $.42 .53 .63 .69 .74 .79 .84 .94 1.00 1.10 1.16 1.29 1.40
earn $ 1.03 1.20 1.35 1.55 1.67 1.82 2.00 2.23 2.52 2.56 2.73 2.33
Investment Quality TRENDS 7440 Girard Avenue, La Jolla, Calif. 92037

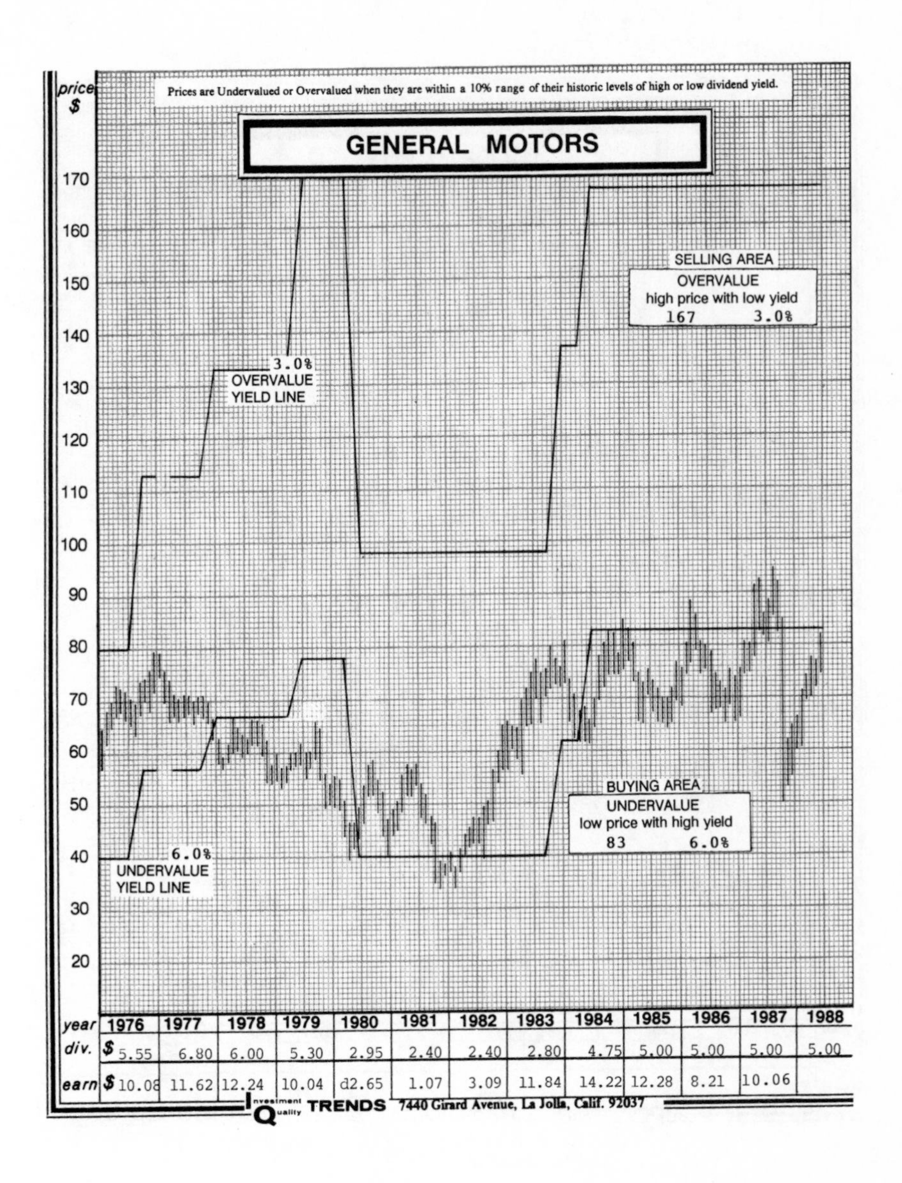

year	1976	1977	1978	1979	1980	1981	1982	1983	1984	1985	1986	1987	1988
div.	$ 5.55	6.80	6.00	5.30	2.95	2.40	2.40	2.80	4.75	5.00	5.00	5.00	5.00
earn	$ 10.08	11.62	12.24	10.04	d2.65	1.07	3.09	11.84	14.22	12.28	8.21	10.06	

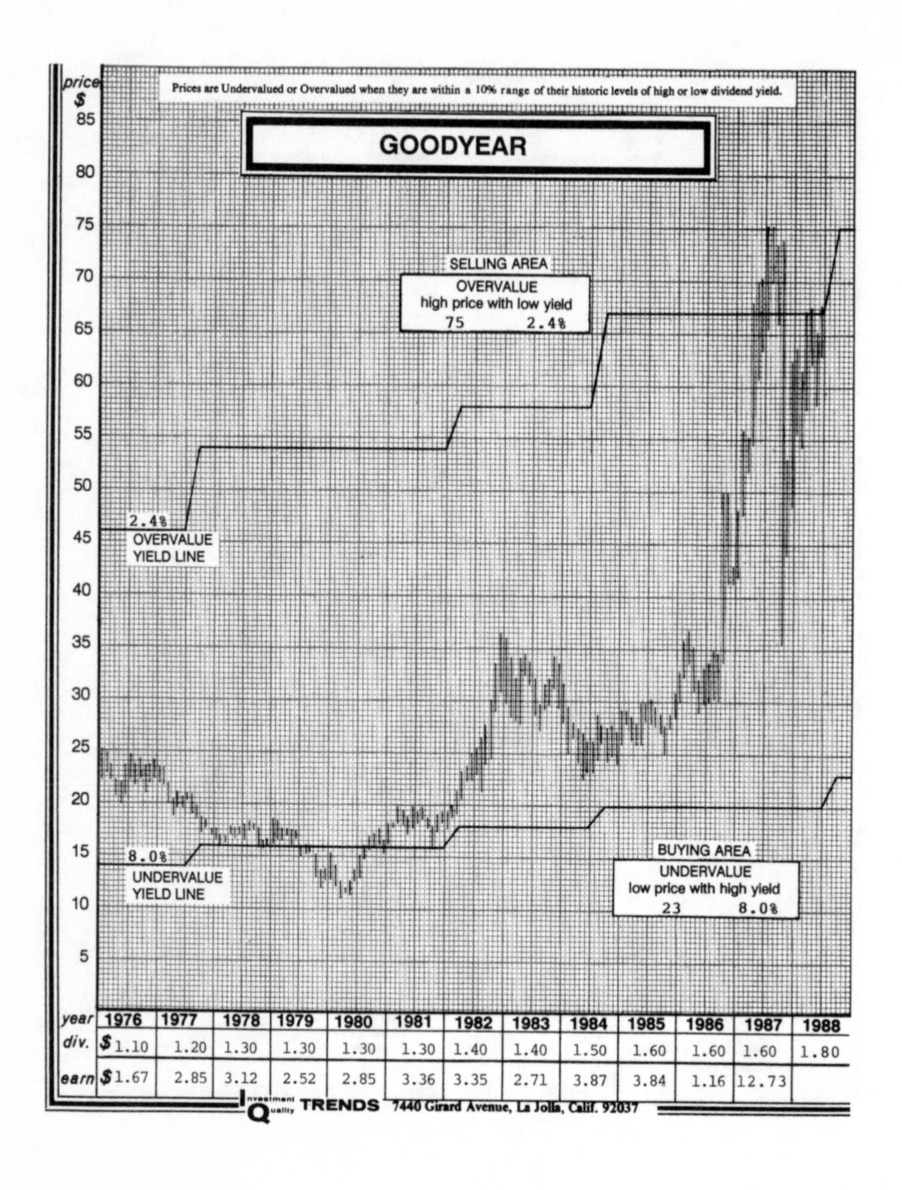

year	1976	1977	1978	1979	1980	1981	1982	1983	1984	1985	1986	1987	1988
div.	$1.10	1.20	1.30	1.30	1.30	1.30	1.40	1.40	1.50	1.60	1.60	1.60	1.80
earn	$1.67	2.85	3.12	2.52	2.85	3.36	3.35	2.71	3.87	3.84	1.16	12.73	

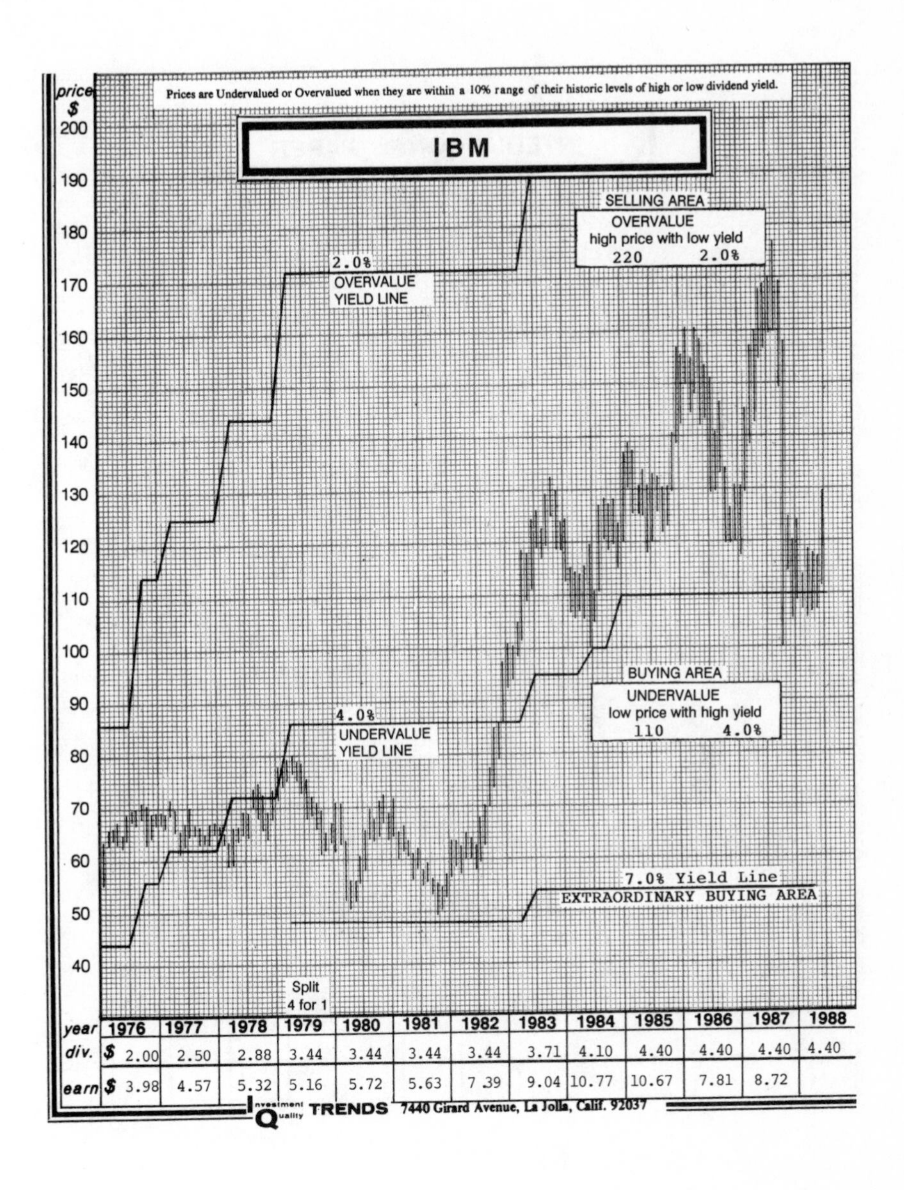

year	1976	1977	1978	1979	1980	1981	1982	1983	1984	1985	1986	1987	1988
div. $	2.00	2.50	2.88	3.44	3.44	3.44	3.44	3.71	4.10	4.40	4.40	4.40	4.40
earn $	3.98	4.57	5.32	5.16	5.72	5.63	7 39	9.04	10.77	10.67	7.81	8.72	

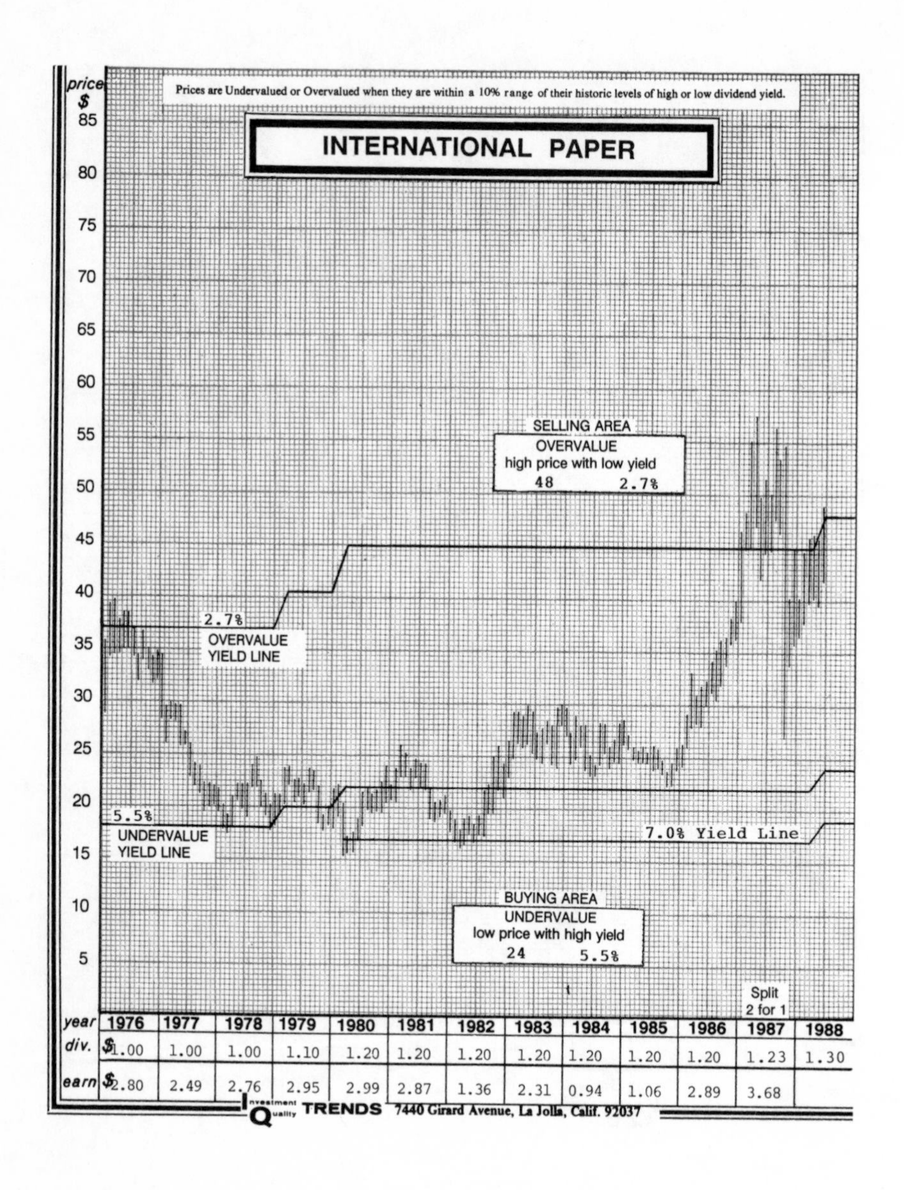

year	1976	1977	1978	1979	1980	1981	1982	1983	1984	1985	1986	1987	1988
div.	$1.00	1.00	1.00	1.10	1.20	1.20	1.20	1.20	1.20	1.20	1.20	1.23	1.30
earn	$2.80	2.49	2.76	2.95	2.99	2.87	1.36	2.31	0.94	1.06	2.89	3.68	

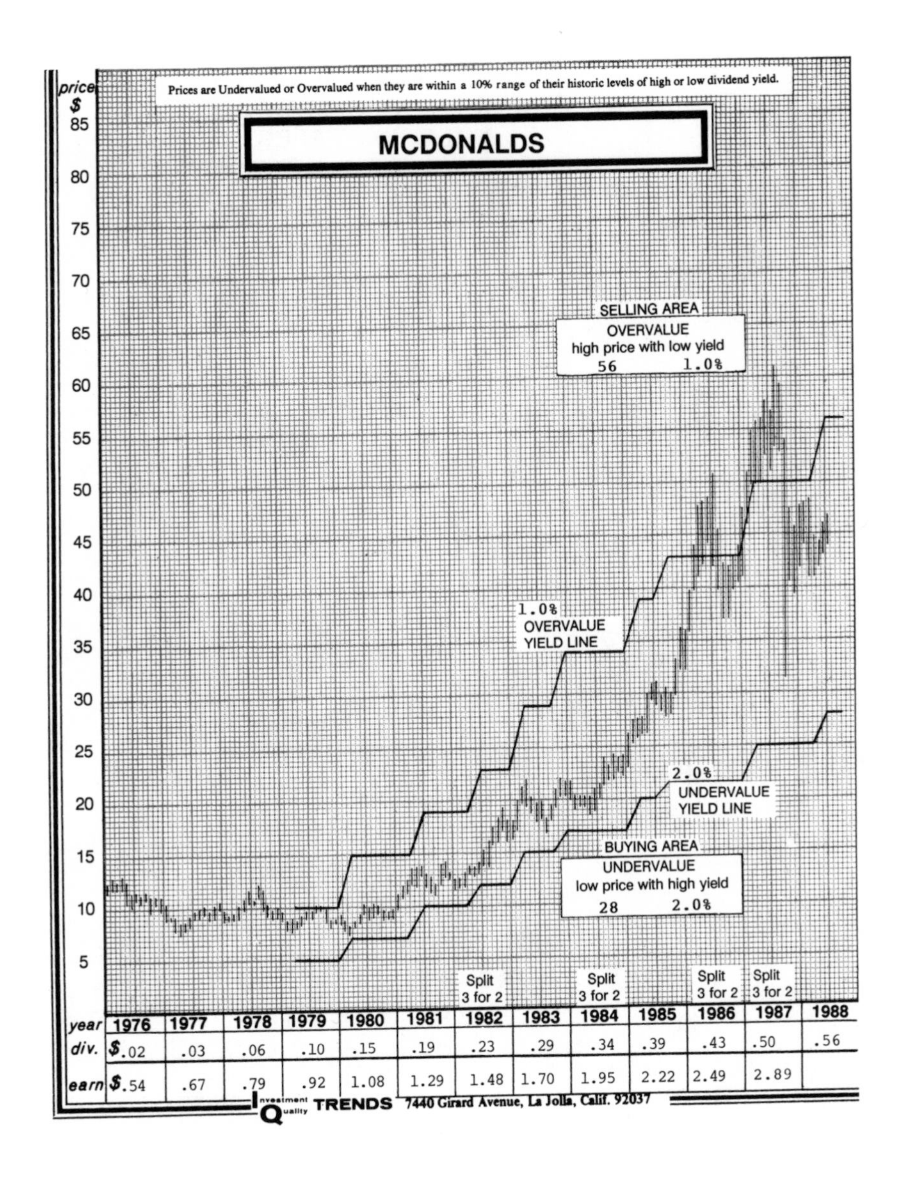
Prices are Undervalued or Overvalued when they are within a 10% range of their historic levels of high or low dividend yield.
MCDONALDS
price $
85
80
75
70
65
60
55
50
45
40
35
30
25
20
15
10
5
SELLING AREA
OVERVALUE
high price with low yield
56 1.0%
1.0%
OVERVALUE
YIELD LINE
2.0%
UNDERVALUE
YIELD LINE
BUYING AREA
UNDERVALUE
low price with high yield
28 2.0%
Split 3 for 2
Split 3 for 2
Split 3 for 2
Split 3 for 2
year 1976 1977 1978 1979 1980 1981 1982 1983 1984 1985 1986 1987 1988
div. $.02 .03 .06 .10 .15 .19 .23 .29 .34 .39 .43 .50 .56
earn $.54 .67 .79 .92 1.08 1.29 1.48 1.70 1.95 2.22 2.49 2.89
Investment Quality TRENDS 7440 Girard Avenue, La Jolla, Calif. 92037

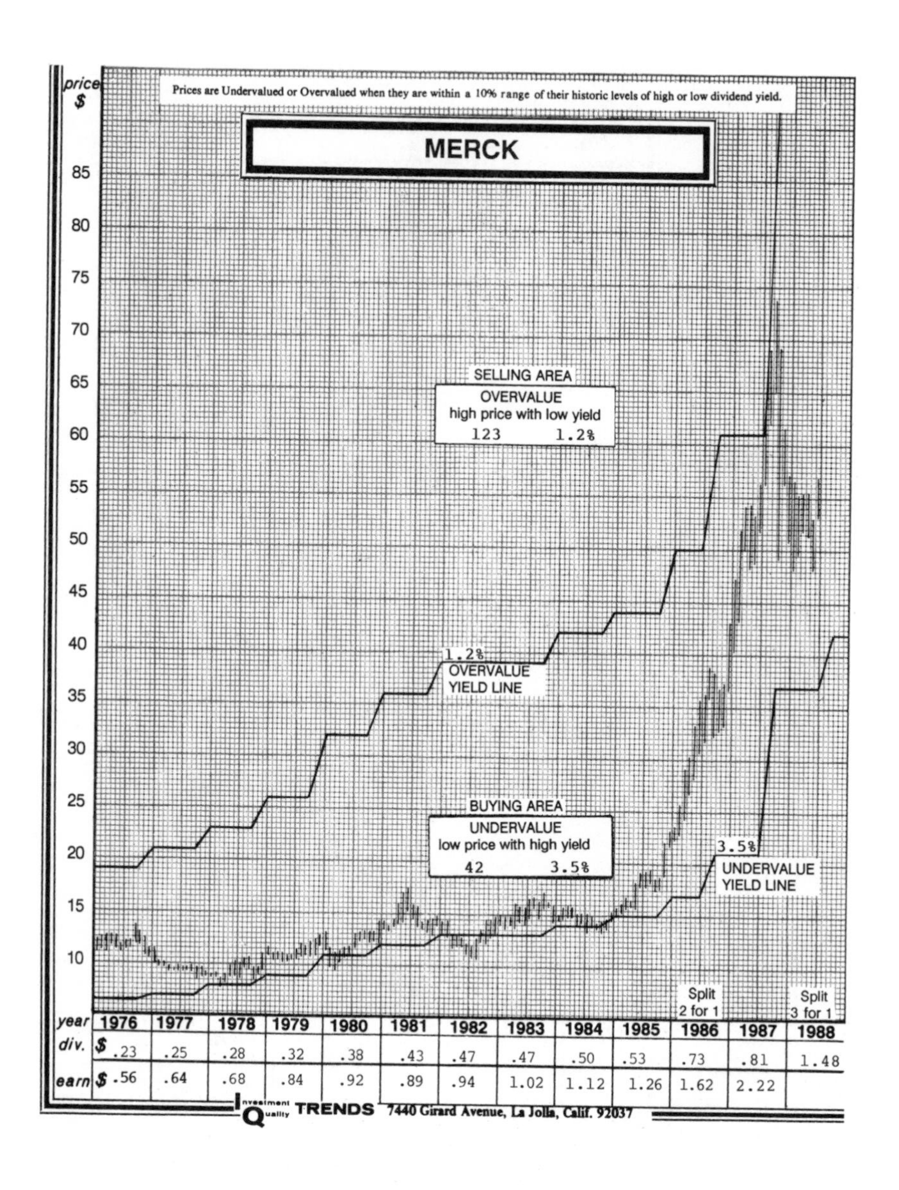

year	1976	1977	1978	1979	1980	1981	1982	1983	1984	1985	1986	1987	1988
div.	$ .23	.25	.28	.32	.38	.43	.47	.47	.50	.53	.73	.81	1.48
earn	$ .56	.64	.68	.84	.92	.89	.94	1.02	1.12	1.26	1.62	2.22	

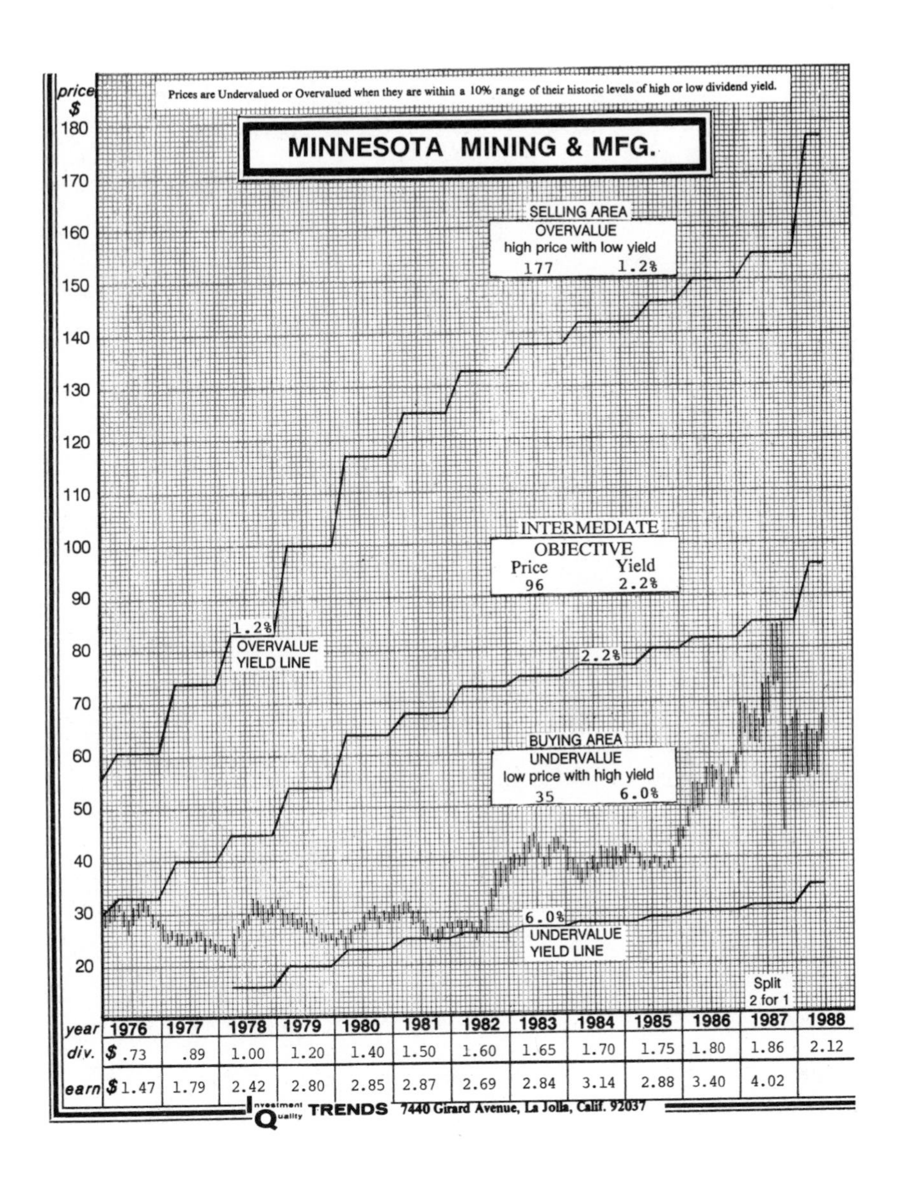
Prices are Undervalued or Overvalued when they are within a 10% range of their historic levels of high or low dividend yield.
MINNESOTA MINING & MFG.
price $
180
170
160
150
140
130
120
110
100
90
80
70
60
50
40
30
20
SELLING AREA
OVERVALUE
high price with low yield
177 1.2%
INTERMEDIATE
OBJECTIVE
Price Yield
96 2.2%
1.2%
OVERVALUE
YIELD LINE
2.2%
BUYING AREA
UNDERVALUE
low price with high yield
35 6.0%
6.0%
UNDERVALUE
YIELD LINE
Split
2 for 1
year 1976 1977 1978 1979 1980 1981 1982 1983 1984 1985 1986 1987 1988
div. $.73 .89 1.00 1.20 1.40 1.50 1.60 1.65 1.70 1.75 1.80 1.86 2.12
earn $1.47 1.79 2.42 2.80 2.85 2.87 2.69 2.84 3.14 2.88 3.40 4.02
Investment Quality TRENDS 7440 Girard Avenue, La Jolla, Calif. 92037

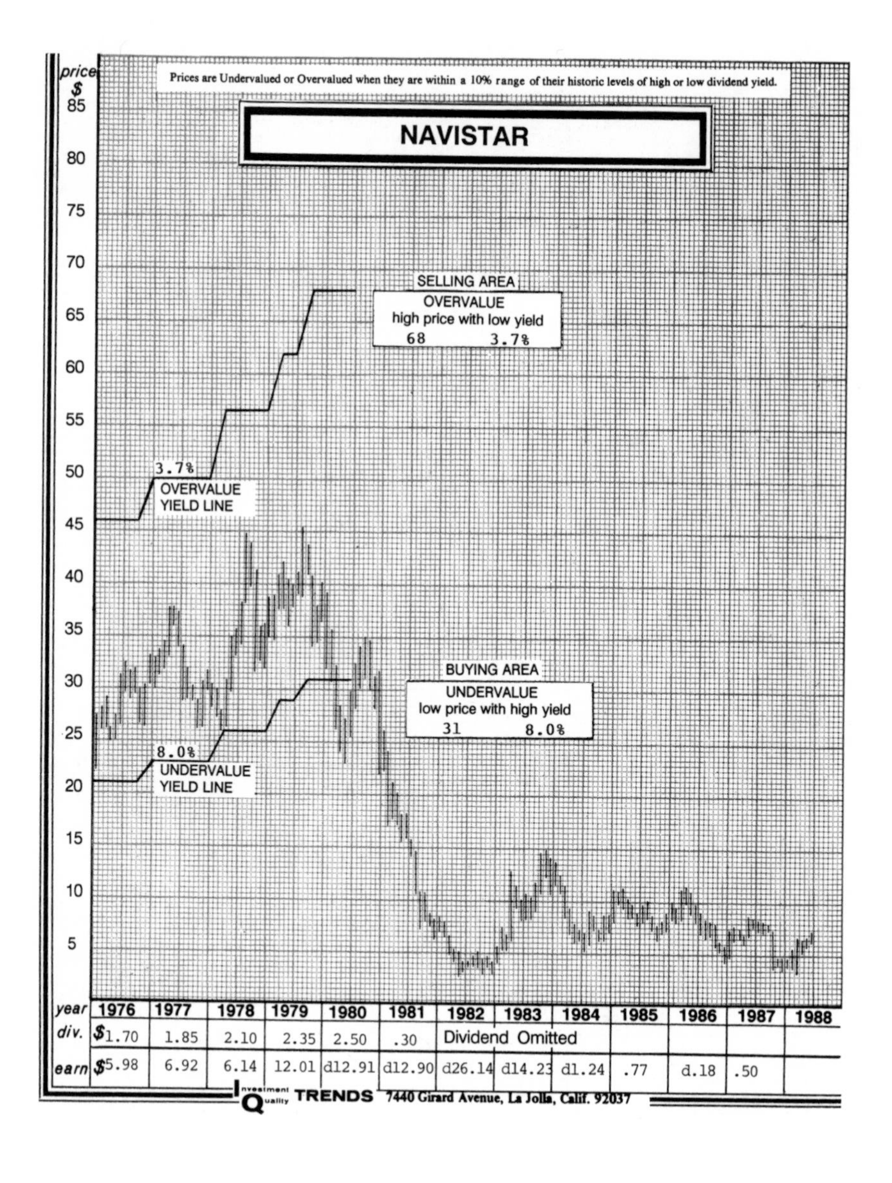
price $
85
80
75
70
65
60
55
50
45
40
35
30
25
20
15
10
5
Prices are Undervalued or Overvalued when they are within a 10% range of their historic levels of high or low dividend yield.
NAVISTAR
SELLING AREA
OVERVALUE
high price with low yield
68 3.7%
3.7%
OVERVALUE
YIELD LINE
BUYING AREA
UNDERVALUE
low price with high yield
31 8.0%
8.0%
UNDERVALUE
YIELD LINE
year 1976 1977 1978 1979 1980 1981 1982 1983 1984 1985 1986 1987 1988
div. $1.70 1.85 2.10 2.35 2.50 .30 Dividend Omitted
earn $5.98 6.92 6.14 12.01 d12.91 d12.90 d26.14 d14.23 d1.24 .77 d.18 .50
Investment Quality TRENDS 7440 Girard Avenue, La Jolla, Calif. 92037

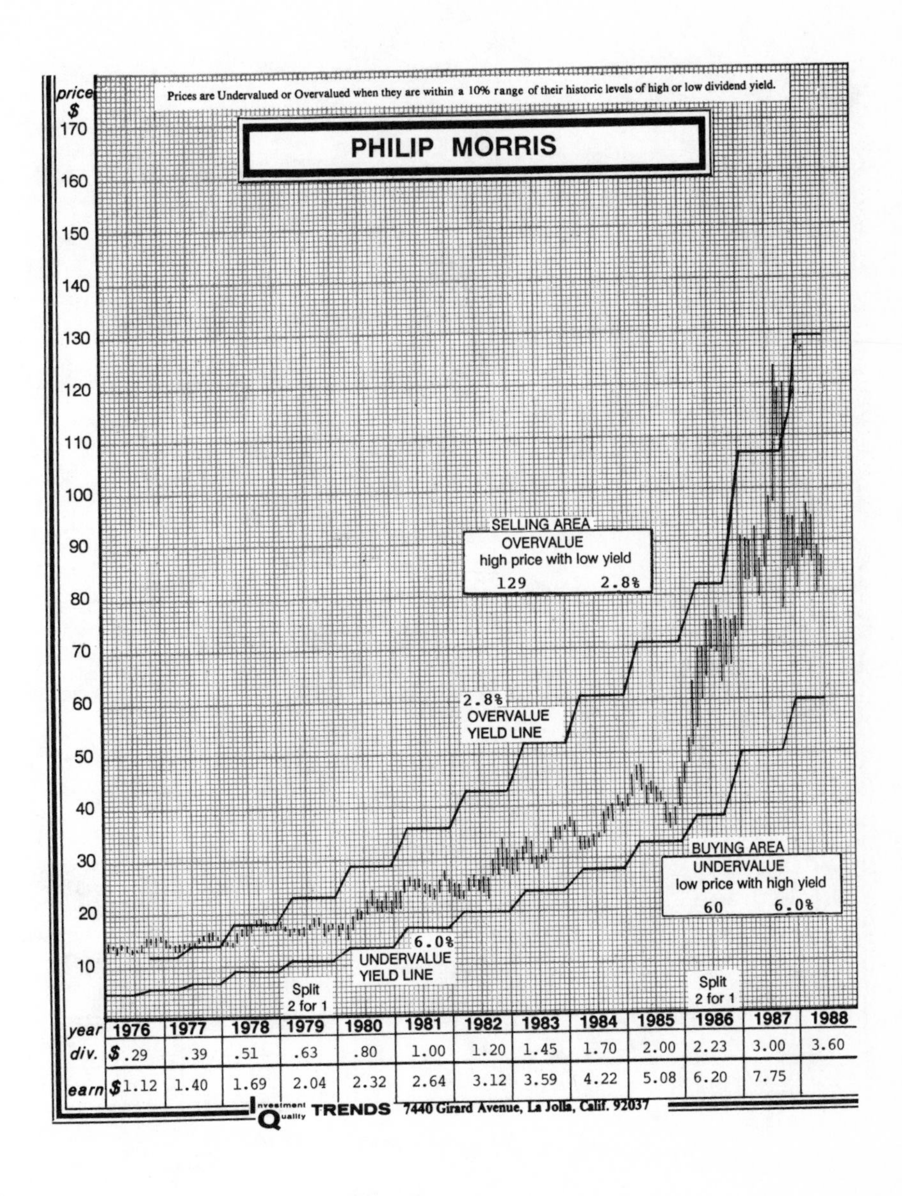

year	1976	1977	1978	1979	1980	1981	1982	1983	1984	1985	1986	1987	1988
div.	$.29	.39	.51	.63	.80	1.00	1.20	1.45	1.70	2.00	2.23	3.00	3.60
earn	$1.12	1.40	1.69	2.04	2.32	2.64	3.12	3.59	4.22	5.08	6.20	7.75	

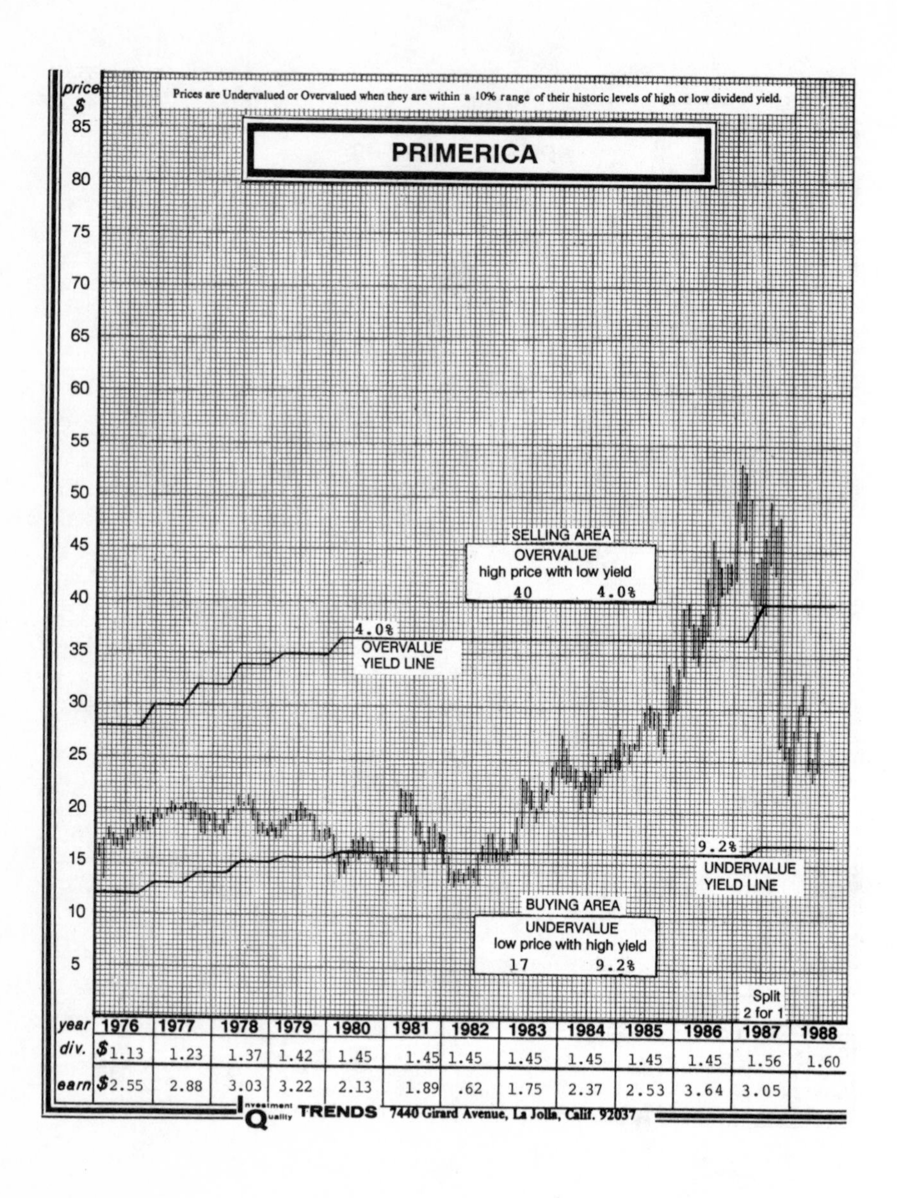
Prices are Undervalued or Overvalued when they are within a 10% range of their historic levels of high or low dividend yield.
PRIMERICA
price $
85
80
75
70
65
60
55
50
45
40
35
30
25
20
15
10
5
SELLING AREA
OVERVALUE
high price with low yield
40 4.0%
4.0%
OVERVALUE
YIELD LINE
9.2%
UNDERVALUE
YIELD LINE
BUYING AREA
UNDERVALUE
low price with high yield
17 9.2%
Split
2 for 1
year 1976 1977 1978 1979 1980 1981 1982 1983 1984 1985 1986 1987 1988
div. $1.13 1.23 1.37 1.42 1.45 1.45 1.45 1.45 1.45 1.45 1.45 1.56 1.60
earn $2.55 2.88 3.03 3.22 2.13 1.89 .62 1.75 2.37 2.53 3.64 3.05
Investment Quality TRENDS 7440 Girard Avenue, La Jolla, Calif. 92037

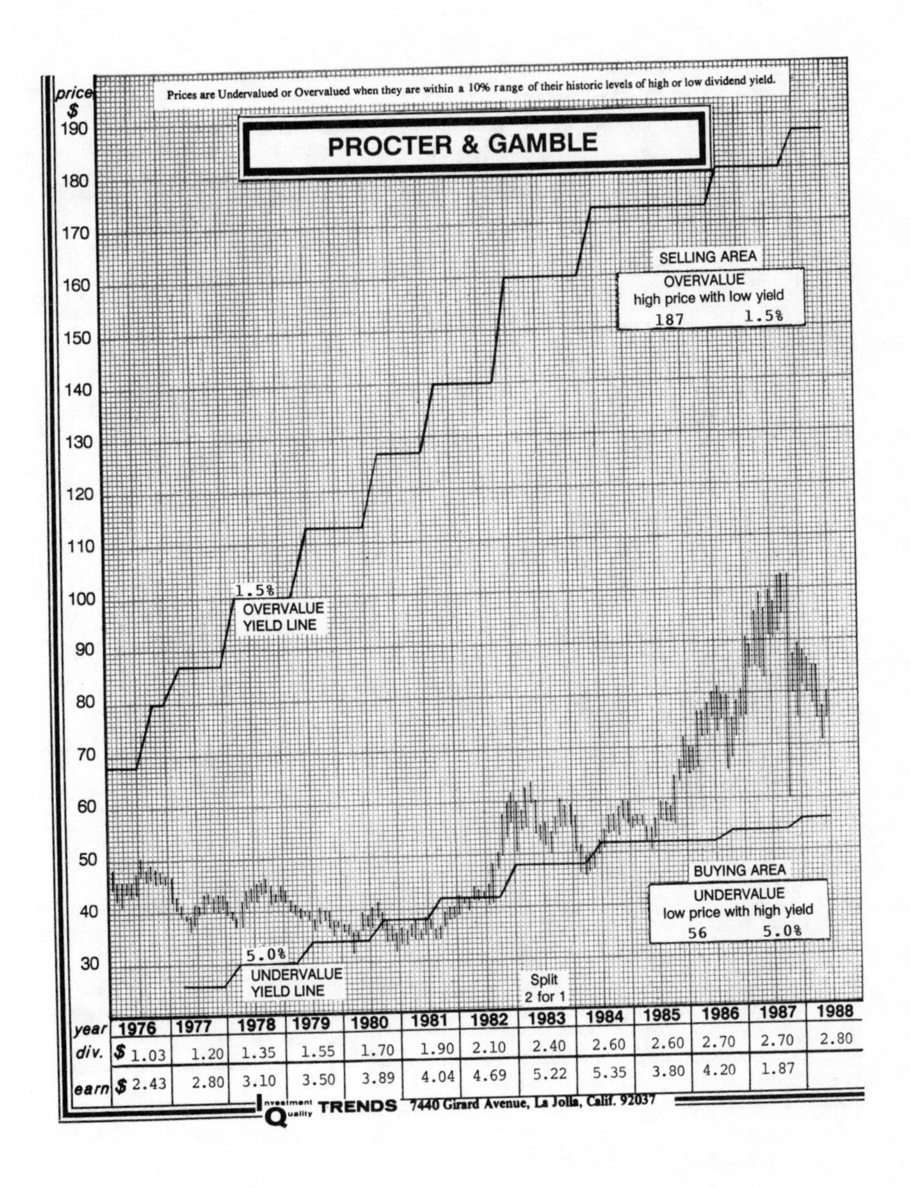
Prices are Undervalued or Overvalued when they are within a 10% range of their historic levels of high or low dividend yield.
PROCTER & GAMBLE
price $
190
180
170
160
150
140
130
120
110
100
90
80
70
60
50
40
30
SELLING AREA
OVERVALUE
high price with low yield
187 1.5%
1.5%
OVERVALUE
YIELD LINE
BUYING AREA
UNDERVALUE
low price with high yield
56 5.0%
5.0%
UNDERVALUE
YIELD LINE
Split
2 for 1
year 1976 1977 1978 1979 1980 1981 1982 1983 1984 1985 1986 1987 1988
div. $ 1.03 1.20 1.35 1.55 1.70 1.90 2.10 2.40 2.60 2.60 2.70 2.70 2.80
earn $ 2.43 2.80 3.10 3.50 3.89 4.04 4.69 5.22 5.35 3.80 4.20 1.87
Investment Quality TRENDS 7440 Girard Avenue, La Jolla, Calif. 92037

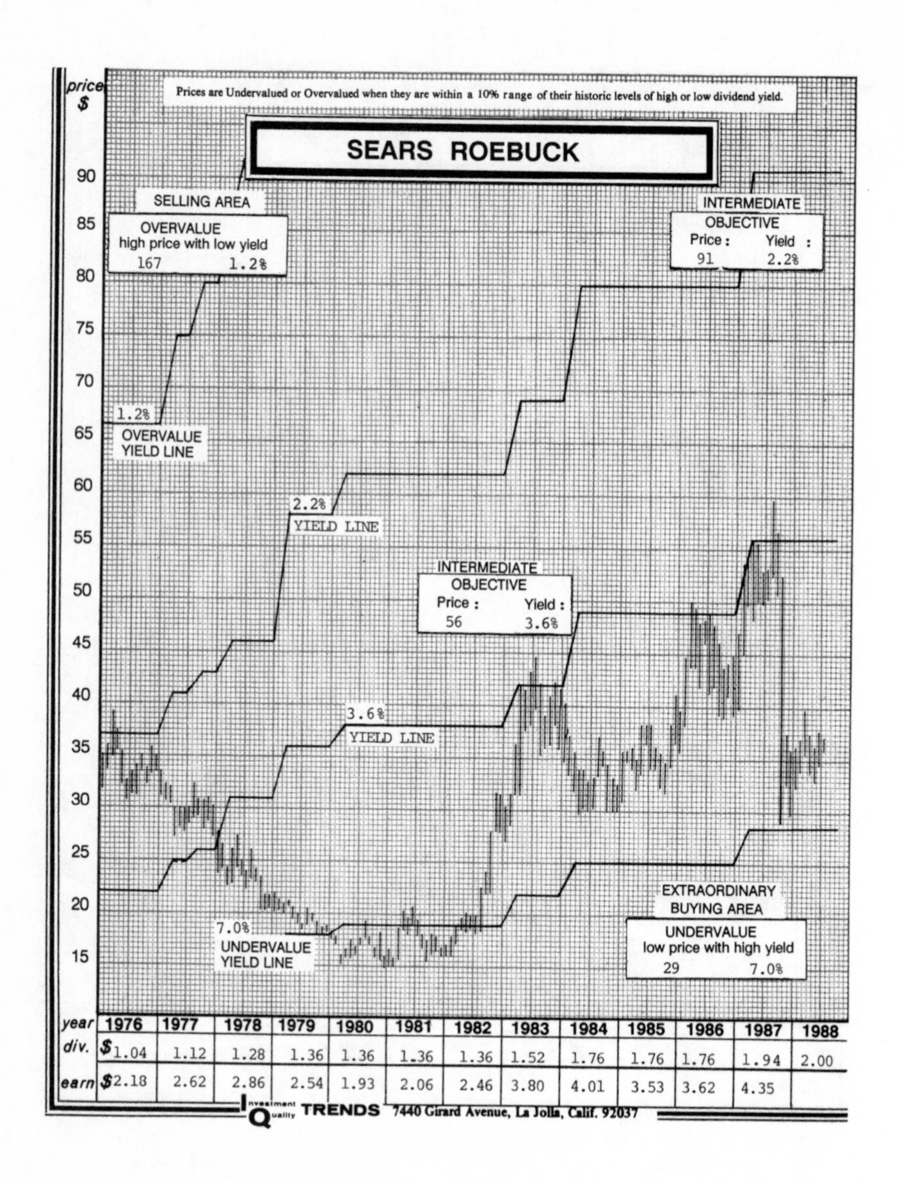
price $
Prices are Undervalued or Overvalued when they are within a 10% range of their historic levels of high or low dividend yield.
SEARS ROEBUCK
90
85
80
75
70
65
60
55
50
45
40
35
30
25
20
15
SELLING AREA
OVERVALUE
high price with low yield
167 1.2%
1.2%
OVERVALUE
YIELD LINE
2.2%
YIELD LINE
INTERMEDIATE
OBJECTIVE
Price : Yield :
91 2.2%
INTERMEDIATE
OBJECTIVE
Price : Yield :
56 3.6%
3.6%
YIELD LINE
7.0%
UNDERVALUE
YIELD LINE
EXTRAORDINARY
BUYING AREA
UNDERVALUE
low price with high yield
29 7.0%
year 1976 1977 1978 1979 1980 1981 1982 1983 1984 1985 1986 1987 1988
div. $1.04 1.12 1.28 1.36 1.36 1.36 1.36 1.52 1.76 1.76 1.76 1.94 2.00
earn $2.18 2.62 2.86 2.54 1.93 2.06 2.46 3.80 4.01 3.53 3.62 4.35
Investment Quality TRENDS 7440 Girard Avenue, La Jolla, Calif. 92037

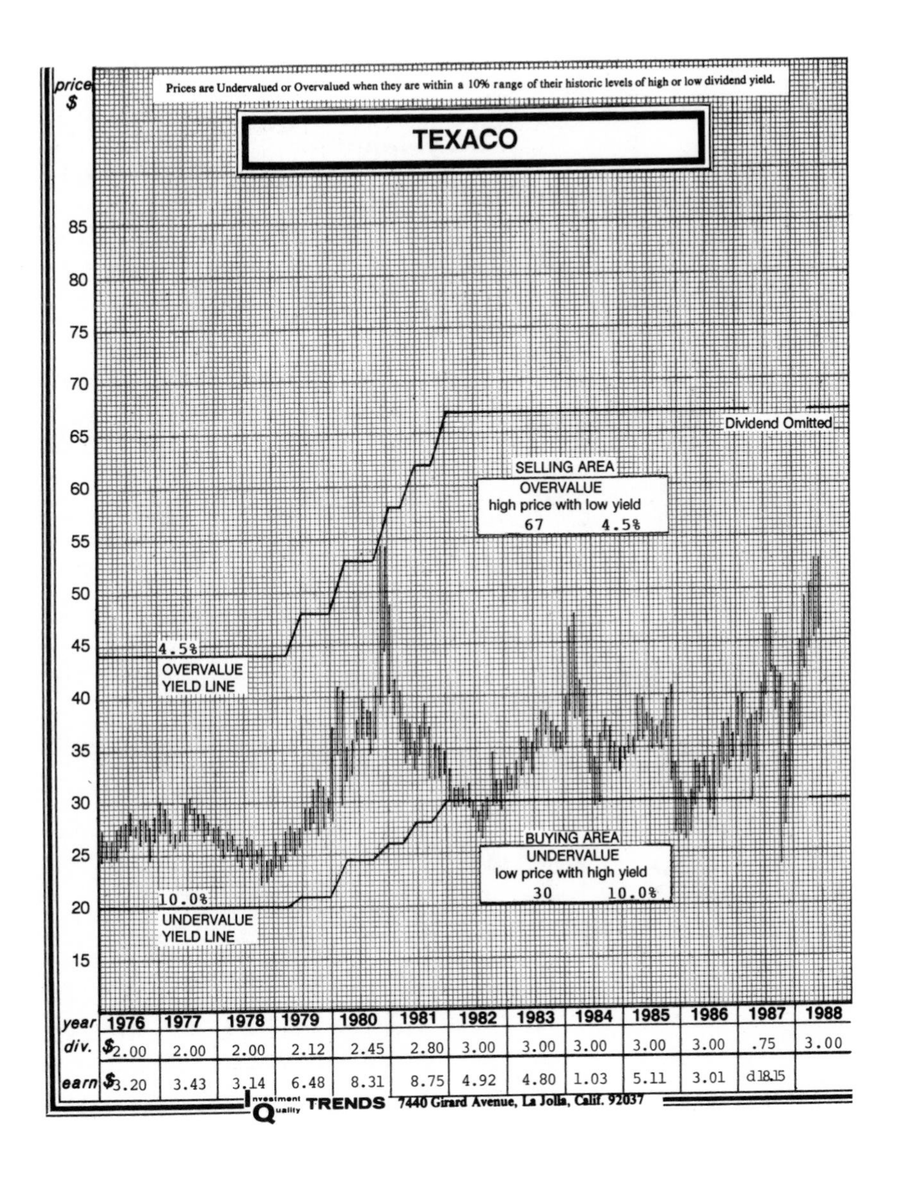

year	1976	1977	1978	1979	1980	1981	1982	1983	1984	1985	1986	1987	1988
div.	$2.00	2.00	2.00	2.12	2.45	2.80	3.00	3.00	3.00	3.00	3.00	.75	3.00
earn	$3.20	3.43	3.14	6.48	8.31	8.75	4.92	4.80	1.03	5.11	3.01	d18.15	

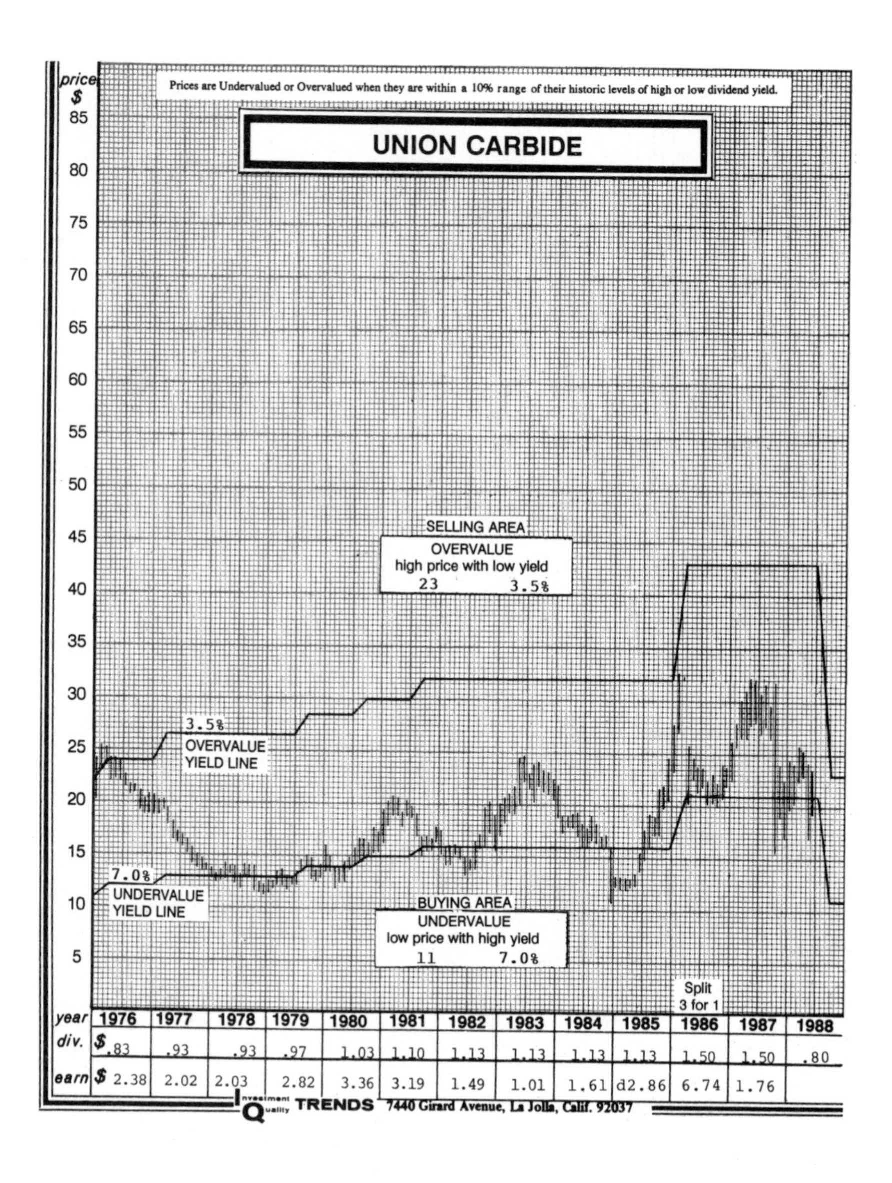
Prices are Undervalued or Overvalued when they are within a 10% range of their historic levels of high or low dividend yield.
UNION CARBIDE
price $
85
80
75
70
65
60
55
50
45
40
35
30
25
20
15
10
5
SELLING AREA
OVERVALUE
high price with low yield
23 3.5%
3.5%
OVERVALUE
YIELD LINE
7.0%
UNDERVALUE
YIELD LINE
BUYING AREA
UNDERVALUE
low price with high yield
11 7.0%
Split
3 for 1
year 1976 1977 1978 1979 1980 1981 1982 1983 1984 1985 1986 1987 1988
div. $ .83 .93 .93 .97 1.03 1.10 1.13 1.13 1.13 1.13 1.50 1.50 .80
earn $ 2.38 2.02 2.03 2.82 3.36 3.19 1.49 1.01 1.61 d2.86 6.74 1.76
Investment Quality TRENDS 7440 Girard Avenue, La Jolla, Calif. 92037

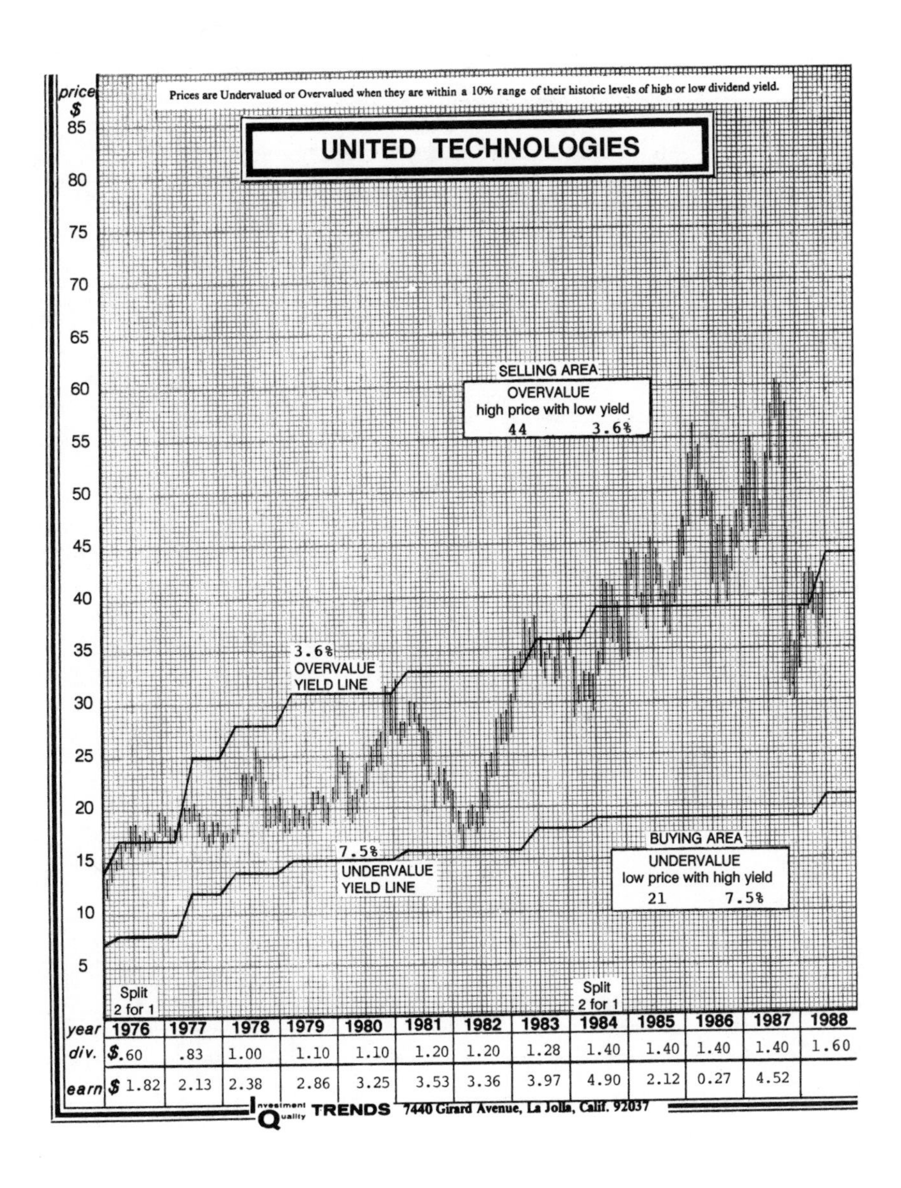

price $
85
80
75
70
65
60
55
50
45
40
35
30
25
20
15
10
5
Prices are Undervalued or Overvalued when they are within a 10% range of their historic levels of high or low dividend yield.
UNITED TECHNOLOGIES
SELLING AREA
OVERVALUE
high price with low yield
44 3.6%
3.6%
OVERVALUE
YIELD LINE
7.5%
UNDERVALUE
YIELD LINE
BUYING AREA
UNDERVALUE
low price with high yield
21 7.5%
Split
2 for 1
Split
2 for 1
year 1976 1977 1978 1979 1980 1981 1982 1983 1984 1985 1986 1987 1988
div. $.60 .83 1.00 1.10 1.10 1.20 1.20 1.28 1.40 1.40 1.40 1.40 1.60
earn $ 1.82 2.13 2.38 2.86 3.25 3.53 3.36 3.97 4.90 2.12 0.27 4.52
Investment Quality TRENDS 7440 Girard Avenue, La Jolla, Calif. 92037

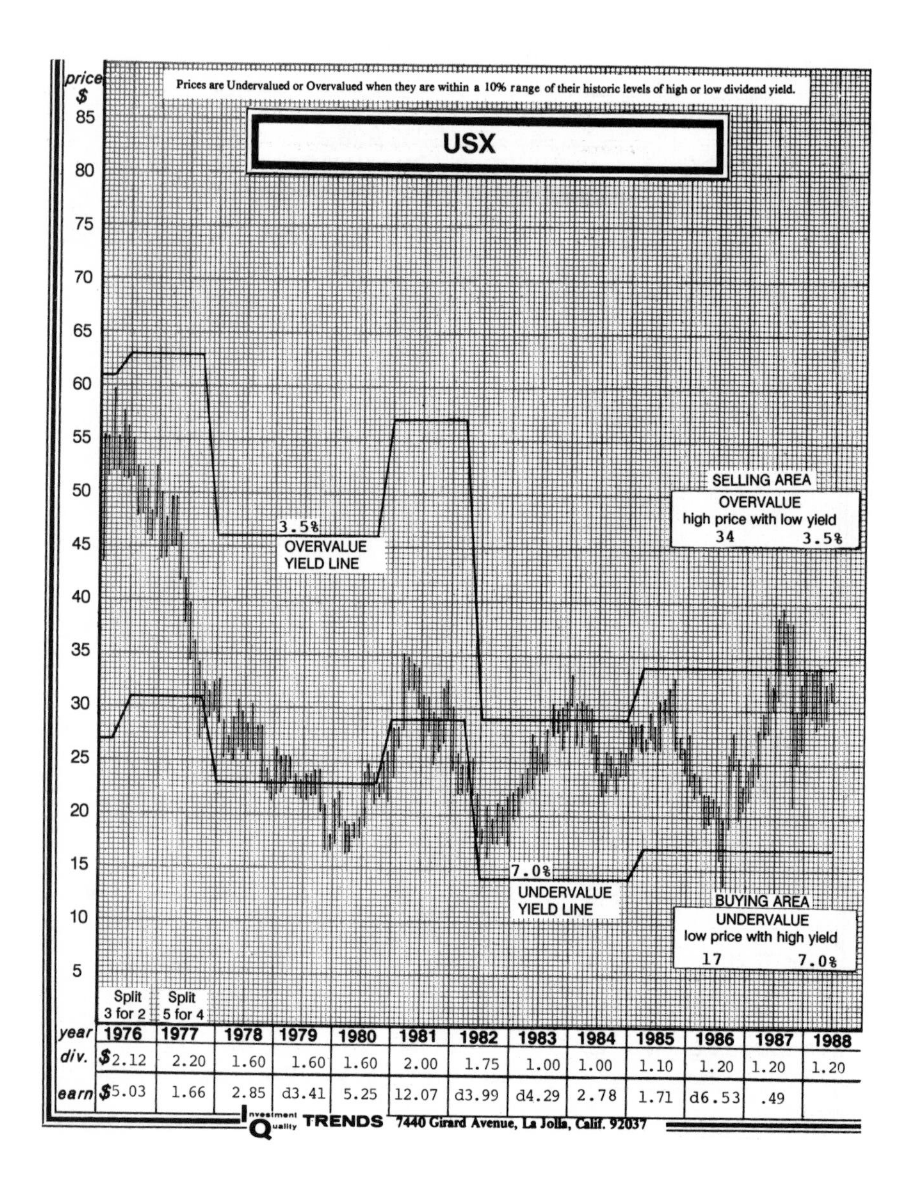

year	1976	1977	1978	1979	1980	1981	1982	1983	1984	1985	1986	1987	1988
div.	$2.12	2.20	1.60	1.60	1.60	2.00	1.75	1.00	1.00	1.10	1.20	1.20	1.20
earn	$5.03	1.66	2.85	d3.41	5.25	12.07	d3.99	d4.29	2.78	1.71	d6.53	.49	

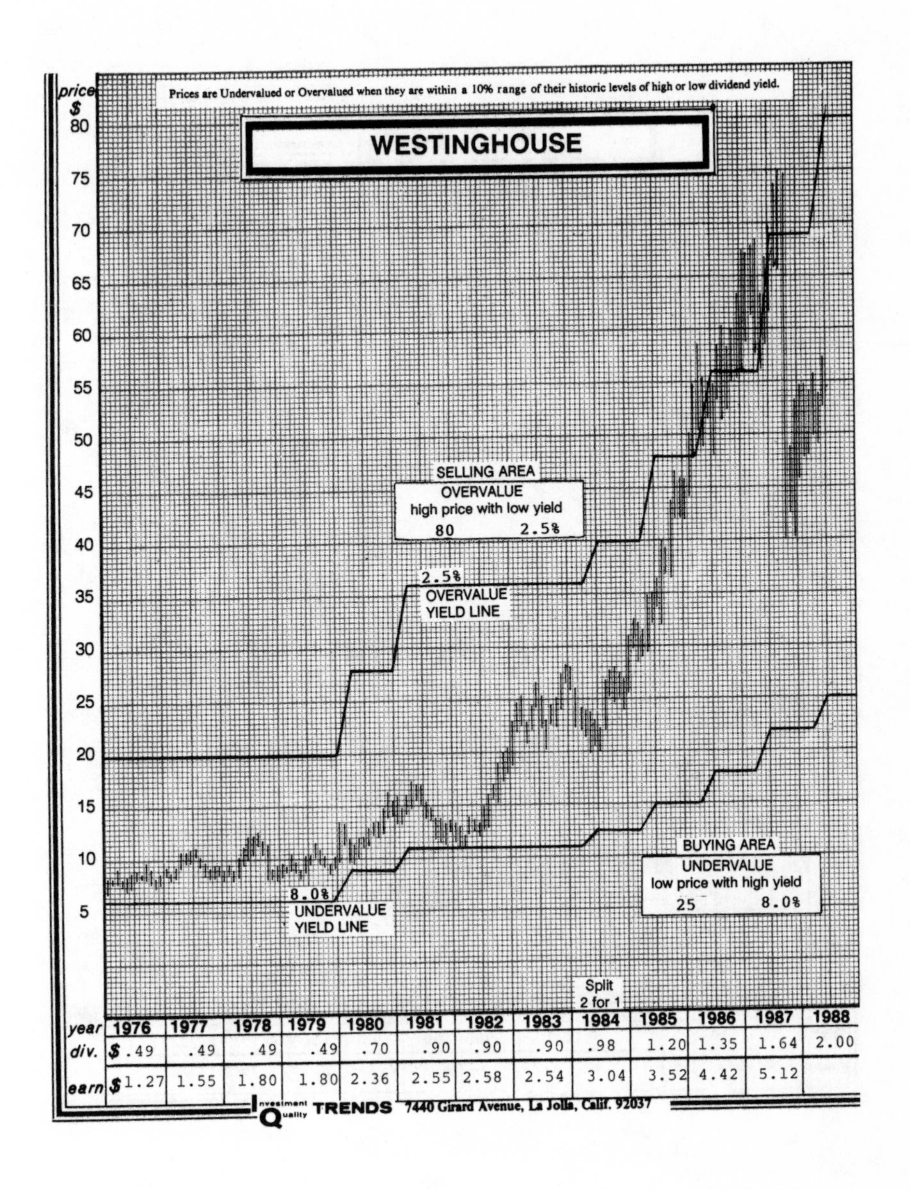

Prices are Undervalued or Overvalued when they are within a 10% range of their historic levels of high or low dividend yield.
WESTINGHOUSE
price $
80
75
70
65
60
55
50
45
40
35
30
25
20
15
10
5
SELLING AREA
OVERVALUE
high price with low yield
80 2.5%
2.5%
OVERVALUE
YIELD LINE
8.0%
UNDERVALUE
YIELD LINE
BUYING AREA
UNDERVALUE
low price with high yield
25 8.0%
Split
2 for 1
year 1976 1977 1978 1979 1980 1981 1982 1983 1984 1985 1986 1987 1988
div. $ .49 .49 .49 .49 .70 .90 .90 .90 .98 1.20 1.35 1.64 2.00
earn $1.27 1.55 1.80 1.80 2.36 2.55 2.58 2.54 3.04 3.52 4.42 5.12
Investment Quality TRENDS 7440 Girard Avenue, La Jolla, Calif. 92037

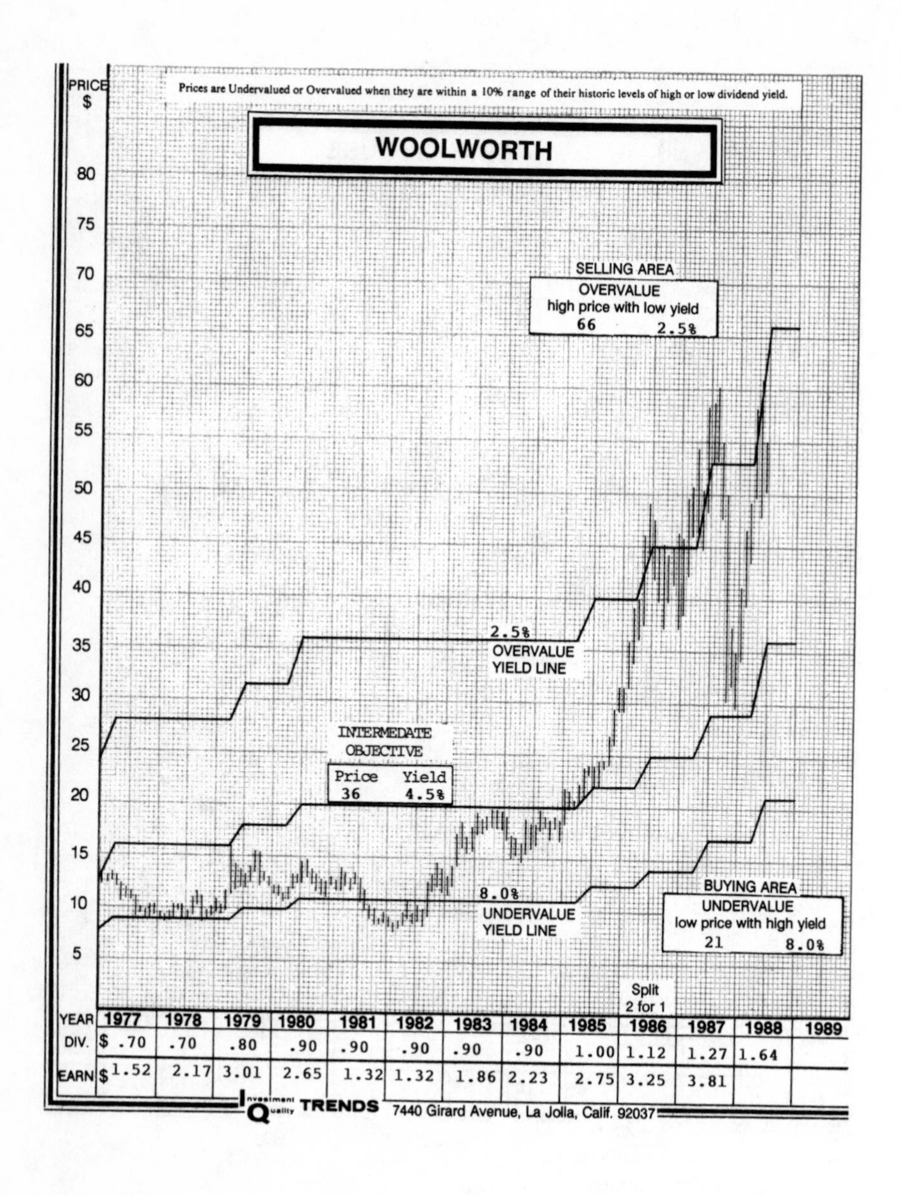
Prices are Undervalued or Overvalued when they are within a 10% range of their historic levels of high or low dividend yield.
WOOLWORTH
PRICE $
80
75
70
65
60
55
50
45
40
35
30
25
20
15
10
5
SELLING AREA
OVERVALUE
high price with low yield
66 2.5%
2.5%
OVERVALUE
YIELD LINE
INTERMEDATE
OBJECTIVE
Price Yield
36 4.5%
8.0%
UNDERVALUE
YIELD LINE
BUYING AREA
UNDERVALUE
low price with high yield
21 8.0%
Split
2 for 1
YEAR 1977 1978 1979 1980 1981 1982 1983 1984 1985 1986 1987 1988 1989
DIV. $ .70 .70 .80 .90 .90 .90 .90 .90 1.00 1.12 1.27 1.64
EARN $1.52 2.17 3.01 2.65 1.32 1.32 1.86 2.23 2.75 3.25 3.81
Investment Quality TRENDS 7440 Girard Avenue, La Jolla, Calif. 92037

Index